Praise for

"Seek ye First the ...

One man's journey with th. o Jesus

"Wherever you may be on your spiritual journey at this point in time, this autobiography will encourage, enlighten and open your mind to so many personal possibilities.

"Brian Longhurst has managed to acquire a profoundly personal relationship with Jesus and Papa which, unlikely as it may seem to those of us who have not yet remembered who we truly are, involves two-way communication of both extraordinary and almost matter-of-fact conversation.

"I believe that this book has the power to change lives, especially for those of us who are either unsure or completely unaware of the journey that we are all undertaking.

"Brian makes no claim to be extraordinary, in fact quite the opposite. Everything he has experienced is available to each and every one of us. That, for me, really is the most wonderful prospect that his writing offers."
— *Ian Condie, United Kingdom*

"Brian Longhurst has dedicated himself to Truth and the living Jesus more than most men ever do – and the results are astonishing. I know that you will enjoy Brian's autobiographical account of his devoted quest, as well as the many humorous and always touching anecdotes that he shares from his life of commitment to our 'elder brother'. Thank you, Brian, for your willingness to seek first the Kingdom!"
— *Rev. Julie Gillespie, Texas, USA*

"Seek ye First the Kingdom..."

"Seek ye First the Kingdom…"

One man's journey with the living Jesus

Brian Longhurst

SIX DEGREES PUBLISHING GROUP

PORTLAND • OREGON

Six Degrees Publishing Group
5320 SW Macadam Avenue
Portland, OR 97239 USA

Second Paperback Edition 2012

ISBN: 978-0-9856048-1-3
Library of Congress Control Number: 2012940619

Inquiries may be made by emailing Permissions@SixDegreesPublishing.com

Unless otherwise indicated all Scripture quotations are extracts from the Authorized Version of The King James Bible, the rights in which are vested in the Crown. Reproduced by permission of the Crown's Patentee, Cambridge University Press.

Grateful acknowledgement is made to the following for permission to reprint previously published material: Foundation for Inner Peace, Glen Ellen, CA, USA *A Course in Miracles,* Second Edition, Copyright © 1992.

Author's note: In quoting portions of *A Course in Miracles,* I have bracketed words added by me, and have underlined, emboldened and italicised some words for emphasis.

Published in the United States of America
Printed simultaneously in the United States of America and the United Kingdom
1 3 5 7 9 10 8 6 4 2

Cover design: Lana Carolan

Publisher's note: While the author and publisher have made every effort to provide accurate Internet addresses at the time of publication, neither the publisher nor the author assumes any responsibility for errors or for changes that occur after publication. Further, the publisher does not have any control over and does not assume any responsibility for author or third-party websites or their content. The views expressed in this book are not necessarily those of the publisher.

DEDICATION

This work is dedicated to all who observe the unserviceableness of Earth-life institutions – political, civic, commercial and religious – who have an aching longing in their heart and soul for truth, peace, goodwill, trust, honesty, freedom, openness, and a deep, inner *knowing* that things don't have to be the way they are – that indeed they can, *very easily*, be immeasurably better.

To all such, herein is a message of hope: there *is* a better way, and each and every one of us can make a *real* difference in helping to transform ourselves and the world into a New Era of spiritual enlightenment – the Kingdom of Heaven on Earth.

CONTENTS

Foreword by Michael J Roads   *xi*
Preface   *xv*

Introduction   1

Part One

1: Early Days and a New Beginning   11

2: A Momentous Rejoining   22

3: Stirrings Within   32

4: Romance Blossoms   41

5: The Rescue Work Begins   50

6: Family Life – Here and Beyond   70

7: Deepening Understanding   84

8: The Rescue Work Shifts Up a Gear   105

9: Friendship, Angels and Revelations   118

10: Tapestry Fragments   134

11: The End of the Beginning   153

Part Two: Vignettes

Vignettes   169

1. "Stand in the Holy Place; Stand in the Lowly Place"   171

2. Hal/Sitting Bull   174

3. Buffalo Bill   179

4. First Encounter with the Holy Spirit   180

5. The Free Gift of Forgiveness   183

6. Goddess Theresa   186

7. Broken Ankle at Crickley   191

8. *Seeds of Redemption*; Charles   196

9. Fleas; "Don't give up!"   200

10. An Open Letter   206

11. The Crucifixion: "I did it to get your attention."   224

12. The False Doctrine of Sacrifice as the
    Path to Salvation   231

13. A Mass Rescue and Healing   238

14. "There is no light of discernment."   243

15. Animals and Eternity   246

16. Peter: "I came to clear the way for her."   249

17. Religious Mythology   251

18. The Not-So-Distant Shore   252

19. Ted's Passing, Rescue and Going Forward   256

20. From Breaking Rocks to Breaking Bread   267

21. Laser: Amplifying the Light for the Kingdom   272

22. Jim, Ship's Doctor   279

23. Exorcising Possessing Spirits   283

24. Religious Misperceptions of Duty   292

25. The Gathering of the Clans   294

26. Tyndale the Translator   297

27. Jesus in Bedrock Hell Fastening the
    Escape Ladder to the Floor   300

    Afterword   313

    Acknowledgements   319

    About the Author   321

FOREWORD
An Introduction to the Author

As a spiritual teacher who has travelled the world for the past twenty years, I get a lot of correspondence from many people. When my wife, Carolyn, and I received an email from Brian a few years ago, it was simply one of many. When I read his email, and realised that this man claimed a friendship with the living Jesus, a trickle of apprehension crawled down my spine. Most mental facilities have a few inmates claiming either to be Jesus, or at least to be on good speaking terms with him; not to mention the Jesus cults! Then I learned that we would be meeting him on our next tour.

I confess, our meeting was nothing like I expected. I imagined a goofy looking man, who, when he was not chatting with Jesus, would probably be singing hymns in a high, nasal voice. You know what I mean; another version of a typical English eccentric. The reality was very different. We met, Brian and his lovely wife, Theresa, in a village pub in Cambridgeshire, and I had immediate difficulty in reconciling my image of Brian with the real person. In reality, Brian is a very handsome man – and this from another male! – who has a huge sense of humour, which, I admit, is probably a mite more colourful than my own. He was nothing like I expected. I had met with him intending that this was the one and only meeting, but it was not to be. With surprising ease, he charmed and laughed his way into the hearts of both Carolyn and myself, and I heard myself happily agreeing to stay at their home for a few days on our next year's tour.

Even after meeting him, in retrospect I was not eager about staying with them. (Sorry about this, Brian, but truth will out!) Surely he would revert to type, and I would be hauled out of bed at about five o'clock in the morning with the expectation of a few long and drawn out prayers, or at the very least, a chat with Jesus, or a hymn or three. Happily, I was wrong again. We all arose after a good night's sleep at a respectable eight o'clock, and listened to Brian's jokes and chatter as he showed us what was available for breakfast.

As I came to really know and love Brian, I realised that he is a very humble, joyous man, who simply has a relationship with Jesus that is very real for him. And he does not deny that reality. I gradually realised that my whole approach to Brian had been based in my church oriented Christianity. Growing up in a C of E family, I was compelled to go to Sunday school for a few years, until Mrs. Harper, the teacher, decided that Sunday school would be far better without me. That was when I knew there is a God!

After bell-ringing for the Sunday service, I liked to slip unseen out of the church, and I usually managed this, but I was forced to stay and sit through enough services that I found them lifeless, boring, and mind-numbingly repetitive. I become very disenchanted with church and all it stood for. And yet, I accepted that there is a God. Many years later, after I had emigrated to Tasmania, the island state of Australia, there came the day when an unexpected, life-altering question hit me; Who am I? That moment forever changed my life.

The reason Brian intrigued me – and continues to do so – is because after my abrupt and startling question, I was overwhelmed with a biblical quotation; "Seek ye first the Kingdom of Heaven, and all else shall be added unto you." For myself, and everyone I knew, we were seeking first all that could be added unto us ... and if there was any time left over, maybe a Sunday morning, that much time we spent seeking the Kingdom of Heaven. As far as I am aware, it was Jesus who suggested the reverse ... and knowing in my heart the Truth of his words, this is what I did. Where it led me, and what was added unto me is not for these pages, but it was my *living* this profound Truth, spoken by Jesus, that changed my life. Note that I say, *my living it*. Jesus did not just say, "The Truth shall set you free." An incomplete quote. The more complete, and thus, meaningful, quote is, "*If you live the truth as I tell you,* you will know the Truth, and the Truth will set you free."

Brian lives his Truth. He is an extraordinary, ordinary man

with the courage to live his Truth. He does not seek attention, neither does he avoid it. He is funny, outgoing, and so very easy to be with. I offered to write this introduction for Brian's book because I consider it very important that you, the reader, connect with the type of man he truly is. This is no pious, holier than thou, man. This is a robust, laughing, chuckling man who makes a joke of his deep and wonderful relationship with Harry. Harry, you might ask; who is Harry?* Jesus H. Christ! Remember him? Brian has this irreverent, yet utterly devoted and loving relationship with a living Jesus that, to me, is totally unique. I have grown to love Brian, to believe in him, and to deeply respect his lifetime journey with his very dear friend, Jesus.

Brian is very real, connected with Heaven and Earth. This is rare. Read his book, enrich your life, smile often, and grow in awareness of spiritual reality.

Michael J. Roads, Queensland, Australia.
Author, *Through the Eyes of Love; Book One*
Through the Eyes of Love; Book Two,
Through the Eyes of Love, Book Three
A Glimpse of Something Greater

---

* Of this reference to me calling Jesus 'Harry', a word of explanation seems warranted as to how this came about:

During the 1948 Presidential election campaign, Harry Truman delivered a speech attacking the Republicans. During the speech a supporter yelled out "Give 'em Hell, Harry!" Truman replied, "I don't give them Hell. I just tell the truth about them and they think it's Hell." Subsequently, "Give 'em Hell, Harry!" became a lifetime slogan for Truman supporters.

When Theresa and I study *A Course in Miracles* together, and come to any bit that is soaringly beautiful, inspiring, uplifting, enlightening, affirming, I say, "Give 'em **Heaven**, Harry." Since many in the military (and elsewhere) use the expletive 'Jesus H. Christ!' the name Harry seems, tongue-in-cheek, appropriate, and is used with love, honour, respect. — B.L.

PREFACE

We are all, every living soul in this earthly life, *Citizens of Eternity, sojourning in time*. Most of us have become so engaged in the 'sojourning in time' part of this Truth that we have forgotten the *Citizens of Eternity* part of it. Happy is the soul who chooses to commence, here in the earthly life, a journey back into remembrance of who he (or she) *really* is. This is a journey that can begin at any age and at any moment. All that is required in order for it to begin is to *choose* it, and that choice will be determined by the *desire*. If the soul truly and earnestly *desires* to begin that wonderful, adventure-ful journey, there will be a longing in the heart, which is the seat of the soul; a tugging at the heart-strings for an awakening to an awareness and experience of that 'something beyond' that has been lacking thus far from their sojourn in time.

"nothing from the Source of All will coerce any of us into embarking upon a journey for which we are not yet ready."

Once that desire rises to the surface of the consciousness, the step that will begin that journey is the active making of a conscious, committed *choice* for it to begin; for nothing from the *Source of All* will coerce any of us into embarking upon a journey for which we are not yet ready. No other *outward* action needs to be taken, for that act of choosing, triggered by the heart's desire, will set in motion the cosmic process which will *automatically* begin our unique, individual, personal journey. This has nothing to do with our Earth-mind understanding, but is of the Life Force, which is pure Spirit – the very Life Essence of the Creator – and cannot be controlled or manipulated by physical, mental or emotional acts of ego self-will. From then, our Higher Self, which is one with the Spirit of Truth, or Holy Spirit, and has mostly lain quiescent during our Earth-consciousness waking hours, will begin to become active in the events of the Earth physical and mental awareness. This will be experienced in various ways, including events of synchronicity.

The beginner will soon start to see things from a new perspective, and wonder why he never before noticed them, in the way that he now suddenly does. There will be dreams of a type not previously experienced, and gradually, imperceptibly, as a plant growing, the 'pilgrim' will begin to find that his whole awareness, life, experience, understanding is undergoing a metamorphosis. This can be a new and strange experience – and for some, a trepidatious one. Let such nascent travellers on the road back to our true home – Eternity – take comfort in the certainty that the Source of All, the Creator Spirit, God, is benign, unconditional, *Perfect* Love. In truth there is actually nothing to fear but fear itself. The Bible is full of loving admonition along the lines *Fear not, all is well*. Jesus constantly exhorted his followers and the people of his time in this manner. As the wise adage says, *Fear knocked at the door; faith answered and there was no-one there.*

Another well-known saying is apposite for such a momentous time in any person's life: *When the student is ready, the teacher comes.* For the reality is that we are all, without exception, lovingly and caringly watched over by and from the Realms of Light. Psalm 139 speaks of this at length and most poetically . . .

> *O Lord thou hast searched me and known me. Thou knowest my downsitting and mine uprising, thou understandest my thought afar off. Thou compassest my path and my lying down and art acquainted with all my ways. For there is not a word in my tongue but lo, O Lord, thou knowest it altogether. Thou hast beset me behind and before and laid thine hand upon me . . .*

* * *

That which follows is the story of one such Citizen of Eternity who, from an early stage on his sojourn in time, began to have glimmerings of that 'something beyond'. He went through periods of trying to ignore it – trying to 'hide amongst the trees of the garden' – but he felt the call, deep within himself, and knew that in truth there was really nowhere to hide; that the *All-Seeing One* was everywhere. Apprehensive as this made him, he knew there was no alternative but to come out and face the reality of which the Spirit of Truth was whispering into his awakening mind: *It's time to begin the journey, the quest for Eternal Truth.*

"Then will begin a journey, an adventure,
which will surpass all our imagining
by its sheer, glorious, wonderful magnificence."

In all outward appearances nothing particular marks him out from the rest of us, and this is clearly portrayed in his narrative. The fact is that we are all actually *far more* remarkable than almost all of us are aware. The reason for this is that we are all God's children, *created in His likeness.* What could possibly be more remarkable than that? When Jesus said '. . . *the works that I do shall he (who believes) do also, and greater works than these shall he do . . .'* (John 14:12) he was speaking prophetically. At some deep level, that still, small voice within us all is calling. If we hear that voice and, in faith and trust, open the door, in will come the Spirit of Truth and fellowship with us. *Then will begin a journey, an adventure, which will surpass all our imagining by its sheer, glorious, wonderful magnificence.* On this journey we may not always be comfortable, but we will never be bored. And it will go on, becoming step by step more joyful, fulfilling and rewarding . . . unto all Eternity.

---

* Wherever the male gender is referred to in a manner such as this, Ladies, please be assured that the female of the species is always similarly and equally intended for inclusion throughout this writing; that the masculine pronoun is used for brevity and language-flow and that no discrimination or bias is intended against the female gender.

INTRODUCTION

This, being a somewhat unconventional story, calls for a somewhat unconventional introduction. It has been my observation over many years that Jesus of Nazareth and the vast, fractured, schism-ridden institution that has arisen purporting to be in his name has been perceived in a number of different ways by humanity at large. Having considered how best to express this observation, it seems apposite to do so by way of an allegory.

This allegory was given to me inspirationally in a manner with which I was previously familiar: I was awakened in the small hours of the night and heard the words being spoken. They were so imaginatively impressed into my mind that I was easily able to write them, verbatim, after waking several hours later, well after dawn had broken. Here it is:

The Caterpillars and the Butterfly

An allegory of human spiritual life.

There lived in a beautiful garden large numbers of a particular creature who crawled about, eating the vegetation, perceiving themselves on the one hand as being superior to all the other creatures in the garden and yet on the other hand perceiving themselves as lowly, wretched and unworthy of being loved. They had many mythologies, and squabbled endlessly about whose mythology was the only right one, which caused many rifts, divisions and schisms between them.

"not only was he the light but they also were the light"

One day a beautiful butterfly came into their presence, soaring in the sunlight, radiating magnificent rainbow-colours from his wings; so much so that he was seen as the Light of the

1

World. Wherever he went he attracted followers, who marvelled at his magnificence and the wonders he performed in their midst. He spoke in a way they had never heard before. He told them that not only was he the light but they also were the light; that the wonders he performed, they also would perform – and even greater things – if only they could believe. He said he was their brother and, in reality, they also were beautiful butterflies, capable of soaring in the light and radiating magnificent rainbow colours. He also said they need not concern themselves with all their mythologies and divisions; they are merely asked to love the Creator and each other as themselves.

Many believed what he said, but others scoffed at his words. The scoffers said among themselves, "He says he is our brother, yet it is evident there is nothing remotely similar between him and us; he has only six legs and two wings and lives on ambrosia, whereas we have many legs, no wings and eat the vegetation. Clearly he is off his head and has no idea what he is talking about."

Even those who believed him didn't fully understand him and instead perceived him and worshipped him as a God, saying they were still lowly, wretched and unworthy of being loved . . . and he was high and exalted and eternally beyond anything they could ever dream of being.

Nevertheless, he told them that if they could imagine his words were like bread, and the love that he outpoured upon them was like wine, they could imbibe this as sustenance at a higher level of vibration than the vegetation they believed was their source of life and nourishment. This would then enable them to see themselves as they saw him, and the higher vibration would transform them, too, from within themselves, into magnificent, soaring butterflies. He also shared another analogy to help them grasp this enlightened understanding: that he was as a vine, tended in the garden by the good husbandman, and that if they could imagine themselves as being branches in the vine, they could draw their uplifting life energy through him, thereby enabling them to fulfil their own glorious, radiant potential.

Many did as he said, but because the light of their inner awareness was dim, they were only able to follow his guiding as an outward ritual. Only very few were able to discern the spiritual reality within his stories. Those who did went by themselves, or perhaps with one or two of their closest, most trustworthy friends, into a secret place, away from the clamour of the world around them, wherein they contemplated his words deeply within their hearts and minds – just as he had counselled them – and gave thanks for all the wondrous gifts he had brought into their lives. In the silence of their own within they received the enlightenment he had promised that was sustenance for their souls, and this enabled them to see themselves just he had said they would.

Those who were only able to perceive his words at an outer, ritualistic level began to quarrel amongst themselves as to who was the greatest among them, or whose interpretation of his words was the most accurate. They made ever greater numbers of rules and doctrines about these interpretations, even though the butterfly had plainly said there were only two 'rules'. This caused further divisions between them. Some broke away from the group structure that had been established in his name, claiming the group no longer truly represented him and his teaching, and was full of corruption and self-serving. In time there arose squabbling even within the breakaway groups, causing yet further divisions. All these groups and the breakaway groups called themselves the *This* denomination or the *That* denomination and even though their holy writings told them that their Creator had called them by their name, all these breakaway groups had chosen to de-nominate themselves.

All the squabbling over who was right and who was wrong in their understanding of the butterfly's wisdom caused many of the creatures – who had at first enthusiastically joined the groups set-up in his name because the stories about him seemed so resonant with their hearts and minds – to become disillusioned with the groups, and they stopped attending their meetings.

Some of those who stopped attending decided that the whole story could not be true and went back to eating the vegetation, and even any old, decaying matter they found in the garden, embracing any elaborate theories placed before them by those who posited a 'better idea' than the butterfly (or those who claimed to be representing him). This led to more and more confusion in the garden and more and more division among the creatures.

Those who had never believed the butterfly (or the groups who claimed to be representing him) said to those who had left the representative groups, or who moved from one group to another, vainly seeking a more perfect portrayal of the butterfly, "We told you so; it was all too far fetched to be plausible in the first place."

But those few who were able to see past the imagery of the butterfly's stories to the truth they contained, and followed his advice to enter alone, or in groups of only two or three, into a secret place, and there to attune with him, and he would be there in their midst, found that his words took on a level of meaning that brought his wisdom into a new dimension of reality for them. This enabled them, in their own inner discernment, to enter into a place of being just as he had described. There they found an inward peace, joy, love, tranquillity and spiritual illumination of the eternal realities, about which the butterfly had spoken, that was far, far beyond anything to be found in the groups who had de-nominated themselves.

* * *

Of course we all know what happens to caterpillars. They eventually stop eating the vegetation, enter alone into a secret place, away from the clamour of the world around them, and there, in the solitariness of their own within, recreate themselves in the image and likeness of the Butterfly. Then they emerge and soar magnificently in the sunlight, radiating glorious rainbow colours for all to see. They live off ambrosia, giving thanks, by virtue of their very beauty, to the Creator for the joy and wonder of Life.

* * *

This allegory of the Life of Humanity indicates that the spiritual awakening of mankind is barely begun, other than for a precious few, who long ago entered into their secret place, within, just as the Master counselled. However, we are now in the most exciting moment in the history of humanity, when an exponential increase is taking place in the numbers of those who are entering in and are recreating themselves from the within into the without into glorious, fully spiritually awakened, soaring Beings of the Light.

Those who have faithfully followed Jesus of Nazareth through the many denominational church institutions see these realities

4

from the perspective presented by them. These organisations have compiled closely formatted and structured forms of words and procedures that serve their perceptions, and they maintain rigid, tightly controlled dogmas and doctrines based on Scriptures that have been altered many times, by people with their own ego-driven agendas, over the millennia since Jesus walked the Earth. Reincarnation, for instance, as a belief system was removed from Church Canon in 553 CE at the Second Council of Constantinople by the then Christian Church authorities. There have been numerous other additions, deletions and alterations before and since, which in combination, have drastically altered much of the original message of Jesus as presented by scripture and the religious denominations established in his name.

Yet Jesus wasn't rigid in the way he spoke of the Kingdom of Heaven. He constantly spoke in parables – allegories – which he knew would be interpreted by each individual according to where he was on the path of Spiritual awakening back to the reality of Eternity, and that is just as he intended it because that is the nature of parables, or allegories, and it served his objectives well to teach in this manner. Any individual who is sincere in his commitment to spiritual truth will, during a lifetime, undergo an evolutionary process in his understanding of the meaning of any of these parables. This clearly indicates that to have rigid dogmas and doctrines on any aspect of Truth, or the teachings of the Master Jesus, is of the intellect, not of the Christ-Mind awareness, and is not serviceable to the spiritual awakening of the mind of the individual, from its own within, where it makes its connection with the Creator, in Whose likeness we are created. As the apostle Paul puts it: *Not that we are sufficient of ourselves to think any thing as of ourselves; but our sufficiency is of God; Who also hath made us able ministers of the new testament; not of the letter, but of the spirit: for the letter killeth, but the spirit giveth life* (2 Cor. 3:5-6).

Jesus was unequivocal about entering alone into the 'closet' for communion with the Father and that when two or three were gathered in his (Jesus') name he would be there in the midst with them. It is in the interest of many religious institutions to promote the perception that congregations should be as large as possible, for pecuniary, evangelical and doctrinal reasons; but when an individual within such a congregation becomes drawn by the Spirit *within* to enter alone into his closet, and there ponder sincerely and earnestly the true, mystical dimensions of life, he will begin to receive illumination direct from the Spirit of Truth. Such a seeker will experience there a peace and joy not of this Earth, and will awaken to eternal realities that will place him in the awareness that the congregational churches are no longer able to be the source or channel of his spiritual sustenance because he will have outgrown them. He will also find that they will have no desire to hear of his inward, mystical experiences.

"we will do greater things – if only we can believe"

Jesus was also unequivocal that we are (all) the light of the world and that the things he did, we – if only we can believe – will do also, and greater things. He came to remind us of this eternal truth and to demonstrate it, so that we would have a living example – a template – of the magnificence of our true, spiritual being to follow and emulate.

It is inevitable that this will happen eventually to us all because that is our fundamental, essential nature, having been created in the likeness of the Creator. Within us is a spark of God Awareness that was given to us at our creation, and this spark, like a seed, contains the complete blueprint of and for all that we have the potential to become. It is only a matter of when, rather than if, that we move back into full awareness, remembrance, of that. We are all at free choice to begin to make that journey at any time, including right NOW.

In writing the story of one's own experiences one is open to allegations of arrogance, vivid imagination and bias. There will be those amongst the readers of this story who will say this is an affront to Christianity. There are those (and I have received many messages to this effect) who will say this has opened their eyes to a greater truth about Jesus of Nazareth, who have been searching for some more realistic, meaningful representation of who he really is than has for centuries been portrayed by orthodox religion. There will be others who cannot decide.

Into whichever category you fall, I ask of you two things: 1) Please listen to your *heart* and your *feelings* as you read. Your heart and your feelings are your soul, your higher, true Self speaking, communicating with you. If your heart and soul resonate with this story, you will feel good about it. Some may find that they feel good about some parts of the story and not so good about other parts. 2) Please read the *whole* story before deciding.

In December 1995, I was given this message by Jesus:

". . . Be not surprised that many souls are lost,* for the light of my spirit was deliberately snuffed out from the Church of Earth by those who sought riches of Earth before riches of eternity. But it is not possible for the Father's purposes to fail, and the light shall be shone in the dark places until all the shadows of death and fear shall have fled away. Rejoice greatly at this, my beloveds, and sing the New Song, that my little ones may hear, and dance the dance of freedom. That which I have purposed in you shall prosper according to the wisdom of the Father. Be not anxious for any detail; all is well."

After this, any doubts I may have entertained about whether to proceed with making public the message that this account of my experiences places before you, the reader, must be removed from serious consideration. This writing is my rendition of the New Song. May it produce a pleasing, informative, enlightening counterpoint with renditions of the New Song by other singers.

You will see that this message, above, and the various messages received from the Realms of Light that are recorded in this story tend to reflect a mode of speech similar to that of the King James (KJV) Bible. I have been asked why such should be the case and conclude 1) that will not actually be the case between dwellers in the Realms of Light, because communication between ascended, enlightened beings can best be described as telepathic, or mind-to-mind communing; or better yet, simply, of one mind; 2) it is a way of communicating with those of us here in time and place that has many qualities that are serviceable (at least to me!) to clarity of understanding, with careful use of words to convey concise meaning, whereas today, language and grammar usage has tended to become somewhat less so, so people don't always say what they mean or mean what they say (is it any wonder, therefore, that the world is at loggerheads!?); 3) I love the poetry of the KJV Bible, (whose New Testament was almost a direct copy from the William Tyndale New Testament translation of one hundred years earlier); 4) because I grew up with the KJV Bible and used it subsequently for study purposes, it is a mode with which I am both familiar and very comfortable.

Our guides, teachers, loved-ones and inspirers in the Realms of Light are always concerned for our peace of mind and wellbeing, and so I believe this is a. for the comfort of the person (me) experiencing the encounter, and b. the way that which is being sent is received and translated through the filtering mechanism of my mind. My awareness of such communications has undergone somewhat of a metamorphosis in the last few years and the Tudor-style English has substantially diminished, save when sometimes employed to make a particular point or convey levity suitable for the moment.

Nevertheless, in late 2005, a few months after substantially completing this writing, I was brought to *A Course in Miracles* (ACIM), a book dictated by the Master Jesus to Helen Schucman, and have been deeply and profoundly moved at finding that the form of language the Master has used with me over the decades (see 'Diary of a Christ Communicant' at www.honest2goodness. org.uk) is similar in many respects to the language structure used by him in dictating ACIM. It is also equally clear and deeply and profoundly affirming and validating that the message of ACIM is broadly reflected in the events, experiences and messages that have filled so much of my life's Path since the 1960s.

In the section at the back of ACIM entitled "Clarification of Terms: 5. Jesus – Christ" it says:

"Is he [Jesus] God's only helper? No, indeed. For Christ takes many forms with different names until their oneness can be recognized. But Jesus is for you the bearer of Christ's single message of the Love of God. You need no other. It is possible to read his words and benefit from them without accepting him into your life. Yet he would help you a little more[t] if you will share your pains and joys with him, and leave them both to find the peace of God. Yet still it is his lesson most of all that he would have you learn and it is this:
There is no death because the Son of God is like his Father.

Nothing you can do can change Eternal Love. Forget your dreams of sin and guilt, and come with me instead to share the resurrection of God's Son. And bring with you all those whom he has sent to you to care for as I care for you."

The whole 'question of Jesus' and how he is represented – both to existing believers and to non-believers – can be and often is, in today's world, a contentious issue, frequently causing disagreement. Almost any formulaic representation will be disagreeable in one respect or another to one person or group, or another. It is my profound hope that at least some parts of this writing will be helpful and meaningful to each reader and that even if other parts are not, that those parts that *are* beneficial will have made the reading worthwhile. May the *Source of All* inspire and illumine your heart and mind as you read, so that you might be helped to find the way on your own path to Eternal Reality within these pages.

– Brian Longhurst

---

* It should be noted here that this is not indicating that such souls are 'lost' for all eternity, but simply that they have lost their way on the Path back Home to Eternity, or Heaven.

† In reality, an *immeasurable* amount more.

Our birth is but a sleep and a forgetting:
The Soul that rises with us, our life's Star,
Hath had elsewhere its setting,
And cometh from afar:
Not in entire forgetfulness,
And not in utter nakedness,
But trailing clouds of glory do we come
From God, who is our home.

From "Ode: Intimations of Immortality"
William Wordsworth   1770-1850

Part One

1: Early Days and a New Beginning

I was born into a multi-generational farming family the day before D-Day, 1944. My father, Pop, worked for his dad for several years after he and my mother, Ma, were married before he eventually took various jobs on other farming estates. In the late 1940s he became manager of a dairy and arable farm on Ashdown Forest in Sussex. We lived there for seven years. It was an idyllic environment for my brothers and me to grow up in; we had seven thousand acres of backyard for us and our imaginations to run free – the farm plus all the rest of Ashdown Forest – exploring the woods, streams, lakes and wildlife.

During our time at Old Lodge Farm, as it was named, I had a number of experiences which I did not understand at the time but which I now see were prophetic. One was a dream, which came over and over, on multiple occasions during our time there. In it there was a tube, similar in shape and size to a toothpaste tube. The top was screwed on tightly. I knew, in some inner-knowing way, that if the top was ever opened, the contents would get out and this would cause death and destruction wherever it went, and there would be little anyone could do to stop it. This caused me great concern in the dream.

Needless to say, the top *was* opened and out came a 'worm' of what looked to all intents and purposes like toothpaste. It kept coming and coming endlessly, mile after mile, 'worming' its way all over the countryside and all over the world, and everything it touched was contaminated, defiled or destroyed, whether plant, animal, soil or anything. It was unstoppable, and nobody was able to put the lid back on. At the age of about six or eight, I had no knowledge of Greek mythology and had never heard of Pandora's Box, but truly this was its equivalent, in tube form.

In the early 1950s, the age of petrochemical agriculture (and petrochemical just-about-everything-else) had barely begun, and had as yet made little perceptible impact upon the environment. The intervening years have seen such pervasive contamination of and damage to the ecosphere of Earth by man-made molecules and other destructive activities of mankind that many scientists and environmentalists believe we are on the brink of global catastrophe. Increasing numbers of ordinary citizens, I amongst them, share this view, but those who have assumed authority over us in the form of the world's governments are still being much too slow to listen and respond actively to the wishes of the people, even in – and perhaps especially – the so-called democracies.

Nevertheless, there is much good news in this regard, for many environmentally-damaging chemicals *have* been withdrawn and this is prompting many new and environmentally-compatible, sustainable approaches to crop-production and other endeavours of man. These are starting to come to the forefront of human awareness and this is showing signs of beginning to accelerate at an exponential rate.

Another 'inexplicable' happening, which came from somewhere very deep within me, was an upwelling soul-awareness of the great, cosmic, universal, creative, intelligent Force, or Being, communing with me. This was intangible, invisible, but built up palpably inside me repeatedly every few months – over a period of several years – until I felt It was silently calling me, filling my every sense to the point where all else was subordinated by it. The only way I could satisfyingly respond to this calling was to go up into the woods, away from all other human contact, and reach upwards to heaven, not just physically with my arms but with my heart and soul, crying out to It to bring understanding of what this was all about, seeking to enter into a state of never-ending union with It.

All things that were of the 'Earth mind consciousness of humanity' were impediments, somehow getting in the way of this communion, and I had to separate myself from them, including the very clothes on my body. I would stand there, 'alone', naked, reaching out in body and soul, heart bursting for oneness; tears of wonderment, joy, love, *longing* pouring down my cheeks, calling out to this Universal Life Force that was invisibly, lovingly embracing me, drawing me upwards into Itself, overwhelming me with Its Love that was far, far beyond the understanding of this pre-pubescent boy. Eventually – after perhaps half an hour, maybe more – the great, insatiable yearning inside me would slowly subside, if never fully, at least to a level where I could 'rejoin the world' of what I now realise is illusory, consensus reality, until the whole process started and built up to a crescendo once more. I have no recollection of just how many times this took place, but it was numerous. It was only in later years, after I began to understand more about the eternal nature of the human spirit and its relationship with the Creator Spirit that I have gradually come to know more of what this was all about. No doubt there is still much more awareness to come as my understanding of eternity continues to grow toward fullness of spiritual awakening.

WE LEFT THE FARM in 1955 and moved into town when Pop took a job selling organic seaweed products to the farming community. Within a few years Pop became the star salesman for the Seaweed Agricultural business. I remember thinking at that time – the late 1950s – 'Whatever happens, I will *never* become a seaweed salesman'. I was embarrassed to tell my peers what my dad did for a living. Yet, little did I know how this perception was to alter and affect the direction of my life not many years later.

IN 1960, AGED SIXTEEN, and with a handful of 'O' Level certificates from school, I got a job as an office boy in an advertising agency in London. For several years I commuted daily on the train to work, lost in the ordinariness and routine of it all, but observing how others much my elder had been doing this for perhaps decades. The thought of that becoming my reality was anathema and I resolved to make a change, somehow, anyhow.

Ma's best friend, who was also my Godmother, had married a Canadian, and after the war moved with him to Vancouver. The thought of going there, getting away from the familiar circumstances and influences that I felt were dragging me into their carousel of sameness and repetition, began to build in me. By summer 1963 I had decided this was a way forward; an 'escape to freedom'; freedom to discover the 'real me' hiding deep inside, that was in danger of inexorably becoming smothered by other people and the influence that their perceptions of what life was all about was subtly having upon me. Somehow, I knew there was more to life than all that and I had to get away in order to make a fresh start, with a clean slate, to discover what was really deep within me, seeking to come out.

"I was floating in the air above and slightly behind a young man. I knew that young man was me."

IN APRIL 1964, AS I STOOD on the deck of the Cunard Line's S.S. *Carmania* waving goodbye to Ma and Pop on the quay far below at Southampton dock, watching them slowly recede into the distance as we pulled out into deep water, I found myself looking down, from a state of complete peace, calm and inner knowing, at a young man, about ten feet below me. I was floating in the air above and slightly behind him. I knew that young man, not yet twenty years old, was me. *How could this possibly be?* At that time I knew nothing of out-of-body experiences, and had no idea what this ship-board event of seeing 'me' from outside myself was all about, and even less idea how much this was a portent of the great mystical and spiritual journey that lay before me.

Yes, I had read the Denis Wheatley novels about psychic matters, resonated with the sense they made to my mind and to my 'inner knowing'; I had dabbled with Ouija boards, through which there had been many communications from 'beyond' which all made perfect sense and which I accepted as a matter of fact, even though some souls in this earthly life warned of the danger of such activities and how they invited dark and satanic consequences. But the communications I had received were all from entirely benign, kindly, well-meaning, good-humoured souls, and I felt no sense of threat, evil or 'the slippery slope to hell', although I do not doubt that such is the experience of others who have similarly dabbled. (This is not intended to be either a recommendation for or a condemnation of Ouija boards; we all have God-given free will to choose, although the advice that has served me well through the decades is, *If in doubt, do nothing.*)

If anything, these experiences had strengthened my sense

of matter-of-fact acceptance of the reality of Eternity and my place – indeed, the place of all humanity – within it. I had had a terrible, breath-taking, heart-stopping fear of death during much of my teen years. The word *death*, it seemed to me, indicated the complete end of life and consciousness, bringing only darkness, silence, emptiness, nothingness. *Forever.* This frightened me so badly I had palpitations, sweating palms and blurred vision every time I thought about it. Awareness of the reality of life continuing beyond this mortal existence on Earth being made real and tangible, through contact with those in that place beyond, was to me a very acceptable, reassuring, natural, sensible and exciting thing. It opened up possibilities that seemed endless, inspiring and utterly desirable. I was definitely eager to find out more, *experience* more, especially as all such experiences to date had been benign.

From earliest recollections of daily morning assembly at school, during which there were always at least one Bible reading, several hymns and several prayers, including the Lord's Prayer, I had accepted matter-of-factly that Jesus of Nazareth, this historical figure, was 'the Lord of mankind, the Son of God, the Christ' (whatever *that* meant); that the miracles he performed were real events – including his own resurrection – and that the God of Abraham, Isaac and Jacob was the one and only, true God of all creation. But this was somehow separate from 'real life' in middle England, where there was beer to be drunk, work to be done (unfortunately), cars to be driven, girls to be wooed, jokes to be shared. So I put God and all His appurtenances 'into a box' and tucked it out of sight, out of harm's way, trying to ignore It (or *Him*, as consensus reality would have it). But *He* never really was quite out of sight, out of mind. He was always there, just slightly out of focus. Well, quite a lot out of focus really, but somehow, never to be totally ignored or forgotten. Not for long anyway.

By about 1963 this 'never quite out of line of sight' God started to move more 'into my face', albeit in a rather indirect way. Right in the middle of the path of life along which I was skipping, blocking my progress so comprehensively that it was no longer dismissible, was this immeasurably large 'billboard', with sky-writingly large letters which read, purely and simply, EITHER THERE IS A GOD OR THERE IS NOT A GOD. This was not God presenting Himself in a confrontational manner. Rather it was, in a sense, me, presenting myself with the age-old question and saying to myself, 'Now is the time to face up to it fairly and squarely; you cannot go on ignoring this all-important issue indefinitely.'

It was axiomatic, incontrovertible – to me anyway – that this God of the Universe IS. I had been trying to live in denial of this, not wishing to be confronted by such an inescapable reality, because acceptance of it would mean that by the standards and values that were a crucial part of my persona, I would require of myself that something meaningful be *done* about it. The frightening question was *What?* Frightening because it would mean, by my then understanding, that I would have to change my lifestyle and *do* something about the fact that this God was not just the God of the Universe but the God of my own, personal life also. That was too close for comfort. After all, if this God had the attributes bestowed upon Him by the perceptions of orthodox religion – He was all-powerful, jealous, wrathful, vengeful, and could squash me like an insect at any moment of His choosing – then I wished to get, and remain, on His 'right side'.

I had no idea how to do this, but again, looking to orthodox consensus for guidance it seemed that the best way to get into God's good books would be to turn my collar round and traipse off to darkest Africa and 'convert the natives'. This may sound glib, pretentious, arrogant, or even, in this time of the new millennium, politically incorrect, but such was my naiveté at the time that I had no other perceptions of how 'serving God' might best be accomplished. However, this prospect did not appeal to me one bit. It did not seem the kind of endeavour with which I felt any resonance whatsoever. Not knowing where to go from there and since by this time I was making arrangements for moving to Canada, that is what I did.

During this several-months-long transitional stage of making the arrangements (writing for jobs, applying for immigration etc.), and then the actual moving from England to Canada, I began reading the Bible, something of which I had not done much in the past. However, I had read enough to know that Jesus was the focal point of the Christian scriptures, so I turned my attention first to the four gospel accounts of his life. This recapitulation seemed to reaffirm my lifelong, unquestioning acceptance that he was the Lord and that the best way to follow/serve God was to follow/serve Jesus. To do this, it seemed logical to get to know him better, and the only way I thought that could be possible was to start going to church again – something I had not done voluntarily since pre-adolescence.

* * *

Having arrived in Vancouver and settled in at my Godparents' house in a suburb called Richmond, in due course I sought out the local Anglican church (after all, being English that seemed the appropriate thing to do!). As I write this, some four decades on, even though I can clearly see the church building in my mind's eye and could no doubt even still find my way there, I can recollect not a single moment or experience inside it. My overall sense is that there was nothing memorable, uplifting or spiritually inspiring about it; not a moment in which I felt actually more in the presence of either Jesus or God within it than when I was away from that building.

After six months the time came for me to branch out on my own and I eventually settled in board and lodgings in Kerrisdale, a middle-class district of south Vancouver. I was still filled with a sense of purpose and commitment to serve God; more than ever, in fact, in spite of the rather non-event experience of attending the church in Richmond. Knowing of no other way to do this than through the church, and having noticed that no more than two or three blocks down the same street from my new accommodation was St Mary's Anglican church, I started attending, with renewed commitment and determination to stick with it. This caused me to soon be recognised as new, young, enthusiastic, committed-to-service blood. I was invited to teach Sunday school to a group of fourteen-year-old boys (no girls; segregation was absolutely the order of the day). This was very much an uphill struggle in which I can make no claim to victory. I was also invited to become a member of the church committee, the voluntary body of congregants who met monthly under the chairmanship of the parish vicar to run the church and all matters to do with it, including the fabric upkeep, maintenance and so on.

I was greatly flattered at this, for I was only twenty years old, a fire burning in me, bright as a magnesium flare, with desire to serve. All the other committee members were at least old enough to be my father and many were easily old enough to be my grandfather. I use the male gender here advisedly as there was not a single female on the committee.

At first I attended these meetings eagerly, anticipating that here, at last, would be that opportunity to serve that my soul had now been craving for the better part of a year. But, to my dismay, there was no spirituality or spiritually-uplifting energy in any of these meetings. They discussed, in an entirely mundane manner only, such matters as the adhesive on the collection-money envelopes, or autumn leaves blocking the gutters and what to do about them. Such discussions could easily take an hour to cover one subject, and often with much more heat than light being generated during the proceedings.

Some of the actual services had moments of more spiritual upliftment than at the Richmond church, especially the hymns, many of which did produce a sense of 'communion with my Lord and with my Creator'. There was also, as I recall, a magnificent stained-glass window over the altar, depicting Jesus in a typical scene as recorded in the Gospel accounts. I do not now specifically recall the scene, but it was probably Jesus at the lakeshore. It was a big window and the illustration of Jesus himself, portrayed in a very realistic way, was actually larger than life-size. As I knelt at the altar-rail to receive the bread and wine of Communion, I would look up at this image and in my heart and mind would be with him, in glorious, one-to-one, *personal* fellowship. Such moments of togetherness were sadly short-lived because although I would gladly have spent hours in this moment with my Lord, other communicants were lined-up behind me to take my place at the rail. I found it difficult to have and to develop a personal relationship with Jesus whilst in the midst of several hundred other congregants, some of whom were coughing, some snoring, some laughing and playing about, and all of whose presence were somehow inhibiting my ability to enter into my closet and fellowship with him there, an experience for which my heart ached interminably.

The overall church experience was immeasurably less inspiring, uplifting, fulfilling or spiritually rewarding than I had envisaged as the anticipated route to oneness with God, and the writing was on the wall that the parting of the ways was not far off. This was sealed when, after missing church for some weeks (having by now moved to accommodation somewhat more distant), I eventually received a phone call from another parishioner.

"Brian," he said, "where have you been? I have been trying to reach you for weeks now. I need to know how much money you are going to give to the church during the coming twelve months."

Roy, the fellow parishioner, made no enquiry for my well-being, either physical or spiritual. The sole interest was money. This accurately reflected my perception of the spirit of the church, whose annual outgoings – including stipends and all fabric costs – were $40,000 per annum and whose annual income was $80,000.

My perception, caused not just by this one event but many others where parishioners were given what was tantamount to *instruction* in how much to give, was that the church was obsessive about money. How far is the church – generally – from the counsel of him whom they claim to be following: "Seek ye first the Kingdom of God and His righteousness and all things shall be added unto you"? The word 'first' in Jesus' admonition appeared to have failed to find its true significance with those for whom the church was so important in their lives, and it seemed to me that the church had become stuck, in their perception, as *ahead* of God and Jesus in their list of whom or what they were supposed to be faithfully following.

However, unknown to me at that time, my heart's desire for moving closer to God and his Anointed Messenger, Jesus of Nazareth, had not gone unnoticed by *Them.*

Teachers of Sunday school used a teacher's manual to guide the lessons. On one particular Sunday I left my copy at the church hall, only realising it as I got home. *Never mind,* I thought, *I'll pick it up next Sunday; it's bound to be there, in safe hands.* After all, if it wasn't safe in church property, where *would* it be safe!?

---

*"Some invisible force took my hand and with it
lifted a book off a shelf before I even saw it there."*

The next Sunday, astonishingly, it was nowhere to be found. Incredibly, there was not a single spare copy in the spare copies cupboard. There was nothing for it but to go to the Bible Bookshop downtown and buy another copy. No problem; the bookshop was on the same street as my office, just a few blocks away. Midweek, I walked there at lunchtime and bought a copy from the kindly lady who ran the shop. We chatted cordially for some time. Suddenly I realised it was time to get back to work, and headed for the door.

As I passed a book case near the exit some invisible force took my hand and with it lifted a book off a shelf practically before I even saw it there. It was called *Between Time and Eternity.* This pushed some buttons deep within me. Anything to do with Eternity, I wanted to hear about it. The dust jacket described the author as a Yorkshire woman who had begun life as an orthodox churchgoer and who had started having unsought experiences of contact from the spirit world. She was taken out of the body to places and events in various parts of the planet about which she subsequently read in *Illustrated London News* and elsewhere. These, and other evidence of the power and authority of those in charge of these events, led her to come to trust them, one of whom introduced himself as her Teacher and instructed her in many matters, all to do with Christian mysticism.

I said to the shopkeeper, "This looks fascinating, just up my street." I looked at the price and counted my money. I had less than was needed to buy it so I said, "I'll come back for it another day."

The lady looked deep into my soul for one of those timeless moments, and I could see she was trying to assess my honesty.

"Go on, take it; you look trustworthy. Read it. If you like it and want to keep it, come back and pay me. If you don't want to keep it, bring it back and no-one has lost anything."

She would have none of my protestations that I couldn't possibly do this, that it wouldn't be right. She told me as a parting comment that the author lived in Vancouver.

One evening after work a little while later, I picked up the book and could not put it down until it was nearly finished but my eyelids were so heavy I just had to sleep – if only I could, so excited was I by her story.

I hurried back to the bookshop at the first opportunity to pay the lady and ask her how I could contact Olga Park, the author, who did not appear to have a listing in the Vancouver phone directory.

"Oh, that's easy," she said. "My husband used to work at the Post Office with Mrs. Park's son, Robert. We can find him in the phone book and he can direct you to his mother."

This was music to my ears. I had resolved in the small hours, as I read her book, that I would contact her and visit her because my head, my heart, even, so it felt, my big toe, were stuffed with questions I just had to ask her about. I was hungering and thirsting after spiritual knowledge, wisdom, truth and experience and it was evident from Olga Park's writing that she had all these. I wanted to learn from her so much it hurt.

Soon, with information from Robert, I phoned Olga, introduced myself, told her I had read her book and was most interested in meeting her, *as soon as possible*. Not many days later I found myself walking up the wooden steps to the door of her little cottage, twenty miles from Vancouver in the woods round the head of Burrard Inlet, the huge natural harbour at whose mouth Vancouver sits. As I walked up those steps and knocked at her door, a profound peace came upon me. This was a magnificent, enveloping, heavenly peace, not achievable by or from any earthly experience or source. It was a feeling that I had 'come home' to the place where I belonged.

2: A Momentous Rejoining

Olga, aged seventy-four in 1965 when I first met her, had come from Yorkshire, via Birmingham, to Vancouver as a young adult with her family in 1910. In due course she married and gave birth to her son, Robert. During the 1920s she attended St Mary's Anglican Church in Kerrisdale, where she was also the personal assistant to the Rector. They shared many ideals about Christianity and established a close spiritual affinity. After several years she and her husband moved to another area and she lost contact with the Rector, but only at the physical level. He had become ill, largely as a result of his own perceptions about spirituality becoming increasingly at odds with the church, and therefore had taken early retirement. Meanwhile, her own awakening to the realities of the spirit world had been progressing – largely unsought but always inspiring confidence that those who were in charge of her spiritual development were under Christ authority and empowerment.

"Olga had experienced many manifestations of Jesus and others from the Realms of Light"

There was a cordial, easy rapport between Olga and me from the first moments that began a years-long association based on our mutual interest in matters to do with eternal truth, mystical/ spiritual experience and love for the living Jesus.

Olga had experienced many manifestations and one-to-one personal awarenesses of Jesus and others from the Realms of Light – including the man who introduced himself to her as her Teacher – over decades, and she had kept faithful, written records of most of these. These contacts affirmed the experience of reincarnation both verbally and more comprehensively by events in which Olga was either taken out of the body or entered into a state that she described as *the dual consciousness,* in which she was aware of both her physical surroundings and body *and* her soul body – which was having its own, different experience – at the same time.

In 1940 she was taken out of the body by the Teacher to a place like a chalet on a mountainside where the Rector, newly and prematurely passed over, sat in a contemplative state. The Teacher told Olga that the Rector was feeling a great sense that his life had been a failure, and all his desires for bringing awareness of, and love for, the Lord Jesus to his fellows in the Earth life had been to little avail. The Teacher said that he needed reassurance which Olga would be able to give him, and that he would be able to see and talk with her, but not the Teacher. She went to him and they spoke for some while, although she brought through to her waking consciousness no recollection of what had been said. Afterwards, the Teacher told her that her words would be carefully considered by the Rector and, in due course, be beneficial to his going forward.

This indeed proved to be so and before long the Rector came to thank Olga for her assistance and tell her that he had now become closely associated with the Teacher, as his student of the eternal realities of Life, as was the case with Olga but he in the etheric and she in the incarnate realm.

Olga later told me that in October 1943 the Rector had visited her during the night, carrying a tiny baby in his arms, which he presented to her. She had had no idea of the meaning of this experience at the time but I had been conceived about then and it was very evident that he had been responsible for bringing me to the Bible Bookshop and getting her book into my hands, ultimately leading to the crossing – or, more accurately, *converging* – of our paths. In a sense, therefore, it could be said that he had fulfilled this prophetic visit of 1943 some twenty-two years later by arranging the circumstances of my meeting with Olga.

During my association with Olga in the mid-1960s our relationship developed into one whereby we had the mutual perception that she was to me 'Godmother Park'; and in a similar fashion, I felt very much that the Rector was my 'spirit-world Godfather'. I quickly developed a very palpable sense of his presence and his particular vibration, often announced by seeing with my *inner eye* the colour of his personal life-energy – a pale, beryl green. Most evenings there would be telephone conversation between Olga and me and I would often see him listening in, or if not actually see him, smell aromatic pipe tobacco. The first time this happened I asked Olga if the Rector had smoked a pipe during his earthly life and she said, "Yes; how did you know?" Although he had laid aside his earthly body before I had incarnated, I felt a great sense of his closeness and solicitousness for my well-being, and this engendered in me an abiding love for this deeply sincere, gentle, caring and loving man. He was always there for me in times of need or doubt, as well as of joy and celebration, but never intrusively so. In due course he became for me 'the Stalwart', and it is by this nickname that I have often lovingly spoken of and with him.

OLGA SPOKE SO MATTER-OF-FACTLY to me about Jesus as being a real, living, 'today', personal presence in her life; how his love, wisdom, guiding, understanding and protection were so uplifting, restoring, inspiring. No-one in church had ever spoken this way, and I wanted *more*. I couldn't get enough. I visited on Friday straight from work until the small hours, Sunday from early afternoon until late, and often midweek straight from work until the small hours, practically every week. I bombarded her with questions about psychic, spiritual, eternal, mystical, metaphysical, esoteric matters endlessly, and she patiently, lovingly, diligently answered. I soaked-up her words of wisdom like a sponge.

Olga told me some time after our first meeting that as soon as she had closed the door upon my departure on that occasion, the Master immediately said to her, "Speak of me freely and unreservedly to the young man; and so that he return again and again, I will fill his heart with joy beyond the pleasures of Earth." I can affirm that she did, I did and he did!

She had a prayer sanctuary at the cottage and at the end of each visit I went to it with her for prayers. She prayed so easily, spontaneously, conversationally. My prayers were rehearsed, stilted, stumbling. My heart was sincere but my mouth didn't know how to adequately *express* the desire of my heart. Hearing her speak so fluidly about Jesus as the *living* Lord, active in a palpable, tangible, purposeful way in her life and in the life of any who sincerely desired it, caused me to grow to love Jesus in a way and with a depth that the church had not been able to do. This became an all-consuming passion for me; I wanted to *experience* Jesus in my life in the same way Olga clearly was doing.

One night in the autumn of 1966, at her sanctuary prayer table before home-time, Olga said to me, "The Master is here and he is speaking to me a message for you. I will repeat it to you and you can speak with him direct. Any reply he gives, I will relay to you. He is saying to you, 'What is your desire?' "

I was considerably intimidated at this experience of him, whom I had always understood to be the Lord of Life, the King of Love, the Prince of Peace, the Son of God, speaking to me and indeed asking a question that I thought might land me in difficulty if I could not come up with the 'right' answer. Not that he appeared to be speaking in a threatening way, but this was, after all, it seemed to me, the 'boss', and one needed to have the right answers for the boss or there might be trouble. So my naiveté and the doctrines of the church had led me to believe.

I said, very hesitatingly, "To serve you, according to your will," or words to that effect. It was a vague and non-specific statement because I had no specific answer to the question, but I believed the whole objective of 'service' was to do the Will or bidding of the Supreme Being and/or His Anointed Messenger, whatever that Will might be.

His reply was surprising to my young, inexperienced ears (can ears be inexperienced? You know what I mean):

"That is not the purpose of your life and being on Earth. You have come into this world bringing with you potential for accomplishing certain things. My purpose is to assist you and guide you in discovering what your potential is so that it might be developed and fulfilled in your earthly life. Consider this carefully, my son, so that you may become aware of this and grow in your understanding of it, that in the fullness of time you may bear much fruit according to that inward desire and potential."

That, at any rate was the gist of his response and that gist has remained with me over the years. Here was Jesus, the Exalted One, saying that *his* job was to assist *me*. I had never heard anyone in the church say anything like this. It was startling in its contrast to all my previous understandings of the relationship of us 'mortal' folk to Jesus, the Christ of God. And yet, somehow, this explanation made so much sense that I could find no argument with it. When you think about it, he is much better equipped to help us than we, him. It was a landmark for me and really cemented my commitment to sticking close to Olga, because this was really 'where it was at'. She had a direct line to Jesus and this was ample evidence of that.

My visits to her cottage continued. She seemed to be a fount of spiritual wisdom, and it was mother's milk to my soul. Her speaking about Jesus cultivated in me a desire to *experience* his livingness as she experienced it. To me, it had become one thing to *know* about him, read about what he said and did, the way he won people's lives, loyalty and devotion in the long ago, and to accept and live, or desire to live, according to his example and the teachings recorded of him in the Gospel accounts. But for me that was like falling in love with some film actress or other, distant, remote person, with whom there could be no touching, holding, exchange of loving expression; no consummation of one's heart's desire for *experiencing* the energy, the aura, the living spirit, the vibration of the pulsing, dynamic Life Force of that person. I craved all of this with Jesus; to have a *truly* personal, intimate, meaningful relationship with him became my all-consuming, active, aching desire.

In my basement lodgings every night I would kneel at my bedside and open my heart to him; tell him of my love for him, my yearning desire to experience his livingness in my life; close, tender, loving, guiding, whatever . . . but *real* to *me* as distinct from second-hand accounts of *someone else's* experience of him.

This must have gone on night after night for months; I do not recall now how long but I do recall very clearly the aching in my heart and soul for this and how it grew until it was almost beyond endurance. Then, on the 24th of January, 1967, after my nightly outpouring, I began to prepare for bed. As I stood in the middle of the room, suddenly he was there, in the corner, manifested, superimposed in the place where stood a beechwood chest of drawers with a mirror on top. He was in the midst of an aura of golden, living sunlight, which radiated out from him more than an arm's length in all directions. He was about three or four paces from me.

As I became aware of his presence he began to move toward

me. It was not a walking movement. He seemed to be above the floor a few inches, and he glided. The movement was relatively slow, certainly unhurried, but as he drew nearer he began to speak. I *heard* him with my ears, I *experienced* his speaking with my soul, with my heart; every cell in my body and every fibre of my being experienced his speaking. There was no part of my being that did not hear him. And every part of my being understood with a total certainty the meaning, at a soul-knowing level rather than an intellectual-knowing level of understanding, what was the true, mystical meaning of those words. The words that he spoke were, I discovered later, from Revelation, chapter 3, verse 20: "Behold, I stand at the door, and knock: if any man hear my voice, and open the door, I will come in to him, and will sup with him, and he with me."

To the best of my knowledge I had not read or heard those words before – so I discovered later – but at that moment they were a timeless part of my being and I knew exactly what they meant because his imparting to me of the words also imbued my mind with the meaning and understanding of them – *his* meaning of them. By the time he had finished speaking he had reached less than an arm's length from where I was standing. His aura of golden, living sunlight had enveloped me, and the feeling of Love – of *agapé* – to my being was so intense, so powerful, so uplifting to my spirit that I felt as if my heart had grown to the size of a football and was going to burst out of my chest cavity. This feeling of all-pervasive, all-inclusive Love was complete, permeating not just my body but my entire aura in an orgasm of the soul, immeasurably more intense than any such physical experience. I was blinded by a waterfall of joyful, rapturous tears and every part of me was alive, electrified, as never before.

His presence was visible in the midst of the light of his aura, which was at least as bright as the sun but did not hurt my eyes at all. With me now fully enveloped by his aura, he stopped. His eyes were radiating the all-knowing wisdom of the ages, and love; personal love as well as universal, unconditional Love. I knew he loved me personally, in a way and with a Love that is utterly beyond any love I had ever known, heard about or experienced in this world. He embraced me, not with his physical arms but with every part of his being – with his total, unconditional, intimate, penetrating, all-encompassing, all-pervasive Love. I was a quivering jelly. Not from fear (how could fear exist in such an exquisitely beautiful, magnificent encounter?) but from being overwhelmed by the power of his Love. The moment of this embrace seemed to be timeless but was probably a few seconds of Earth-time. I remember reading at some later date, in the book of Revelation, chapter 1 verse 16, "... *and his countenance was as the sun shineth in his strength*" and saying to myself, "That is an exact and perfect description of his appearance."

Then the manifestation gradually withdrew and disappeared from my sight. But the power and sense of his presence that was left with me, in me, lasted for at least an hour, probably two. I have never taken any form of hallucinogenic or consciousness-expanding drug, but I have no shred of doubt that this feeling was a 'high' beyond that capable of being induced by any such substance. I had to physically restrain myself from rushing – more like flying – upstairs, outside, onto the rooftops and calling to all the world, "He's REAL! He's *really* REAL!" even though by this time it was well after midnight.

Eventually I slept.

Next morning I could hardly wait to phone Olga, and could barely contain my excitement as I exclaimed, "Something really wonderful has happened; I simply must come and see you straight away after work today!"

I'm sure she must have been on tenterhooks all day waiting to find out what could possibly have happened to be as exciting as my voice must have conveyed. I know my excitement all day was almost uncontainable. I never at any time said anything to any of my work colleagues, but some few weeks later my boss strolled up the lane with me one lunch hour on our way for a bite to eat together and, to my amazement, very hesitantly he said, "You have really changed recently, Brian; you've become so . . ." he searched for a word to express his meaning, "so . . . spiritual."

I forget how the rest of that conversation went but he appeared to have a sense of awe about him toward the change he discerned in me.

That evening, on the 25th of January, I must have driven at breakneck speed to the cottage and burst in, no doubt like a whirlwind, to Olga. I blurted out the news and described the whole experience, including what the Master had said to me. She became very excited, and to my surprise said, "This is a message."

"I know it's a message," I said, probably sounding slightly irritated at what appeared to be a statement of the obvious.

"No, you don't understand," she said. "This is a message not just for you, but a message also for me," and she became even more excited. "There is something I have never told you. Not because I didn't think about telling you, but because I was never authorised to tell you. But this experience of yours is a message of authorisation to me, to tell you all about this. Now is the time."

She went on to explain that many years ago, after years of contact from, and counselling by, the visitor from spirit who had introduced himself to her as her Teacher, he came to her one night and took her out of the body to a place in spirit that resembled a temple or cathedral.

There, before a gathering of a good many witnesses from the Realms of Light, including the Lord Jesus himself, he had instructed her in a form of service of Holy Communion. He had spoken the words, shown her gestures of the arms and hands, shown her when to stand, when to kneel, when to face toward the altar of Lights and of Bread and Wine of partaking (signifying the addressing of the words the Teacher had given her to speak to the Source of All) and when to face away from it (signifying the addressing of the words to – and the inclusion of – others present, whether in the Earth life or beyond). He showed her how to take the bread and consecrate it by blessing and breaking it, just as Jesus did at the Last Supper, and the words to speak in accompaniment to the actions. He did the same for the consecrating of the 'fruit of the vine'. He gave her words and actions for the partaking of the sanctified bread and non-fermented 'wine' (grape juice) and for the partaking of the same on behalf of and as an offering to others, whether incarnate or discarnate, who 'seek after the Light of the Sanctuary of Christ Communion, and of all who have desired our prayers'.

There was much, much more. He explained to her that this was to be, for her, at least for the time being, a solitary communion at the Earth-life conscious level; that it was and would become for her a Mystical Communion with Christ. He said the spirit light generated by the sincerity of her heart, through the uplifting energies created during the service, would attract many from the realms beyond Earth who were lost in dark and dismal places – the 'Wilderness' – who would find spiritual solace in this celebration event, as well as many from the Realms of Light who were in at-one-ment with its message and the desire conveyed by its words and symbolic gestures.

"It was an act of attunement with the mind and spirit of the living Jesus."

But the central purpose and objective of the ritual in which the Teacher instructed her was that it was to be an exercise in unifying the focus of the heart and mind of the communicant in an act of attunement with the mind and spirit of the living Jesus. The words of the ritual were assembled mostly from the words of King David (Psalms), Isaiah, Jesus (the Gospels), Paul and John of Patmos (Revelation), and linked into a cohesive, structured, progressive format by words given by the Teacher during this out-of-body instruction. There were also inspirational hymns included to add to the conduciveness of getting on a spiritually attuned, Christ-Mind wavelength.

The ritual was designed to enable the communicant to gradually ascend to a place of refined, uplifted attunement, and then to enter into a period of silent communion of heart and mind with the heart and mind of the living Jesus. This is to develop the faculty – dormant in those who have become so engaged in the 'sojourning in time' part of their lives that their physical and spiritual worlds are not in a resonant state of peace, harmony and balance with each other – of entering into the *within* part of their mind, where they will have awareness of and fellowship with the Anointed Messenger of the Holy One. This will bring enlightenment and illumination of the eternal realities, of which Jesus is Master, for the uplifting of all who truly seek after God and earnestly desire the Kingdom of Heaven on Earth.

The communicant can speak with Jesus in their mind and have pen and paper ready for writing his response, which comes into their mind as objectively spoken words; a form of communication described by Olga as the *silent voice*, and which I have latterly come to term *mind-to-mind communing*.

Olga explained to me that the words spoken to me by the Master in my basement room were also part of the service in which she had been instructed. These words are the Master's invitation to all who respond to his knocking at the door of their inner awareness, so that he may enter into their lives and have spiritual fellowship, or 'supping' with them of the Bread, symbol of Eternal Life, and the Wine, symbol of perfect, unconditional, Spiritual Love. This was his message to her that I was ready to be instructed by her in the order and meaning of this service of Mystical Christ Communion.

This she diligently did, and from then I went to her cottage every Sunday morning to participate with her in these Communion Devotions. She explained to me that this was an earthly manifestation of a heavenly 'Society of the Mystical Communion of Christ' or SMCC and it was to have no earthly organisational structure or rules or regulations. It was intended as a focus to assist 'all who will' to enter into a state of at-one-ment with the great desire-thought of Jesus – namely, the Kingdom of Heaven on Earth. This was intended to be a solitary or near-solitary activity, in accordance with Jesus' own teachings that we should enter into our closet and when we are alone, to then pray (Mt. 6:6), and also when two or three are gathered together in his name that he would be there 'in the midst' with them (Mt. 18:20). There would *never* be any outward, organised, institutionalised manifestations of it that could be usurped, manipulated, distorted or perverted for the self-serving ways of those who did not have a heart first and foremost for the Truth of Eternity and the Kingdom of Heaven on Earth.

This, at last, was what my heart had been craving since I had first begun seeking in the 'outer court of the temple' – the church of earthly consciousness – in which gathered multitudes of souls without the light of spiritual discernment. Now at last I felt as if I had been brought to the very entranceway to the 'inner court of the temple', which would enable me to move into a state or place of true and meaningful communion with the King of Love, the Prince of Peace, the Lord of Life; Jesus of Nazareth, the mystical, Anointed Messenger of the Holy One, the great I AM.

3: Stirrings Within

This was not the beginning of my journey back into Oneness with the Creator Spirit because, in the eternal scheme of things, who can say when such a journey actually begins, if in reality it ever has a 'beginning', but it was certainly a way-marker of a major new phase of that journey.

As I became more familiar with the Communion procedure over the ensuing weeks and months, I was able to gradually become more aware of the spiritual 'vibes', or power, created by focusing upon and attuning with it. My awareness of those in spirit, whom Olga called the Inner Plane Servers (IPS) of the Sanctuary of Christ Communion, grew, and as my awareness grew, so did my love for, and trust in, them. There is an indeterminate number of such servers, and names are hardly a priority, but some who were very close to me did get to be known, either by name or by some identifying quality or characteristic.

For example, I became aware that the Server with whom I was most closely and readily in tune, and whom I knew as the Rector, had in fact been the Rector of St Mary's Church, Kerrisdale back in the 1920s and early '30s and had passed away in 1940. I also learned that it was he who had conveniently 'removed' – de-materialised – my Sunday-school teacher's manual from there, knowing that I would have to go to the Bible Bookshop to replace it, and that Olga's book was there in the shop, thus enabling him to bring about my meeting with her. This is one tiny example of the empowerment of the Christ-servers of the Inner Plane Sanctuary for bringing about help, progress and enlightenment of those in the Earth life who are known by the IPS to be ready to go forward on the path of spiritual awakening, even when they, themselves, have no such awareness of that readiness. If ever there was a case of synchronicity, for goodness' sake, this was it!

Over a period of some months I experienced many dreams of a nature that indicated my soul-centres of awareness of non-physical realities were growing, or awakening from a dormant state. Also, subtle nuances of images, moving or still, and sound such as music and speaking, as well as taste and smell, like aromatic pipe smoke, perfume of flowers, the unique, personal scent or auric colour of individuals that would enable them to be identified, were impressing themselves into my extra-sensory awareness. The Rector frequently brought to my mind hymns with significant meaning for any particular moment, event or occasion, most of which I had not heard or sung since school days.

The majority of these awarenesses were so subtle that one might be tempted to question whether they even happened, but I learned that if one dismisses such as 'not having actually happened', which most people are prone to do, then there follows a sense of regret at having done so, and the impression fades away, whereas, if one accepts that it *did* happen, the awareness of the event grows, and details, meaning and understanding of the event grow with it. I liken it to photography. If a light-sensitive film is exposed to an image, the image is imprinted on the film, but if the film is not 'fixed' with a chemical solution, it fades away and is lost. Fixing, however, causes the image to become permanently ingrained into the film for longer-term study and consideration. Details not at first perceived in the image then become apparent with extended study.

If a person continually dismisses the awareness of faint impressions on their senses, the facility for receiving those impressions becomes, or remains, dormant; but with an attitude of willingness to accept such initially faint impressions as real, they not only become fixed, the frequency and quality of such impressions increases. It has been my experience over more than forty years that by accepting, and therefore 'fixing' such impressions, they remain available for study, contemplation and recollection over an indefinite period, and immeasurably more can then be discerned from them than would ever be the case from only fleeting consideration and then dismissal.

DURING THIS TIME, 1967, I read a book called *Lychgate* by Hugh Dowding, who was head of RAF Fighter Command during World War II. In it he recounts how he was visited by enlightened souls from spirit, who said they wished him to help them with 'rescue' work. They explained that there were many more souls departing their earthly bodies prematurely because of the war than in times of peace, and that many of these souls were in a state of deep shock, either not realising they were 'dead' or not knowing what to do about it. Such a condition is sometimes referred to as being earthbound.

They explained to Hugh that such souls could not be reached by, or perceive communication from, dwellers in the Realms of Light because they were in a denser state of awareness, often similar to being in a fog – either literally or metaphorically. What was needed in order to bring the help that would be serviceable to such distressed souls was a 'living link', or an intermediary, incarnate soul, who had awareness of the conditions being experienced by the distressed soul and also of those from the Realms of Light who desired to help but who could not be seen by the distressed soul.

Such an intermediary would be able both to see and be seen by the newly departed souls and those from the Realms of Light who were trying to help, simultaneously. That person could explain to the distressed souls their situation: they had died and would benefit from accepting this and being willing to 'go forward' into the place in the spirit realms in which they really belonged, where loving help and guidance would be made available to them, from other departed souls – relatives and other loved ones – who had pre-deceased them. Acceptance of this explanation by distressed souls would enable them to become aware of the presence of such loved ones nearby and so they would then be ready to go with them to the place in the spirit realm where they belonged. Using Jesus' terminology, this would be going to the appropriate 'mansion' within the Father's 'house'. It should be understood that the word 'place' is not literally correct in the context of the etheric, or soul realms, as in the time-and-place sense, because the etheric realms are not 'places' but states, or degrees of spiritual awareness, or enlightenment. To be 'with' another person simply means being on the same mental wavelength that they are on, and that brings the parties into mutual awareness of each other's presence.

The enlightened souls who visited Hugh told him that only incarnate souls of an enlightened potential are able to be such living links because they have the capacity for sensory awareness of the lower astral realms as well as the Realms of Light, but souls in the lower astral realms are unable to perceive higher realms, from where help for them is available. They informed Hugh that he was perfectly fitted for this work and would like to enlist his willing assistance with it. Needless to say, this came as somewhat of a surprise to Hugh, but their sincerity and trustworthiness was indubitable, and he had adequate, innate understanding of spiritual truth to recognise that what they said was so, and he therefore readily acceded to their request.

The example of this work described in Hugh's book that I recall most readily was the case of an RAF bomber that crash landed (or had been shot down) in North Africa during the war. All the crew – about six or seven men, I believe – had been killed by the impact, but none was aware that he had 'died'. Hugh was taken out of his body, which was asleep in bed in England, to the crash site. All the crew were there, remaining close to the wreckage of the plane, waiting for rescue to come and take them back to base. Little did they know that this would be so, but not in quite the way they were anticipating!

They suddenly became aware of Hugh's presence and this caused them some significant surprise because they knew very well who he was. As one of the most senior personnel in the entire Royal Air Force, his face would be familiar to them all, but why would the head of *Fighter* Command be visiting crew in *Bomber* Command – two totally separate divisions of the RAF? And why would he be there in North Africa when they knew he was based in London and would need to be there for close liaison with the rest of the commanders of the Allied forces and the Prime Minister? So, as soon as they saw him they knew 'something was not quite as it appeared'. This was a good thing because it meant they would respectfully listen to this senior officer, and they were already partly prepared for being told something unexpected. He was able to explain to them in a kindly but authoritative way what had really happened to them and it was now time for them to become aware of, or awake to, the spirit world into which they had been suddenly projected by the plane crash. One by one their 'eyes opened', and once past their initial astonishment, off they went with their now-visible-to-them loved ones.

All this is fairly straightforward stuff to those of us in the earthly life who accept this reality, however hard to believe it might be to those for whom this is totally new. Although I knew the broad brush of this before I read Hugh's book, there were many details which were eye-opening for me, and some tragic cases were included in the narrative.

But the real impact of this book upon me was that it awakened a profound and soul-wrenching compassion for such 'lost souls', some of whom had/have been in this limbo place 'between time and eternity' for what would be measured in Earth/linear-time as decades, centuries and even millennia. When I considered just the *known* recorded history of mankind over, say, four thousand years, with the details of warfare, bloodshed, torture and man's general inhumanity to man, and the sheer terror and agony beyond imagining of those experiencing being eviscerated, burnt at the stake, crucified – as were many tens of thousands during Roman times – and all manner of other fiendish torture 'for the good of their souls' by the Spanish Inquisition and all the other 'holy' wars (an oxymoron if ever there was one) and divisions, not to speak of political wars, genocides and mayhem, I felt as if my soul was experiencing an agony and anguish that reached out into all Eternity.

Something that was far bigger than I am and yet that *was* me – or at least, I was a *part* of it – in some metaphysical, metaphorical sense, felt as if all the awfulness, torment, fear, pain and panic experienced by every soul at the moment of terror (however short or prolonged such a moment might be), was something that I was vicariously experiencing. What I felt was not exactly the actual *physical* pain of their experience but the emotional and mental anguish of such souls. To me, this experience was unendurable, and every fibre of my soul reached out, as if calling out to the Universal Mind, '*No*, this cannot be allowed to continue. We *must* bring this awfulness to an end, and replace it with peace, relief, release, freedom, succour, love, balm to all these wretched, tortured souls, so that they might have an end to the endlessness of their distress.'

This became part of my very *being*; a huge, unquenchable desire of my heart and soul. I had no understanding of how I could 'do' anything for what assuredly must be untold millions of such souls experiencing such indescribable distress. Again, I had no awareness that my heart's desire had been 'heard'; the word from Isaiah 65:24, "*And it shall come to pass, that before they call, I will answer; and while they are yet speaking, I will hear*", was not then known to me. Yet, unbeknown to my Earth-mind consciousness, the answer to the prayer of my heart's desire was already on its way and would begin to become manifest in my life within a year.

MEANWHILE, I TOOK a leave of absence from my job in Vancouver and spent a month touring around North America, and then three and a half months in England. During that visit home I telephoned Hugh – now Lord – Dowding, who lived in retirement in my own home town of Tunbridge Wells. He was delighted to hear of my having derived such value and personal benefit and growth from his book, and invited me for tea. He and Lady Dowding made me most welcome. There was not a shred of pretentiousness, but rather, an aura of spiritual humility, love and respect for all living things emanating from them both and pervading their entire home. It was evident that here, truly, was a soul well chosen for this rescue work and of whom it could be said, "*His ways are ways of pleasantness and all his paths are peace*" (Proverbs 3:17).

The outcome of my enjoyable visit with Lord and Lady Dowding was that somehow, the reality of the existence and distress of these myriad souls, in realms unseen to Earth-life awareness, became more palpable to me, and my desire to be serviceable in bringing relief and release to them even more part of me. Still, at that time, nothing outward happened.

IN EARLY 1968 I returned to Vancouver. My inspiring, uplifting and enlightening times of visiting with Olga continued from where they had left off before my extended holiday. I had moved into my own apartment and Olga had recommended, upon guidance from within, that I set up a prayer table, which would be a place where spiritual energy could build up from times of prayer-attunement with the Lord Jesus, God, and in the broader sense, all those from the Realms of Light who are in a state of committed oneness with the Great Desire of Jesus: the Kingdom of Heaven on Earth. The most suitable place for this prayer-table was in a corner on one end of a long, low chest of drawers. Here, the exalted vibrations created by attuning in prayer with the Realms of Light would remain and accumulate rather than be dissipated by the comings and goings of day-to-day activities elsewhere in the room. There, each night I lit a votive candle, knelt in prayer and focused on my heart's desires for the reality of the living Jesus to be part of my everyday awareness and experience.

"I suddenly saw the Master Jesus come floating down through the solidness of the place above me where the wall and the ceiling met."

One night, as I knelt there, having sent out my thoughts and desires, I began speaking the *Kingdom Prayer*, usually known as the *Our Father* or *Lord's Prayer*. Half way through this I suddenly saw the Master Jesus come floating down through the solidness of the place above me where the wall and the ceiling met. He was in a sitting position and he floated down until he was seated on the chest of drawers immediately to my left, no more than a hand's breadth away. This was in itself, for me, an amazing experience, but one which I felt put me in a difficult position. Here am I, directing my thoughts, words and desires to 'God, the Father' – the Supreme Being, the Head Honcho, to whom, it seemed to me, should be accorded my full and undivided attention. Now, unannounced and uninvited – though *always* most welcome – into my flat (by a somewhat unconventional entranceway!) comes Jesus of Nazareth; 'God the Son', as many would describe him. The dilemma was: do I interrupt my speaking to God the *Father* – surely not exactly etiquette with anyone, but least of all with Him – in order to acknowledge the presence of, and make welcome, the Messiah. What to do? My mind was in a state of frozen indecision.

I hardly need have worried, for Jesus immediately saw – anticipated – my dilemma and said, in a matter of fact way, "Carry on; everything's fine. I can wait; there is no rush", and he sat there, his hands clasped in his lap, fingers interlocked, twiddling his thumbs and swinging his lower legs back and forth as they dangled over the side of the dresser. This was astonishing to me – the Anointed Messenger of the Holy One behaving just like any 'ordinary' person – and my focus on the rest of the Kingdom Prayer was somewhat distracted, to say the least.

Nevertheless, I ploughed on and finished, the Master being good to his word and waiting for me, totally relaxed and unruffled.

I turned to him and said, "How can it be that you are here, visiting me when there are so many others needing your help, and whom you also would wish to visit?"

The question was really a double one. Partly it was saying 'Can I be worthy to be privileged by a visit from you, the Lord of all mankind, when there are many others more worthy and in greater need?' and partly it was saying, 'How on Earth do you do that?'

His reply answered both aspects. "I am attuned to all mankind all the time; there is never a moment when I am not with you all. All that is needed to complete the contact is for you to attune with me and we are together, at any time." This seemed to be a principle, along the lines of two-way radio links. If party A is at one end, listening to a transmission from party B on a given frequency, he can hear party B without any trouble. If he wishes to respond and be heard by party B, all he needs to do is open his microphone with transmitter attuned to the same frequency, and speak, and party B will be able to receive from, as well as transmit to, party A.

This was a profound lesson for me in understanding the ways in which commun(icat)ion between souls can take place: *get on the same frequency*. This is, in human soul terms, sharing the same desires. The stronger the desires, and the greater the commitment of those souls to those desires, the stronger will be the connection between them. Therefore, the more truly one seeks after God and the more earnestly one desires the Kingdom of Heaven on Earth, the stronger will be the mind-to-mind, heart-to-heart contact with others of like desire and commitment. This was not exactly rocket science, and made my degree of acceptance of the presence of Jesus as a *living*, palpable reality much more meaningfully possible as an objective truth, rather than 'just me being fanciful; so much wishful thinking; imagination running wild'.

This provided a very solid basis for acceptance of future experiences of contact with and from Jesus and of others in the heavenly Kingdom, operating under Christ authority and empowerment. This was a foundation for growth in mystical, Christ-authorised, spiritually-focused living and being. I had asked Jesus of Nazareth to be my spiritual Lord, guide, protector, and he had accepted my invitation/request. He *never* takes such a responsibility lightly or half-heartedly. Truly, he is the Good Shepherd. During the previous few years I had come to love this Nazarene with an all-consuming passion, by reading about him and hearing about him from Olga. Now, I was *experiencing* the dynamic livingness of the love that he IS, and my heart and mind were responding to that and growing within it.

During this period, when I was in the very early stages of my spiritual journey, back in the 1960s, I said to the Master, "Why don't you just give me the answers to the 'top 10' questions (about the Creator, Creation and Eternal Truth) and then we can really get this show on the road."

Smilingly, he replied, "It doesn't work like that. This is a growing process and you have to be able to assimilate the realities of Eternity (back) into every level of your being. To simply have them on a plate for your mind, which has not yet been made ready to receive them, would not be serviceable to that growing process and would cause confusion because the growth has to be balanced across the full spectrum of every aspect of your being."

It was becoming very clear to me that there is, and can be, no authority like experience. You can accept the experience or the word of another as your own truth, but it is always someone *else's* truth - adopted - until you have the experience yourself; then, and only then, can it become a personal, *living*, empowering truth, and regardless of anyone else's teaching or doctrine to the contrary, that living - *experienced* - truth cannot be nullified. Or, to be more complete, it can only be replaced by one's own further, greater, larger experience of truth. For our awareness of truth is not a static thing. It is a living, growing, organic, unfolding thing. We are always moving forward within truth, and the journey continues until we have become fully awakened into awareness of *all* knowledge of Eternity - just as was Jesus in the long ago. What is the truth, the whole truth and nothing but the truth for us today, is something more than it was yesterday because we have grown, just as branches in the vine, when tended by the good husbandman, continue to grow, so that we may, by opening ourselves daily to receive the Light of Spiritual Truth, bear much fruit.

4: Romance Blossoms

During my time in Canada I had had several girlfriends, and they had each brought various qualities into the relationships. However, none had brought what I was really seeking in such a relationship: spiritual fellowship. That may be inferred by some as meaning a lot of religious, pious, no-fun time in each other's company, but that is not what is implied at all. Rather, spirituality, as distinct from religion, is an abundance of joy, peace, happiness, freedom in and of the heart and mind (not to speak of love!).

It can be experienced anywhere, any time, together or apart (although preferably, together!), at some lavish occasion, or walking in the hills or the woods, or sitting indoors listening to evocative music on a rainy day. In other words, it is a recognition that life and relationships are not so much about what we do together but rather, *who we are* within a relationship. For example, if a woman only finds a relationship fulfilling if the man is always taking her out and spending money on her – and the more money spent, the more fulfilling the relationship – *spiritual* fellowship is clearly lacking.

On the other hand, if just *being* with the significant other, even – and perhaps especially – indoors on a rainy day, brings peace and joy to heart and mind, then there is spiritual fellowship, whether making tender or passionate love, reading a book, listening to music, studying, attuning with eternity or watching the rain. Togetherness, *true* togetherness, is a *within* thing, and spirituality is of the *within*, experienced in one's inner being and radiating outwards from there, irrespective of what may appear to be happening outwardly.

These relationships were therefore, from my perspective, unfulfilling. They did not bring a deep, soul-to-soul satisfying sense of belonging together for the makings of a lasting, spiritually functional relationship.

During my leave of absence in England in 1967, while out

on a walk in the woods in Kent with friends and their dogs one November afternoon, I reflected on the fact that such relationships were not *soul*-satisfying, leaving a deep sense of being like a doughnut: hollow in the middle.

I said to the Lord Jesus, "I am willing to remain celibate in my life on the path of spiritual progress with you if that is serviceable. *However*, you well know that there are as many red corpuscles flowing through my veins as the next man, so if celibacy is not serviceable, please bring me into contact with the right life-partner for this journey."

* * *

In March 1968, back in Vancouver, wishing to exchange written communication with friends and relatives in various parts of the globe, and finding writing letters by hand rather tiresome and time-consuming, I bought a redundant typewriter (remember typewriters!?) from my employer and decided to go to night-school to learn how to type. Armed with a totally unrealistic vision of myself quickly acquiring a typing speed to beat the band, I set off for night-school typing class.

Having initially misread the details of what courses were where, I eventually arrived at the beginners' class a few minutes late. Everyone else was already seated and the class had begun. I made my apologies and quickly found a seat at one side of the room. The desks were arranged so that all those on one side of the room were facing all those on the other, with a gap down the middle. When I had recovered my composure I glanced around the room, in part to acquaint myself with who else was there in a general way and, far more importantly, to spy out the female talent. All but one other attendee were female. *So far, so good.* Most, however, were much older than I, or not 'worth' a second glance in terms of the 'talent stakes'. Aah, well!

But, soft! What light through yonder visage *breaks?*

Across the room, directly opposite and facing me, is a young girl. And she is looking right at me. Smiling. I look back at her and, after holding my gaze for time-no-time, she coyly looks away. Is that a blush I see? I look away but cannot avert my eyes for long. There she is, looking at me again. It is more than a look; it is a *communicating*. There is something about her. Can it be something that seems somehow familiar? Surely not. I have never seen her before in this incarnation, of that I feel sure. And yet, assuredly, something deep within me feels as if I know her.

The class is a two-hour event but there is a short break after an hour and everyone troops out of the room, to stretch their legs, get refreshment, or simply to mingle. I decide this is a good moment to acquaint myself more closely with this young lady. She is in the hallway outside the classroom, chatting with the person who had been sitting beside her. The details are unimportant as to how the conversation began, but begin it did, and we chatted easily and cordially for a few minutes until it was time to resume our places.

Throughout the class's second session more smiles and meaningful glances were exchanged that said, 'I wish to continue getting to know this person.' After the class ended we met up in the hallway and I asked if she would like to come for a hot chocolate with me.

We gave our order to the car-hop at the drive-in and sat half-turned toward each other in the front of my car. She was *very* attractive, no doubt about that. Young, but how young? It could be a tricky game, guessing the age of young women. Women of any age, come to that. I put her at late teens or early twenties. That was good enough for now. But who was she, *inside*, behind the mask we all hold up to the world, until we feel safe enough to lower it and expose the real us behind it? She told me her name was Theresa when we introduced ourselves. She immediately recognised me as English when I apologised for arriving late, and she was eager to share with me that she, too, was English, although her accent seemed about mid-Atlantic as I listened to her speaking. She was from Margate – so we were *both* from Kent, an interesting point in common. She had come to Canada aged not yet eight, with her parents. No wonder her accent was 'half and half'. Surprising and interesting that she had any trace of English accent left at all.

But would this attractive English girl be what I was *really* seeking? Would she be like the others – conscious only at the outer, earth-physical level of awareness, or would she, *could* she perhaps be aware that we are here for some greater purpose and that we can have awareness of that greater reality beyond the immediate? Could it be that she might have a desire to travel the path of progress toward eternal spiritual enlightenment? I was eager to find out the lie of the land. *Grant me patience Lord; but hurry.* I had no real desire for one of those drawn out 'getting to know you' events that, after weeks or months of exploration of the possibilities, lead to what is clearly no real foundation for a lasting and *soul*-fulfilling relationship.

Plucking up my courage and taking a deep breath I looked her straight in the eye and asked, "Do you love the Lord?"

To my delight, a look of surprise that was tinged with pleasure – rather than 'Oh, dear, we have a nutter here, let me out, quick' – flashed over her face.

"Yes, of course," she said, and laughed.

"Oh, good," I replied, feeling very pleased and relieved that this risky litmus test had come out positive. We chatted animatedly about spiritual matters as we drank our beverage, and all too soon it was time to go.

It turned out that her family had been vegetarian for some years, and this was an area of continuing interest for her. Great; I had also been moving in this direction for a while, and only now had the opportunity to begin practising this, having just moved into my own place. She was also well aware of the reality of the spirit world and our ability to have contact with it, because her mother had been a medium for years. Things were looking better and better! Here was plenty of common ground and potential for a relationship to develop into a long-term fellowship and life-long, soul-to-soul partnership.

I dropped her off at her home and drove back to my flat with a keen sense of anticipation. I could hardly wait for the next class, when I would see her again. It was two days hence. *Good; no need to wait for another whole week.* My feelings for Theresa were of great warmth, kinship, tenderness, comfortableness and pleasure in her presence and I could tell that these were reciprocated. Here indeed was a soul without guile.

"We sat next to each other and I could feel the closeness and mingling of her aura with mine."

We sat next to each other in class two nights later, and I could feel the closeness and mingling of her aura with mine. We were bonding at a soul level, even without looking at each other. We only attended a few more classes together and it was obvious to us both that there were rapidly becoming much more fulfilling – and interesting! – ways of spending Tuesday and Thursday evenings for the next couple of months or so. On what was probably the last evening we attended the class, we walked through the rain back to my car a few blocks away. Theresa put her arm through mine to huddle closer under the umbrella. *Bless the rain!*

I unlocked the passenger door for her and we stood under the umbrella beside the car, looking deeply into each other's eyes, each other's souls, in the light of the street lamps, for what seemed like several minutes. Everything said this was the moment for that first kiss. As our lips touched there was a bolt, a wave, of energy that went through me, starting at my lips and surging throughout my being. It wasn't just my body, although that was good enough! It was *all* of me – body and soul. Wow! Those lips were unlike anything I had ever experienced. So soft, so full, so sweet, so gentle, so giving, so full of promise of much more to know and experience; so *eager* to experience more. How long that kiss lasted I have no idea, but it was a timeless moment. There would certainly be more. We both knew we both would be ready and willing for more.

Theresa and I saw each other every day. We *belonged* together. Apart, there was something lacking. I felt aimless if she had other commitments, which, blessedly, wasn't too often. After we had known each other not very long she began coming to my flat after work and we would eat together, walk along the beach, talk, kiss, talk; eagerly recapitulating on the events in our lives while we had been apart, before being re-united in this incarnation. For, assuredly, we knew each other. We had *always* known each other. It became impossible to think of a moment in eternity when we could have been without each other.

* * *

A couple of years previously I had taken a former girlfriend out to Olga's cottage, keen for her to experience Olga's spiritual wisdom and enable her to grow in understanding of matters eternal and invisible, which she had always had difficulty in doing. As we drove away afterwards, Cheryl said to me, "Gee, what a cute little old lady." *That was all she saw.* I knew that marked the end of the prospects for this relationship.

As Theresa and I drove away from Olga's cottage after *her* first visit there, she said, "Wow! What a wonderful soul; so full of life, insight and wisdom" and she was bursting with enthusiasm for the encounter. Here indeed, was another positive outcome to what was, for me, a further, crucial litmus test!

*   *   *

Our relationship continued to blossom, and the thought of being separate from her was alien to me. The sense of belonging together, and completeness that I had with her, would certainly have left a vast hole in my life without her. There were numerous instances of telepathy between us, so attuned to each other had we rapidly become.

However, not all was sweetness and light. Theresa had come from a violent and abusive family environment. She was physically, emotionally and sexually abused from earliest childhood (although I had suspected the sexual abuse for a number of years, it only came out fully into her conscious recollection long after we were married). This had impacted and deeply traumatised her, and like most of us, she held up her mask to show herself to the world as a 'rational, well-balanced human being'. The trauma of such experiences goes deep inside and is internalised, even to the point where the conscious mind deliberately 'forgets', as an act of self-preservation, when the pain (emotional or physical) is too much to bear.

But of course, the mask cannot be held up to everyone all the time, and in a close relationship such as ours had already become, there are moments when it slips and 'irrational' behaviour comes out. Although my parents' marriage was not a good one in many respects, our home life was not abusive and indeed, mostly loving, so I like to think of myself as reasonably emotionally balanced and rational. Therefore, irrational behaviour, which, by definition is 'illogical', is something I was not very good at handling, and this was a long-term cause of misunderstanding between us. Nevertheless, our relationship was mostly good, and very loving, there being a soul bonding between us that was able to withstand the *slings and arrows of outrageous fortune*, and not long after we met, the Master said to me, "I have brought the Little One to you to be your Companion of the Way." Alleluia; there *is* a God, He and Jesus love me and They *do* answer our prayers!! God was in his Heaven and even if *all* was not right with *our* world, this was a terrific start as far as I was concerned. And it sure knocked the socks off celibacy!

* * *

From time to time during that summer of 1968, Theresa and I would visit her parents (she had moved into her own flat shortly after we met), more because Theresa felt a sense of daughterly duty than out of a desire so to do. But I was becoming increasingly aware of the negative, oppressive atmosphere in their home, and this made me less and less comfortable about such visits. There was a psychic black cloud enveloping the place that could practically be cut with a knife and I felt very sure this was affecting Theresa, who was a bundle of nerves when the time came for one of these visits. It was like walking into a place of spiritual darkness.

After one particularly unpleasant visit I said to Theresa, "I'm not going there again. If you feel you must, out of duty, so be it, but I don't believe it is good for us, so unless it is essential, let us stay away."

I could tell Theresa was not happy about my decision; not because she didn't agree with me, but her fear of her parents and their domineering, manipulative, controlling ways caused her deep concern about their reaction once it became clear she also was not making her occasional visits. For her, such a prospect was even worse than continuing to go there.

---

*". . . send out a blessing; it will act as a buffer,
neutralising the negative psychic energy"*

Not many days after telling Theresa this, early one Saturday morning, as I was emerging from a deep sleep, I heard a man's voice speaking to me. It was the Rector. "If there is a deep divide between you and others and you send out a blessing to them, it will act as a buffer between you, neutralising the negative psychic energy, and there will no longer be discord between you. A cordial association will then become possible," he said. His speaking had begun during my sleep and continued into wakefulness, and I realised that he had arranged this to be sure that I would bring the message through into my waking consciousness. I lay there musing upon what had been said. It made a lot of sense so I decided to try this immediately. Still lying in bed, I sent out a blessing for peace and goodwill upon all Theresa's family.

Instantly I saw them all, gathered as if to have a group photograph taken in front of their house, and my blessing left my navel like an umbilicus of translucent-white living substance, about as thick as a finger. It streaked toward them, and a pace or two in front of them it opened out like a funnel, encircled and joined up behind them, enveloping them all completely as if inside a balloon, creating a buffer between them and anyone – including me – outside the balloon. Needless to say, I was considerably astonished and greatly excited. I knew this was a 'real' experience and that my blessing had done just as I had heard the Rector telling me it would do.

Theresa worked as a dental nurse on Saturday mornings, but as soon as she arrived at my flat at lunchtime that day I said to her, "Come on, we're going to see your folks."

She was about as astonished as I had been earlier.

"I thought you said you weren't going there any more," she replied, with a hint of relief in her voice that at least she would have me to help her cope with what had been, for her, decidedly unnerving visits.

"I did say that, but something amazing has happened and the situation has changed now, so there won't be any more bad vibes."

On the way there I told her what the Rector had said, and how I 'knew' things would now be totally transformed.

Even as we walked up the steps to the front door, Theresa feeling slightly apprehensive, and holding my hand for dear life, the transformation in the atmosphere emanating from the household was palpably apparent. The unpleasant, negative, oppressive energy had given way to a peaceful, welcoming, friendly aura. We glanced at each other, grinning from ear to ear.

All this 'spiritual stuff' works! It has real, tangible earth-meaningful value and benefit; it's not just glib, trite, airy-fairy platitudes! Theresa's parents were warm, effusive, smiling. The TV was switched off! They engaged in friendly, sincere, caring conversation, made a cup of tea. Nothing like this had happened on preceding visits. A miraculous transformation *had* taken place, just as deep in my inner being I *knew* it had.

Not a word passed between us about this until several hours later, when we had got into the car to drive away. Even then, it was all so wonderful; a blessed relief to Theresa, and a grand affirmation to me of the reality of this other, all-encompassing, precious dimension in our lives, about which the world around us had no awareness. We drove home so absorbed in our thoughts and quiet thanksgiving that little was, or needed to be, said.

I continued to send out blessings to Theresa's family from time to time and her parental home environment remained largely transformed for the better from that day forward until we left Vancouver eighteen months or so later.

5: The Rescue Work Begins

On Wednesday, the 5th of June 1968, my twenty-fourth birthday, I awoke to the news that Bobby Kennedy had been assassinated. The following Sunday morning Theresa and I drove out to Olga's for our Communion Devotions. By this time Olga, now seventy-seven years old, had handed over the role of 'officiant' to me. As I stood before the altar, facing outwards (toward any souls 'in this life or the next') offering the consecrated bread and wine for the students of the Sanctuary of Christ Peace, to *all who seek after its Light* and to *all who desire our prayers*, suddenly I was overshadowed by Bobby. I *knew* that I looked like him; I *felt* like him and it was as if there were cobwebs over my head. As I ran my fingers through my hair to instinctively brush away the feeling of cobwebs, my hair felt exactly like I knew his hair would feel. My own hair is very fine and straight but Bobby Kennedy's hair was thick, wavy and wiry – a totally different texture and feel. As this was going on and without my saying a word, Theresa looked at me and her expression became very startled.

"Bobby Kennedy is overshadowing you. Your features have disappeared and his are there."

"Bobby Kennedy is overshadowing you," she blurted out. "I can see him. Your features have disappeared and his are there."

Theresa's knowledge of such things was gleaned from her family background of her mother being a spiritualist medium for many years, so although she was startled, she readily knew and understood exactly what was happening.

The feelings I was picking up from Bobby were of confusion. He knew he was 'dead', but he didn't know what to 'do' about it. He was still earthbound; stuck in the etheric counterpart of the

Earth life, in part at least, because of the sudden and traumatic way he had been catapulted from his body. I believe he knew he was lost and was desperately trying to find his way, looking for help. No doubt there was a beacon of spirit Light radiating from Olga's sanctuary of Christ Communion and this had been seen by Bobby, who had been drawn to it, not really knowing what it was but being attracted by the fact that here was Light and he was in sore need of Light.

The fact that this sanctuary of Christ Light was in British Columbia, Canada and Bobby had been murdered in Los Angeles, some twelve hundred miles away, has no significance in the spirit world. There, 'travel' is instantaneous; by either thinking about where (or with whom) one wishes to be, or by desiring a certain thing or condition, one is instantly transported to such. Further, Jack, Bobby's older brother, who by this time had been in spirit for about four and a half Earth-time years, will have known 'the ropes', will have been well aware of the plight of his newly passed-over younger brother. They were/are very close and he will, assuredly, have been in a position to help Bobby, even if Bobby was not, at that stage in his transition, aware of Jack being close by. This could have been in the form of a response to Bobby's urgent plea for help, even if he was unaware of anyone being close.

We spoke to Bobby, explained what had happened, and blessed him in the name of Jesus, counselling him to ask Jesus to help him, and that this would either bring Jesus himself, or someone sent under his authority to help him. After a few moments, during which I had the feeling that this counsel was sinking in – bearing in mind that Bobby was in a state of deep shock and bewilderment – he was suddenly gone.

*　*　*

Later that month I had one of those dream experiences that are very real and that I interpret as events taking place out of the body during sleep, although they can just as readily take place other than during sleep time. In this experience, Olga, Theresa and I were enjoying a most pleasant Sunday afternoon cup of tea, along with (of course!) English biscuits, in my flat. It was a bright, sunny afternoon and we three English folk were in our element. But there was a fourth person there, equally enjoying the fellowship and joining in the conversation. This fourth person was Jesus of Nazareth. By now, of course, I knew very well who he was, and he was so *real*, but at this still relatively early stage in my relationship with him, I still felt slightly unsettled. I loved him with all my being, and his very existence was manna for my life and soul, yet here, right in my flat (again!) was the *mighty Lord*, and I was not sure how to address him, behave toward him, or act in his presence, especially in a social setting. He was so obviously relaxed and enjoying himself, but I was somewhat tense and uneasy . . . feeling somehow on the outside, looking in.

"There was a flash of puckishness in his eyes and in the way his mouth moved as he smiled. Then he spoke: 'I am the avenger.' "

I wanted to join in the relaxed atmosphere of fun and pleasantness of the situation but this was proving difficult, feeling so on edge. Clearly this was no good and something had to be done to redress the situation. With some trepidation I said to him, "How should I address you; by what name or title should we call you?" He looked at me and there was love, tenderness, understanding in his countenance. But there was more, also; there was a sparkle of fun, a twinkle of humour, even a flash of puckishness, betrayed both in his eyes and in the way his mouth moved as he smiled. The moment was fleeting but completely unmistakable. Then he spoke: "I am the avenger." That was all he said, but he knew the impact those four words would have upon me. This was the 1960s! *The Avengers* was a global-phenomenon TV series about the British secret service. This was the era of James Bond; when derring-do with style, with flair, with bowler hats and furled umbrellas and figure-hugging leather trousers on karate-kicking, breathtakingly gorgeous ladies, was all the rage. I knew it only too well and he knew this was the image that word would instantly bring to my mind – as indeed, it did.

How the scene, the experience, ended I did not bring through to my waking awareness, but that was enough to have a huge effect on me. It jolted me to the core. Later, I looked up the word *avenger* in the dictionary and also in the Bible concordance.

The dictionary said 'avenge' meant to *inflict retribution, exact satisfaction, on behalf of (person, violated right, etc.)* According to my then understanding of Jesus' 'job description', that seemed to be as apposite as possible.

The concordance showed several New Testament references to 'avenge' and 'avenger':

> Lk. 18:7,8: *And shall not God avenge his own elect, which cry day and night unto him, though he bear long with them? I tell you that he will avenge them speedily.*

> Rom. 12:19: *Dearly beloved, avenge not yourselves, but rather give place unto wrath: for it is written, Vengeance is mine; I will repay, saith the Lord.*

> 1 Thes. 4:6: *That no man go beyond and defraud his brother in any matter: because that the Lord is the avenger of all such, . . .*

> Rv. 6:10: *And they cried with a loud voice, saying, How long, O Lord, holy and true, dost thou not judge and avenge our blood on them that dwell on the Earth?*

> Rv. 18:20: *Rejoice over her, thou Heaven, and ye holy apostles and prophets; for God hath avenged you on her.*

> Rv. 19:2: *For true and righteous are his judgements: for he hath judged the great whore, which did corrupt the Earth with her fornication, and hath avenged the blood of his servants at her hand.*

There are a number of other places in Old and New Testaments where the word *avenge*, or various derivatives, are to be found, but those shown above – all of which were new to me at that time because I was not extensively familiar with the Bible scriptures – clearly indicate that Jesus was well familiar with them when he used the word to describe himself to me.

My perspective on such matters now has grown somewhat, and I prefer to see the word and its application in the context of Jesus of Nazareth as being a person who *puts right that which is wrong, or is not serviceable to the well-being of all.* In a broader perspective it could be described as *restoring to balance that which is out of balance (with the perfection of the Creator Spirit's eternal scheme of things)*, which helps to remove the rather negative shadow around the word avenge caused by the etymological association of it with *re*venge.

I now see that words like 'right' and 'wrong' are subjective judgements rather than absolute, unchangeable, fixed realities. We are all continually creating our own reality, and that changes, evolves on a moment by moment basis, until we have remembered fully who we really are and returned to our rightful inheritance of perfection in the Kingdom of Heaven. In the interim, as we journey back toward that Place of Being, it is a growing, ever-becoming process, just as is the growing of any organism – a baby in the womb, a lettuce in the garden, or anything else. It is something more, something greater in 'this moment' than it was in any 'previous moment'. We may all say, for example, 'killing another person is wrong and that is an unchangeable truth', but history is full of killing where the killer justifies his actions as being 'righteous'.

For instance, the loving spouse – whose partner is terminally ill, in pain, whose quality of life is less than zero – motivated by tender love and compassion, helps them to end it all. The law of the land may see that as a crime of murder – although this is under careful scrutiny and review now and it does not seem unreasonable to consider that the law may well be changed at some not-too-far-off date, even as it already is in some jurisdictions.

If we are rigid and inflexible in the posture that the ending of another's life is murder under any and all circumstances, then it prohibits the expression of this so-vital a quality of the higher nature of humanity known as compassion toward another's suffering. And if that suffering, terminally ill person wishes to end their suffering and is accepting of death as the only feasible way to do it, it could be reasonably viewed as an act of great compassion to assist in this release. An act of compassion is an act of love, which enables a going forward in remembrance of our eternal, spiritual reality. Denial of such an act for reasons which may be based on self-imposed, restricted perception could therefore be construed as denying oneself an opportunity to grow spiritually. This is neither a statement for nor a judgement against euthanasia, but is an example of how attitudes are often taken for or against a particular matter without consideration being fully and fairly given to all sides and angles of the issue.

Further, in the eternal perspective there is no such thing as 'death', since living things, including humans, are not essentially bodies, but spirit, functioning in the physical world *through* the vehicle of a physical body. It is, therefore, the *spirit* that is the livingness of each being and the spirit does not die when it lays aside the physical vehicle through which it has found expression, because life is God – pure and perfect Spirit – and God is indestructible.

* * *

Later in that summer of 1968, I was becoming more and more disenchanted with the world of advertising. I felt one was expected to say what it was expedient to say rather than how it really is. I was waking up feeling sick and getting home from work at the end of each day with a migraine. Clearly, it was time to move on; *you couldn't have a conscience and be in advertising.*

My former boss had been headhunted to run the British Columbia operations of Canada's biggest chain of office supplies retailers, and he kept phoning to ask me to join him there. The idea did not appeal to me. My heart and soul were set on activities that would 'fulfil the inner man' and somehow the prospect of peddling paperclips and glue to the local businesses did not seem to offer much chance of achieving this goal! Nevertheless, my present employment was becoming unbearable and Paul kept on pestering me to join him. It seemed at least an escape-hatch to something tolerable, even if not inspiring, and I had always got on very well with Paul. Finally I accepted his offer, and at eight o'clock on my first Monday morning as a sales rep for Willson's Stationers, found myself sitting at the desk allocated to me in the large sales office.

There was bedlam going on all around me as the other twenty or so reps greeted each other and discussed the weekend's events or other matters of varying import. I knew no-one, so sat there, silently wondering what I had got myself into. Instantly I heard a voice, loud and clear, speaking from a couple of paces away to my right, say, *Don't worry, you won't be here for long.* What a greeting on my first day in a new job! This was a voice from the spirit world, but it was as clear as if spoken by any of the others bodily present in the room. Moments after that, the meeting was called to order by the sales manager and my new 'career' was under way.

* * *

At the end of one evening in August 1969, after I had driven Theresa home, we sat in the car talking. She had been telling me of her years of nightmares – sleeping and waking – caused by intrusions from earthbound spirits. In one of the experiences she was in a Nazi death camp and the all-pervading, nauseating, terrifying fear was smothering her senses like a pall. As we discussed this I was suddenly aware of the features of another woman overshadowing Theresa's appearance. No words could adequately describe the look of stark terror in her eyes. There was a pleading, begging cry for help in them. I instantly knew this dear soul was the cause of Theresa's experience. This lady, of whom I had the impression that she was a Dutch Jewess and whom we now believe to be named Rachel, had been living this terrible nightmare for, in Earth, or linear, time, well over twenty-five years; no doubt, without a single moment's respite.

Theresa had no awareness of being overshadowed; all she knew was that she was experiencing everything this lost, tormented soul was experiencing, and had no idea why, nor any awareness of its origin. Without saying a word to Theresa I began speaking silently to this lady, explaining that she was now departed from the earthly life, that she was 'stuck' in the events prevailing at the time of her demise and was, perhaps unwittingly in her sheer panic, overshadowing Theresa; that this was no longer necessary because she could call upon help from the Realms of Light and help would *immediately* be sent to her; that even if she was Jewish and not of the 'Christian' faith, she would do well to call upon Jesus of Nazareth for that help and that either he himself would come or he would send other help under his authority and she would then be instantly released from her torment.

She looked at me with a look that portrayed partly disbelief and partly a desperate *desire* to believe what I had said. I assured her, still silently, that this was absolutely true and that she should now call upon this help without further delay. With barely a moment's hesitation she was gone. Theresa, who had no knowledge of this silent communion, and who had herself been in terrible distress, let out a gasp and a sob of relief, for her torment had ceased at that exact, selfsame moment. I explained to her what had taken place.

The next evening, as we sat in the car outside her home again, the lady suddenly came back. This time there was a heavenly radiance about her and her face was full of joy and gratitude. Truly she had been released from her torment. She returned to express her appreciation for the guidance I had been able to impart the previous evening and to let us know that she had received the help, just as I had assured her she would. There was also a vibration indicating deep and profound regret for the distress with which she had unwittingly burdened Theresa. Our visitor was now soaring in rapture. I *felt* the thanks and the blessing outpouring from her heart. Then, in an instant, she was gone again.

The following day Theresa told me that Rachel had come to her as she knelt at her prayer sanctuary before bed, to thank her. Theresa said it was as if Rachel had 'kissed her soul'.

We have had no further awareness of contact from her, although I dare say she has never forgotten the help given, and has been, or even still is, sending her blessings and help in some way to us. I am in no doubt that she is now able to help others to find release from similar experience and that such service brings joy and fulfilment to her life. Such a prospect is blessing enough for us that we may have been contributory in enabling it. Anyone who thinks that earthbound souls who 'possess' the bodies of incarnate souls are all 'evil spirits' is sadly mistaken. This lady had no evil in her; just fear beyond imagining and a desperate need of help. The most helpful things she could be given were love, compassion, understanding; a rational, meaningful explanation of what was happening to her, and what she could do to bring this condition to an immediate and blessed end.

In a so-called civilised world, full of the clever, the proud and the scornful, the lack of awareness and understanding of such matters, although documented in untold numbers of books around the world, and available to all, is truly of epic proportion. The church equally has access to such documentary evidence and is resolute in its commitment to keeping its congregants and its ministers in ignorance about it. That is sad enough, but what is immeasurably more sad and unserviceable to humanity is the way the church has persuaded the populace at large, and particularly its congregants, that *all* contact with the spirit world is evil and that any such is the work of Satan, luring God's children into a snare.

No wonder church attendance is at an all-time low and falling in Britain and much of the rest of the world. Even in countries where it is not falling, the narrow, exclusivist attitudes of the Catholic Church and many of the various schismatic Protestant denominations runs entirely counter to the embracing, inclusive, unconditionally-loving example and teaching of Jesus. How applicable are his words to the Pharisees for all too many of today's religious leaders: "But woe unto you, scribes and Pharisees, hypocrites! for ye shut up the kingdom of Heaven against men: for ye neither go in yourselves, neither suffer ye them that are entering to go in" (Mt. 23:13). How much a reminder to us of the unserviceableness of denominational religions are the words given to a Light-seeker in Australia: "*. . . I have called them by their names but they have de-nominated themselves.*"

* * *

Theresa and I were married a few weeks later. We lived in the upstairs half of a house that had been converted into a self-contained apartment. Life was not quite idyllic but it had much to create an overriding sense of joy and contentment. I was newly wed to my darling Companion of the Way, and my relationship with my dearly beloved Jesus was growing all the while into an ever more palpable reality. What more could any living soul ask for?

One morning, not long after we were married, Theresa strained a muscle in her back, making it difficult to lift her arms above her head. After her morning shower before going to work she was unable to dry her hair by herself. Her hair was very short (Mia Farrow-style, for those who can remember!) and her usual practise was to merely towel it dry. On this occasion I did the honours. This was done with speed, loving tenderness and dexterity such as I had never known. Her hair was fully dry in no time at all and there was absolutely no doubt it wasn't I who had been in charge of the towel, but Jesus, coordinating the procedure through me. So personal is his love for us – all of us – that he had come to give this intimate demonstration of his caring in such a heart-filling way as we will never forget. We both felt powerfully, wonderfully uplifted and exhilarated by his visit and his loving, solicitous contribution to our new family unit. Truly, he loves to surprise us with joy.

On another occasion, after we'd come home from work and prepared our evening meal, we sat at the table to eat. As I was about to give thanks for the good food and bless it to our health and strength, the same voice that I had heard in the Willson's sales office on my first morning there, spoke, this time from my left, a couple of paces across the room, *Prayer is an attunement, not a pleading.*

In December that same year, Pop, who had been to New Zealand to help the commercial development of the seaweed products there, stopped in Vancouver for a few days on his way home. On his last night with us Theresa's parents had invited us all out for a meal. Theresa sat between Pop and me, and between courses Pop moved his chair back, and reaching behind Theresa, tapped me on the shoulder. "Why don't you come back to England and join the firm?" he said.

Before I could speak Theresa blurted out, "Oh, yes *please!*"

I was flattered of course, but wasn't sure what to say. I had placed my life into the care of Jesus, and was committed to living under guidance from him. He had given no indication that this, or anything like it, was on the cards. It was my understanding at that time that to take precipitate action without first receiving some indication from 'above' was putting myself out on a limb, placing myself outside the Master's protection and guidance. I asked Jesus for his input in this matter but received nothing whatsoever. Not a word, feeling, dream, vision or 'throw-away line' from anyone else that hinted at any sort of affirmation one way or another. Never had I felt such lack of any sense of contact when I could most have used it. After all, this would have been a big move geographically, a total change of direction career-wise and would, of course, have removed us from direct contact with Olga, a constant source of spiritual fellowship and mentoring, and in spite of a fifty-four-year age gap, a real joy to be with.

Meanwhile, Pop returned to England, and when we went back into work at the beginning of 1970 the vibes there had undergone a radical change. As we walked through the front door (Theresa had recently joined Willson's in their telephone sales department) it was like being slapped in the face, the change was so palpable, and the whole atmosphere had suddenly become unbearable. I felt as if this was like stepping out of the advertising frying pan into the stationery fire.

"Why have you led me into this?"
"I don't lead you *into* these things;
I lead you *out* of them."

I felt let down by the Lord and said to him, "Why have you led me into this?"

His instantaneous reply was, "I don't lead you *into* these things; I lead you *out* of them."

I heard him very clearly and was in no doubt about what had been said, and who had said it, but I was in grave difficulty over it. It most certainly did seem as if he *had* led me into it because when I got into bed on the night I had accepted Paul's job offer, the Master said, "Well done, Little One." I had taken that very much as his seal of approval on my course of action. Now, barely fifteen months later, the job had gone very sour on me.

Over the years I have come to realise that in the eternal scheme of things there are what appear to us from our Earth-life, finite perspective, many subtle nuances, and when we are starting out along the path of spiritual awakening, our ability to see and understand these apparent subtleties is very limited. Truly, earthly consciousness and perception are very literal-minded. With the benefit of time my discernment of these eternal realities has grown and I now see that there are several Laws of Creation, to which the Lord Jesus has referred on a number of occasions to me as 'the Principles of Life of the Father' (PLFs), which apply in a situation such as this.

We have free will to live as we choose and to decide in which direction to move at any and every moment. A single step does not radically alter the overall direction of that journey, which is ultimately guided by our own desire, deeply embedded in our heart and mind. Jesus and all the others from the Realms of Light who love us and are there to help us – including those of us in the Earth life who love and choose to follow the Lord Jesus – never impose their desires or choices upon us against our own will. They *always* honour our choices and decisions and will help to redirect us if we have taken a step that is not in the general direction of our life's journey and we have consciously chosen to co-operate with them and allow ourselves to be guided/redirected by them in such an event. That redirection may be by the outworking of circumstances rather than by their speaking.

I had taken the Master's words "Well done, Little One" as meaning that this was *his* choice for me. The reality, I now perceive, was that this was not the case. He was simply saying that my decision to *move on* was something with which he was pleased, for my sake, not because it was his objective for me. This was a *stepping-stone* by which he could lead me *out* of the world of advertising. When the time came for me to move onto the *next* stepping-stone, he would, by the authority over my life that I had given him by my committed willingness to be guided by him, once again lead me *out*. Never mind that each stepping-stone is not in itself our ultimate objective. Suffice it to be a way out of that from which we have become ready to move. Life in the illusory realm of time and place is a journey of sequential steps, each one being an experience in itself. It's illusory because time and place are temporal, not eternal, and only Eternity can be reality. Each experience can start as being positive and exciting, but in due course it has served its purpose and it comes time to move on. This is growth. It is like the baby in the womb. At first it is comfortable, roomy and secure. But as the baby grows, it starts to feel confined and its freedom restricted. Eventually that place becomes like a prison and it is time to move on to the next phase, or stepping-stone, of life's journey. Unfolding, sequential, creative experiences mark our route back Home to God.

* * *

Soon after Pop got back to England he wrote confirming that

the company was interested in employing me and asking for my response, indicating interest or otherwise, so that a formal offer of employment could be made. But still there was no word of guidance or direction from the Lord. I was in a complete quandary. Theresa was really excited about the prospect, and so was I, but I felt it was only appropriate to make such a major move in accord with the authority and directing of Christ, under whose guidance I had voluntarily placed myself.

To decide independently, it seemed to me, would remove me from that authority and the protection it afforded from the world's snares and pitfalls, into which I had no desire to fall. Days turned into weeks and Pop wrote again, expressing some surprise at my lack of response. So, under pressure to do something, I sat down at home after supper with pen and paper, not having the faintest idea what to say. I asked the Lord for guidance and began writing. It appeared to be rambling, taking no direction and I was aware of no inspiration coming in at all.

" . . . the guidance was there even though I was
completely unaware of it"

After writing maybe a couple of hundred words and still not knowing how to answer Pop's invitation, I put down the pen and decided to at least read what had so far been committed to paper, if but to see if it was complete gibberish and worthy only of consigning to the 'round file' and starting over again. At first it seemed to be a somewhat circuitous line of approach to the subject but after a while, having explained that there were a number of commitments that needed our attention – such as finishing off the repayments for Theresa's loan for university studies (that would take a few more months) I read the words . . . *but this is the direction towards which we will be working.* I was absolutely flabbergasted. I had apparently written that – meaning that we would be bringing our affairs into order in Canada so that we would be in a position to return to England to take up the job offer – without having any conscious awareness of having done so. This clearly indicated to me that the guidance was there – *in my own within* – even though I was completely unaware of it, and that this was the way forward.

It would take us some months to get everything in order, and it was the spring of 1970 by the time my official job offer had arrived and I had responded affirmatively to it. In April we went with great excitement to the travel agent to book our sea passage home via the Panama Canal, departing in November and arriving about a month later. We had had our annual holiday before we got married, so there had been no chance for time away on honeymoon. We asked the travel agent if we could have a table for two in the dining room on board ship, as we would be treating this month-long voyage as our honeymoon. He was delighted at the idea, and gladly complied with our request.

Meanwhile, Theresa, who had had all sorts of 'female troubles' since adolescence, and also a rotated pelvis as a result of being walloped in the base of the spine in her late teens by a hit-and-run driver, and had been told by more than one medic that she would never bear children, had fallen pregnant! Having understood she could not conceive, we had taken no contraceptive precautions. By January of 1970 she was several months pregnant, but all was not well. She began to feel ill physically, but more sinister, she felt a serious and distressing sense of unease about the baby, and that something was wrong with its development. Her physical state was much more than just routine morning sickness. I was becoming deeply concerned and asked the Rector for his help and guidance as to what to do in this frightening situation. He immediately said in a very kind but firm and authoritative way, "Do nothing. All is in our care and we will attend to this matter." A day or so later, on a Saturday, I went off to do the weekly grocery shopping, leaving Theresa lying on the sofa in some pain and distress, trying to get some rest.

When I came back she was in a state of great excitement.

"As soon as you went out, the Rector came in with a number of other people from spirit," she reported. "I was lying on my side, trying to get comfortable, and one of the men came up to me and rammed a huge hypodermic into my buttock. I felt the sharp pain of the needle going in and then the serum being injected. It was such a real experience that I checked afterwards and the red mark where the needle went in is visible."

She showed me, and there, large as life, was indeed a red mark from the injection.

Within a few days Theresa started to experience uterine discharge, not just of blood but of fragments of human tissue. A further few days and a lifeless, partially developed foetus, badly deformed and disintegrating, came fully away. It was a boy.

Theresa's periods had always been very erratic. She frequently went many months without one, and often they were very slight. On other occasions they ran one into another with hardly a break between. Having had surgery to remove a grapefruit-sized ovarian cyst in her teens, and been told she would never bear children, and since she was allergic to the pill we hardly knew what to do, but with her history it came as no surprise when she had no period for several months after the loss of this foetus. As summer turned into autumn and we were getting excited about our upcoming journey back to a new life for us and career for me, she began to get strange feelings in her abdomen, and by September we agreed she should visit the doctor.

After a while he came out to me in the waiting room and enquired, "Mr. Longhurst?" When I replied in the affirmative, he stuck out his hand and said, with a huge grin on his face, "I don't know whether to clout you round the ear or congratulate you; Theresa's five months pregnant – you're going to be a dad!"

* * *

As we boarded the ship and gave our names to the crew member ticking us off on the passenger manifest, Theresa was six months pregnant, and very obviously so. The crewman looked at her bump very pointedly, eyed us both up and down and said in a voice that could be heard by all around us, "Oh yes. You're the *honeymoon* couple!"

In those days the norm was to get married and *then* produce a family, and as far as he read the situation we were only just squeaking in under the door for that order of events. So it was, no doubt, for all the other passengers and crew who had witnessed this little encounter.

During the voyage home, on a number of occasions, I saw a little boy from the spirit world. He was a toddler, just stivering about, and clearly had not been walking very long. He had curly, blonde hair and mostly wore a navy blue toddler's trouser-suit. He was radiantly happy and clearly belonged with us. He was never far from us and looking to us as one's own child would look to its parents. I *knew* his name was Peter David. It seemed logical to me that this was the soul-body of the child Theresa was carrying within her, and I was over the moon about this. After several sightings I mentioned this to Theresa.

"Oh, I am so glad you have been seeing him too," she said. "I didn't like to say anything in case it was just my wishful thinking."

She also had seen him numerous times, and described him and his clothing identically to my observations – including the name!

That was it. This was definitely our son, Peter David, due to arrive in this world in only a few more weeks.

In early February 1971, the baby finally arrived, after a long and exhausting (for Theresa!) delivery. It was a girl! I was so astounded when the intern in charge of the delivery announced this that I said, in a state of utter disbelief, "No, it can't be; you must have made a mistake!"

But his amused reply was unequivocal, "I'm awfully sorry but she just ain't got what it takes!"

Yet, that was not the end of the Peter David saga. Theresa and I continued seeing him. On one occasion, a few months later, as I came home from work at the end of the day, there he was, his little head just visible above the windowsill, looking out of the window at me, waving to his daddy. Theresa and I saw him independently of each other on a number of further occasions and after some time it finally dawned on us that this was her *first* baby who had not made it through into the earthly life. It was our new daughter's older brother, visiting us from the spirit world. What joy that was to our hearts to know he was alive and well, with no deformity and full of the joy, exuberance and energy of life and love. Here was a classic case of knowing these things intellectually, so none of it should have been a surprise to either of us, but the actual *experience*, affirming all that we knew in *principle* was true, was so much more meaningful, wonderful and *joyful to* us. In a way, it is rather like saying that to know something in theory is a two-dimensional thing but to *experience* it adds extra dimensionality to it, bringing it into a living, pulsing reality.

There are millions of couples around the world whose children do not make it through into this life, either by miscarriage or termination. About one in five pregnancies ends in miscarriage, so that is a lot of souls who never make it through to this world. With miscarriage there is almost always going to be grief and distress for the bereaved parents who have lost a much desired and longed-for child in their lives. For those choosing to terminate a pregnancy, for whatever reason, there will almost always be guilt added to all the other feelings. For most, having no awareness or denying the reality of the living soul of the little one, who will naturally gravitate toward the parents he had chosen to provide his vehicle of expression, is depriving the parents of some very helpful and beneficial easement of their grief and guilt. This is such an unnecessary deprival. Such denial is not a spontaneous or natural state of being but one created by centuries of being conditioned by dogmas and doctrines of institutionalised religion dominating society. Alternatively, knowing, *experiencing* that their offspring is actually alive and well and loves them and desires familial fellowship with them, would bring great comfort, if only they were aware.

This domination has been based on inculcating fear into the minds and hearts of the populace, not unconditional love. Is this what Jesus desires for his brethren in the earthly life? It is also worth considering that the soul of the little one will be profoundly confused by the fact that his parents are ignoring him, acting as if he doesn't exist, when the simple sending out of love and blessings toward the one they love and miss (or feel guilty about), even if they have no perceptual awareness of him, will be a massive healing aid to all.

This is not intended to be an advocacy of actively seeking such awareness – that should always be a free choice – but it is not a blanket condemnation either. Rather, it is a cry from the heart to all in such a situation who feel the presence of the souls of their loved ones – offspring who don't make it to term or much beyond, or older generations who have returned to the etheric realms after a full sojourn in time – to acknowledge and allow such feelings, even if they do not include, or lead to, a sensory awareness of the departed soul, to accept and welcome those feelings and/or awareness as being the blessing for all that they actually are. Such a change of attitude can and will move us away from the fear of 'death' that so pervades today's society, and into a much healthier understanding of the eternal continuity of life. This will, assuredly, be one more significant and substantial step forward towards the Kingdom of Heaven on Earth.

* * *

In the spring of 1971, I was busy getting into my stride as a seaweed salesman and Theresa was busy making a home for us and our new baby daughter. Due to complications, she had had to stop breastfeeding after only a month and had switched the little one onto baby formula. When she was about three months old, I had gone away to West Sussex for a few days on business; my first time away overnight since she was born.

"Theresa snatched her up and this jerking motion caused her to gasp and start breathing again. It probably saved her life."

Early the first evening Theresa decided to go and have a look at her, asleep in her cot. To Theresa's horror, she was blue and had stopped breathing. She snatched her up and this jerking motion caused the baby to gasp and start breathing again.

It probably saved her life.

We were living on the top floor of a Victorian terrace and Theresa had no car of her own, so she tore down to the ground floor of the building with the baby in her arms and frantically bashed on the door of the young New Zealand couple who lived there. Fortunately, Janine was in.

"My baby's dying, please help me," yelled Theresa.

Immediately Janine was galvanised into action. Still barefoot, she grabbed her car keys.

"Come on," she said, "where's your doctor?"

Within minutes they were at the doctor's surgery, which was attached to his home. He saw them straight away.

Taking one look at the baby he said, "Can you drive her to the hospital? It'll be quicker than waiting for an ambulance. I'll phone ahead and tell them to expect you."

Janine raced them to the hospital, where doctors and nurses grabbed the little one from Theresa's arms.

Herein is a further story of how greatly we are helped from

the Heaven Realms, here on Earth. Neither Theresa nor Janine knew exactly where the hospital was, although Theresa had an inkling of the general direction because that was where she had had the baby twelve weeks earlier. But because I had driven her there – at night – and had driven her home nine days later, and because she was a newcomer to the area, as was Janine, Theresa had only the vaguest idea of where to go. They found their way there with no detours, however, but that was not the end of the story. The hospital was a mass of separate buildings set in a vast site, with lanes in all directions and signs that were at best inadequate and at worst, misleading. In spite of this, they drove unerringly straight to the paediatrics unit, even though they had no conscious awareness of where it was. Truly they were under very close guidance, because minutes of further delay could have been decisive to the outcome.

The senior paediatric consultant, Dr. Jacoby, was there. I knew him because his son, Richard, had been at school with me and I had once helped Richard when he had badly injured his hand while we were out cycling together. I had called his dad from a payphone and he had come and rescued Richard, and expressed his profound thanks to me for helping his son. Now it was his turn to help my infant daughter. After checking her heartbeat and finding it to be racing out of control at over three hundred beats per minute, he immediately injected digitalis straight into her heart! This stabilised her heart rate and undoubtedly – again – saved her life, although she was to spend the next several days in intensive care. The doctors told Theresa that if she had arrived at the hospital just five minutes later than she had, they would not have been able to save our daughter's life.

After a few days I returned from my business excursion to an empty home, knowing nothing of these dramatic events, since at that time we had no telephone and Theresa had no way of contacting me because I was travelling about and staying at bed and breakfasts wherever I finished up at the end of each day. I was feeling sorry for myself, with a migraine, and went to bed. An hour or so later Theresa came in alone.

"Where's the little 'un?" I asked, and Theresa immediately burst into tears.

As soon as she told me what had happened and that she was

still in intensive care, I leapt out of bed, the migraine instantly vanished, threw on some clothes and off we flew to the hospital. There was the tiny, twelve-week-old with tubes and wires all over her body, looking as fragile as could be; but as soon as she saw me she began to perk up and not long afterwards was allowed home.

It turned out that the baby formula was too rich for her to digest and was going rancid in her intestine. This was poisoning her system and had set her heart racing. Much longer without the digitalis and it would have burnt out. Blessedly, she made a full recovery, with no lasting heart, digestive or brain damage.

6: Family Life – Here and Beyond

Later that same year we moved to a flat in a big, old Georgian mansion out in the country. This move came about by way of another synchronistic event. I was in the local health food shop talking to the proprietor about some aspect of wholefood when an elderly lady intervened. She said she had overheard the discussion and proffered some advice, stating during the conversation that she was the cook for Lord and Lady Dowding.

"Oh, I know Lord Dowding and her Ladyship; I had tea with them a few years ago," I said.

Needless to say, our conversation developed and I mentioned that we were looking for somewhere to live. The lady introduced herself as Edna and said that the flat next to hers was coming up vacant and could be ideal for us. Rental accommodation was sparse, so this flat was a godsend.

Edna proved to be a splendid neighbour, helping us greatly with vegetarian and wholefood recipes and ideas (the Dowdings were vegetarian), cooking fantastic meals for us from time to time and doing the odd spot of babysitting. It was here that our second child was born, forty-nine weeks after her older sister. So much for Theresa's infertility! We tried all manner of the latest contraceptive devices, but it seemed like I only had to take my socks off and she fell pregnant! In spite of all our precautions, she conceived three more times. Had we actually brought six offspring into this world, Heaven knows how we would have coped!

Theresa's health was very fragile – she had contracted brucellosis from infected milk in Scotland in 1973 and this almost killed her. Brucellosis causes spontaneous abortion, or miscarriage, in cattle, and the same appeared to be the case with Theresa. Generally poor health and especially female troubles meant that none of the three subsequent pregnancies lasted even half way to term and eventually led to her having a hysterectomy a few years after that.

* * *

There was a further synchronistic event involving Hugh Dowding, more than twenty years later. As part of our business activity we exhibited at various trade shows. One of these shows was booked at what was, during World War II, Duxford Aerodrome, near Cambridge – an RAF and US Air Force fighter base, now part of the Imperial War Museum. The exhibition was in what had been the Officers' Mess, now tastefully refurbished as a conference and exhibition facility, but retaining the atmosphere of its original purpose.

I arrived on the appointed day with our exhibition stand and equipment, flat-packed for ease of transportation and assembly. We were pre-booked as stand-space 22 and I took our equipment to that marked-out spot. There was another exhibitor's stand already erected there. I found the organiser, who studied the floor-plan.

"Oh," he said, "there is a mix-up, but we can re-schedule you to stand 27."

I arrived at space 27 and there, hanging on the wood-panelled wall at the back of the space was a portrait in oil of Air Marshall Lord Hugh Dowding, looking as he might have during the war. If there had not been a mix-up, Hugh's portrait would have been hidden behind some other exhibitor's stand, never to be noticed by me.

As I stood, transfixed for a long moment frozen in time, looking at the portrait, Hugh's eyes sparkled smilingly at me and he was right there, bringing his love, blessing and personal joy straight into my heart. It was a very precious and treasured moment for me. I always marvel at how these serendipitous 'little' events are organised by our friends and loved ones in spirit, just to let us know that they are not as far away as we in the Earth life may think. Hugh had, unwittingly – synchronistically – been an *enormous* influence on my life, opening it up to the spiritual service of helping lost souls, massively more of which service was much later to become a central part of our lives, and here he was, after that service phase had become fully operational, bringing this reminder that he was still very much with me, even though I had not 'seen' him since 1967. Is it any wonder the term *stalwart* seems so apposite to describe such true and timeless (as well as tireless) friends? Assuredly, not just friends, but brothers in the Sonship of God.

THERE WERE SOME very negative psychic energies in the mansion to which we had moved, emanating, so it seemed, from the ground floor, and the children were highly sensitive to them. When our younger daughter was only six months old I awoke in the middle of the night from a deep sleep, with a dreadful feeling in the solar plexus of pervasive evil, but having no idea why. As I lay there wondering what was going on, I became aware of a ruckus in the baby's room, just down the hall from our bedroom. It sounded as if her cot was being violently thrashed about, hitting the walls and floor. I leapt from bed and hurtled into her room. The cot was completely collapsed, dismantled and lying in a disorderly heap on the floor. The nuts and bolts holding it together were unscrewed and removed from their sockets. She was lying, dazed, still half asleep, on the floor across the room. This act of violence, in which her cot had been shaken until it had come apart – or, perhaps more probably, had been deliberately dismantled – and the six-month old lifted and moved out of it and across the room, came from an unseen source. Some would call this the work of poltergeists, but I have always understood poltergeists to be *mischievous* spirits. Whatever did this was well beyond mischievous, for I had been wakened by a combination of the noise and the nauseating, fearful vibration of *malevolence* clutching at my midriff.

During the three years we lived there numerous other incidents indicated that ungodly energies permeated the place. When our older daughter was just three she woke up one night screaming in terror. I raced to her bedside and cradled her in my arms to calm her down. She was eventually able to tell me that an ugly, frightening old woman had come and was saying horrible things and threatening her with harm. I told her that the Lord Jesus was our friend and protector and that he had power over situations such as this. Calling on his name and authority, I commanded the old crone to go and never to return. This calmed our daughter and she assured me that the harpy had indeed departed. I told her that at any time unfriendly spirits might come calling, all she had to do was reach out her hand, call out to Jesus to hold it and ask him to guard and protect her, and that he would instantly be there, and she would have nothing to fear. Within minutes she was asleep again and there were no more such visits from the old hag.

THE YEARS ROLLED BY and we moved several times, eventually managing to get a mortgage to buy a house. I had become the top sales representative for the company and for three years consecutively earned enough commission to pay off the mortgage, but the company had got into various kinds of difficulty and I never received a penny of these earnings. It was a stressful and worrying time in our lives, although we always had a roof over our heads and food on the table, even if sometimes only by the skin of our teeth! My brother asked if I felt bitter about being deprived of what was rightfully mine. It would not be true if I were to say I was not entirely happy about it but I could honestly say I was not bitter.

"If I am bitter, whose gut is it going to rot?" I said to Mike. "Only mine, so what's the point?"

Over the years I occasionally pondered the 'what ifs', but by and large it was simply a case of getting on with life, and the matter became increasingly consigned to the memory archives.

In 1977 the company was sold and most of the sales force was let go. The new owner wanted me to move to Cambridge, where his headquarters were located, to be his sales manager. He told me he was going to teach me how to become a businessman. This seemed like a wonderful new beginning and we eagerly welcomed this, but our enthusiasm was to be short-lived. This new employer was a bully who treated everyone – staff, suppliers, even customers – like something you wouldn't want to step in. He was true to his word about teaching me how to become a business man, but not in the way he intended it.

"To behave toward our brothers in a way we would not wish them to behave toward us is dishonouring them, and in so doing we dishonour ourselves."

I resolved from observing and experiencing his behaviour toward his fellows that this was not the way I ever wished to behave, in any circumstances; whether in a social, domestic or work setting. Regardless of the circumstances, our fellows are our brothers, created by God, the Creator Spirit, in His likeness. To behave toward our brothers in a way we would not wish them to behave toward us is dishonouring them, and in so doing we dishonour ourselves, because in the eternal scheme of things we are all One in the Sonship of the Father Creator. To dishonour any living being is to bind us to them in a karmic debt, and this holds us – as well as them – back on the path of spiritual progress. An entirely unserviceable situation is thus set in motion, and this has to be brought back into balance, however long it takes. And if we are unaware of the cosmic laws in effect, and of which we have been in breach in that incarnation, then subsequent incarnations will be required to correct the imbalance.

As time went by it became increasingly clear that, much as I loved the products and the job, the oppressive work environment was rapidly creating conditions wherein the reasons for going began to outweigh the reasons for staying. During this time two work colleagues and I looked very seriously into the prospects of moving to Norway to set-up our own seaweed processing operation there. Plans moved ahead and came near to fulfilment; we had arranged financial assistance from the Norwegian authorities, I had given notice and left my employment and we had sold our house preparatory to moving to an island halfway up the west coast of Norway.

"Having that 'blind trust' provides a measure of peace and well-being in the most distressing moments."

But the hand of duplicity intervened, and at the last moment our plans were dashed to ruins. I was out of work, living in rented accommodation to which the owners were due to return from abroad in only a few months, with a wife and two school-age daughters to support, with no job and no apparent prospects. It was a bleak moment, but after all the years of *experiencing* the

Lord Jesus, I was able to call upon some of that knowing-beyond-all-doubt of his living, personal, loving presence in my life and the reality of his beneficent, protecting power, to help me maintain my equilibrium. I had an inward sense that all was going to be well and that this was, in some way I could not then clearly understand, the Master once again leading us *out of* a situation.

Having that 'blind trust' gives one something to hold onto; it provides a measure of inner peace and well-being in the most distressing moments. The fullness of the measure, or the degree of discernibility of it, is directly proportional to our own degree of blind trust. A limited level of trust affords us only a limited amount of peace and comfort; a larger amount of trust affords a proportionally greater level of inner peace and tranquillity. In our Earth-life journey we tend only to come to any degree of trust by actually experiencing the trust*worthiness* of the person or situation in which we are willing to place our trust. Placing trust in a complete stranger, about whom one knows nothing, could be considered foolhardy. Over the better part of two decades I had been *experiencing* Jesus as loving, caring, a real friend and help in time of distress (as well as in times of joy). Without the certainty provided by that experience, something akin to blind panic could very easily have enveloped me at that time.

With Theresa's loving support also and keeping in mind the Master's oft-repeated counsel, "If in doubt, do nothing," we did that. Still, in my earthly consciousness I could think of no prospects. Days and weeks went by and the date for having to move from our rented house loomed nearer.

One day, with time on my hands and our situation weighing on my mind, I decided to start clearing out some of the stuff we had brought with us when we sold our own house. I had substantial quantities of trade magazines, mostly un-read, and other paraphernalia from my erstwhile employment, so set to sorting through it to discard non-essential items. There were several recent issues of a journal covering arid-zone agriculture which I had not read, so before throwing them out, I started looking through them. There, in one of them, was an article about a new product claiming to conserve water by improving the ability of soils to retain it, which indicated that crops could be grown where previously they could not, such as in deserts, or could be grown better than before in marginal-quality soils.

This article pressed my buttons. Here was something with which I truly resonated; some new technology to really do some good in the world. And the company was UK based, near Manchester. I thought maybe I could apply to be their UK distributor, since they seemed to be focusing their attention on arid parts of the planet. I felt sure there was plenty of scope for improving efficiency of water-use in commercial horticulture, landscaping, re-forestation and the like, even in temperate climates, and I knew lots of people who might become customers or even wholesale distributors. I called the company and told them of my ideas, saying I would like to apply for a sales agency. They invited me to visit, for a chat.

As I got into the car to drive to Manchester on the appointed day, instantly the Master was there with me, in the passenger seat, larger than life – as was so characteristic of him. His relaxed, reassuring presence and the love emanating from him welled me up with reciprocal love for him and gratitude for the unwavering constancy of his friendship, support and solidarity, and *suddenly* I knew, beyond doubt, with a knowing which is not of intellectual thought processes but of the higher part of our mind, the part that is one with Christ, that these people were actually going to *employ* me. Not just a commission sales agency but a salaried staff member. Here would be a chance to rebuild my life, work and provide security for my beloved family again. The journey to Manchester was more like air than road travel, and I had no need of a plane for this kind of flying; my very soul was soaring to the heights of Heaven.

Sure enough I drove home afterwards with a firm offer of a job as Sales Manager. The car reverberated with songs of rejoicing and thanksgiving, from heart and soul as well as voice. I felt I knew what Handel must have experienced as he received the inspiration for the Alleluia Chorus from *Messiah*.

Amazingly, after just a few months the Company became insolvent and we seemed to be back in the mire. But I had made good contacts in that short time, and almost immediately set up a new business with several new associates, and we soldiered on.

By this time we had bought a house in Wiltshire and I was working from home, with most sales contacts being by phone. It was a struggle, but we were making progress.

"suddenly I was aware that there were four children
standing at the foot of our bed."

One night at bed time Theresa and I had just put out the light and were settling down for sleep when suddenly I was aware that there were four children standing at the foot of our bed. To our right was the oldest, a boy of about twelve. Next to him, a girl of about nine, then a boy, about eight, and last but not least, a girl, about seven, all lined up in order of descending height – and presumably therefore, age. I sat up, startled by the suddenness of the apparition, but unafraid – the vibes were entirely benign.

The oldest child said, "Hello, Dad, it's me, Peter. Sorry if we startled you. Diana, Christopher and Jessica are here with me. We have come to let you know that we love you and Mum and our sisters in the Earth life; we are well and happy and are never far away. Every time you think of us or send out love and blessings and goodwill toward us, we instantly have awareness of it. We know you love us deeply and this fills our hearts with joy. We want you to keep in your understanding that even though we are not incarnate, we really are here, and are your loving children. We will always be here for you, and will always love you."

The other three, Diana, Chris and Jessica were not silent during this and added their own affirmations, eager to chip in their own comments. Peter, in characteristic big brother manner, was shushing them, but of course they were determined to be heard also.

As you can imagine, this was a deeply moving moment. Theresa knew something was going on, that there was someone there, and picked up the vibes, even though she didn't see them or hear their speaking, and I quickly explained what was happening. It was a joyous experience for us both, and Theresa, who had felt a great burden of guilt that she had been unable to bring these, our four other children, into this world, was greatly uplifted by it, and relieved of much of her burden.

We shared this experience with our daughters, who were aged

eleven and ten, and they accepted this very much as a matter of fact; a perfectly natural, normal experience, which was, of course, exactly what we wished them to do, since to us that was precisely what it was and is. It was our desire that they should have no fear of such events and experiences; that they should be able to accept such with equanimity.

*   *   *

Some years later, after they had grown up and left home, but had come to visit, this event came into the conversation and they shared with us some of their experiences during our brief, eighteen-month sojourn in Wiltshire. In one, our younger daughter was also in bed, contemplating life as she was settling down for sleep when suddenly she became aware of a little boy in her room. He was standing by the wall between the door and the window. His hands were clasped behind his back and he was leaning against the wall, then pushing himself away from it with his hands, swaying back and forth, all the while looking casually around the room.

As she finished recounting this incident, I said to her, "What happened then?"

She said, "I don't know; I went off to sleep."

At that moment, I instantly knew it was Chris, and as the awareness hit me I heard him say, "I'd come to play."

Here was Chris, her younger brother, alive, well and full of sibling love for his older sister in a normal, healthy way, just as we all are (in spite of the usual rivalry, squabbling and nonsense that go on in every family). He had arrived at her bed time, knowing that she would soon be asleep and that her soul would then be leaving her body and entering the soul realms – his home territory – so that they could spend the hours of her sleep time together.

I said to her, "You never told us that before; I didn't know you had had awareness of your brothers and sisters in spirit."

But without this new, added comment from Chris providing greater insight into what the moment was all about, the significance was veiled from her understanding until this moment, years later.

Then her older sister added, quite casually and matter-of-factly, "Oh, yes, I was aware of Peter being around all the time. I always have been."

It was so normal, so natural to her that she had assumed this was something we would have somehow 'known', so why would she need to even bother mentioning it!?

Theresa's and my awareness of our four offspring in spirit had been fairly dormant since the early years, when we had had those few sightings of Peter as a toddler. I guess we had been so involved with events at the Earth-life level of activity that these more subtle realities had become rather pushed into the wings. However, after that bedside visit in Wiltshire, contact was well and truly restored, and we entered a phase of our lives when contact with 'the gang of four' became very much part of our experience, both in an uplifting, spiritual way, and also very much at an ordinary, down-to-Earth, familial way, and always with love, spontaneity, comfortableness and joy strengthening the rightness of such contact. In this is no 'trafficking with the devil' as so many old-order religionists would have one believe. This was, without a shadow of doubt, 'the love of Heaven' in the most natural, comfortable way imaginable.

This began an era of frequent and meaningful contact with Peter, Diana and Christopher. We came to know each of them as intimately as we knew our two daughters in this world – and actually in many ways better, because contact with those in the Heaven realms is literally at the soul-to-soul, mind-to-mind level, whereas the denser substance of our bodily senses acts as a type of screen, filtering out nuances and subtleties that the soul means, intends and conveys but that are lost in the filtration system of our sensory perception faculties. Also, although I referred to the gang of four earlier . . . in reality, there was no awareness of Jessica at all. Full and total awareness of her – at the soul-to-soul level – came just once, in April 1993, when I was out walking our dog in the nearby city greenspace.

As I paused to 'tune in to the infinite' by my favourite grove of trees, suddenly and unexpectedly, there she was. I – my inner being – knew instantly who it was. She appeared about six or eight paces away, maybe three metres above the ground, amidst the nearby trees. She was radiant sunlight; gossamer, diaphanous; light and insubstantial as a thistledown wafting gently in the breeze. The love that spontaneously emanated, burst forth, exploded from her was so intense and yet so delicate, so personal and so immediately overwhelming that it caused me to gasp out loud, to feel faint with the rush of upliftment with which it filled my heart and soul. She was full of joy that is so far beyond any experience at the purely Earth-mind conscious level that I was almost dazed – and certainly bedazzled – by her vibration.

She was so sparkling, effervescent with this joy that she could not keep still, and was in constant motion, like one might imagine a fairy to be in a children's story. The love was intensely personal, one-to-one, for me, her beloved Dad and I knew it was something she had yearned to do – come and visit me in this loving way – for a long time. The communication was not as I had experienced it from others, including her own brothers and sister in her realm. Rather, it was like telepathy; what I now refer to as *mind-to-mind communing*. I simply 'knew' what she was 'saying', which was in essence:

"I love you so dearly; admire and honour you for all that you are; am with you often, even though you have not been aware of it; have deeply longed for this moment of sharing, but the time was not right until now."

It was a moment that was impossible to measure in Earth time. It was out of time. Then, as suddenly as she had arrived, she was gone.

I was exhilarated, exalted, elated; soaring with the intimacy and intensity of it; yet, as I walked home afterwards there was a nuance also of sadness elusively floating around in my heart and in my head. Over the following hours and days, as I became adjusted to the experience and the personal immensity of it, I came to know in my soul that the sadness was because although it was a most wonderful *Hello* – an introduction and getting-to-know-you at a level and in a way that, other than in exceptional cases, can take many weeks, months or even years between two souls incarnate – it was also a *Goodbye*.

"She was going to reincarnate. She was going to take upon herself another persona, a new Earth-life identity."

How could this be? What could possibly separate us now,

after this most wonderful of encounters? But I really knew the answer, even though it had not been spoken during this exquisite communion between us. It was not what had been exchanged (as distinct from spoken) but what had been between the lines during that timeless moment: she was going away. *She was going to reincarnate.* She was going to take upon herself another persona, a new Earth-life identity. She would no longer be, to my perception, 'our Jessica', other than as with us all in the Earth life: as a seed memory within the overall, eternal aspect of our higher being. Jessica would *never* be lost, gone, disintegrated, but would become part of an ever growing, ever becoming, ever expanding Being of the Light, until she became, as is the destiny of us all, *fully* enlightened and restored to the oneness that we all are within the Sonship of our heavenly Father.

Meanwhile, she would soon become, once again, a citizen of eternity *sojourning in time,* just as we all are during our brief appearances on Earth. But the 'Jessica' part of her would become a dormant, Shadow of Light part of her 'allness' as she took a new vehicle of expression, and thus continue to grow by experiencing new challenges, new adventures, new opportunities to transform adversity into fulfilment, to bring into manifestation some new magnificence uniquely hers, just as is the potential with every single one of us *creative*-created beings in this dimension. But above all it is our objective to heal relationships broken, often over numerous incarnations, so that we all become restored to the oneness in Eternity that is our destiny.

That is our purpose, our reason for being here. And, deep within our soul is the seed memory of all the other identities we are/have been during our multiple journeys into this illusory world of physical experience and back to the *etheric* counterpart of Earth again. So would it be with Jessica. She would always 'be', but just as Jessica was who she was because of all she had been *before,* so who she was now about to become would be that new being because of the 'Jessica' contribution to the greater being that (s)he is going to become.

Jessica had not made it through into the Earth dimension back in 1975. She had grown up in the etheric realm, and had always been close to her Earth-life mum, dad and siblings. There, she had progressed as far as she was able as Jessica, and in order to progress further toward full enlightenment, another *potential*, another *opportunity*, was required, in another persona, just as is the case for us all. She had certainly become a radiant being; perhaps more than I could be fully aware. Her appearance to me assuredly indicated that she had become a *Being of the Light*. Whether this meant *full* enlightenment I have no information but there is no doubt in my mind that however much she may be coming back here to resolve issues for her own enlightenment, she is coming back for the help of others. Either way, this is a joyous and wonderful, blessed, glorious thing.

We are drawn back to the Earth physical because here – and only here, in time and place – can we outwork and resolve the karmic issues that accrue between souls as a result of misperceptions about who we really are. This leads to unkingdomly thoughts, attitudes, judgements, behaviour toward our fellows, leading to largely unconscious guilt, fear and shame. Reincarnating enables opportunities to correct those outstanding issues and grievances, and restore perfect peace, harmony and balance between us. In this way the Kingdom of Heaven can be established on Earth in and through us, the fragmented Sonship, and our restoration to wholeness, oneness in Christ completed. Much more about this later.

Meanwhile, during our sojourning in time, we call into our presence opportunity to grow, experience, help, give, forgive, heal, achieve. This means not just material, pecuniary success, but immeasurably more important, fulfilment of our soul's desire for *spiritual* awakening to the magnificence that we, in our Sonship of the Creator, really are. In this way we recreate, realign ourselves anew in that truth in as many ways as the potential we bring with us into this life can permit; as many ways as our heart desires, all in accord with our birth vision.

All that gets between us and our ability to fulfil our heart's desire is commitment, or rather, lack of it. How *truly* do we seek it; how *earnestly* do we desire it? For so many, the cares of the world, the personal difficulties and the circumstantial obstacles we unconsciously allow to slowly and inexorably get in the way, gradually push our ambitions and *deep-down* motivations to the back burner.

Although our contact with Jessica had been basically limited to the foot-of-the-bed encounter in Wiltshire and now the grove-of-trees experience, the information given by mind-to-mind communing had been massively more. As I later mulled over that exchange, it became absolutely clear that the overriding commitment of Jessica was her all-encompassing, supreme desire, passion, focus, to reincarnate. She had been almost desperate in her eagerness so to do back in 1975 and had not made it through. The ensuing 'years' had not been wasted for her, and no doubt much more had been accomplished in her quest for spiritual awakening during her spell in the etheric counterpart of Earth than we had any awareness of.

But now had come the right time, once again, for this great desire of hers to re-enter the world of material experience, and she had set her face toward this with single-minded determination. Here was a soul on a mission. This time, it was clear, it would not be thwarted. The encounter in the grove of trees had been on a Friday morning in April. At Communion two days later, she appeared, for the first – and only – time, to my awareness, as a young adult, to confirm her commitment to the Lord Jesus for her birth vision of her about-to-be-embarked-upon incarnation. I suspect it needed no confirmation for her own sake but that it was as much to allow Theresa and me to see her demonstration of it, so that we would have that comfort of knowing it to be so.

7: Deepening Understanding

After about eighteen months living in Wiltshire we moved to Gloucester and rented an office in a refurbished Victorian grain warehouse in the dockland area of the city. We bought a house nearby and our material lives continued to progress.

Whenever we moved house and selected a suitable place to set-up our sanctuary of prayer and communion, I always had a niggling doubt about whether the Lord and all our other loved ones in the Heaven realms would (re)establish contact with us in the new geographical location. How unfounded was my doubt – every time. Looking back now I realise of an axiomatic certainty that such contact is nothing whatsoever to do with geographical location. As if we could ever become 'lost' to the Beings of Light in the Heaven realms; like we are driving along in a car and they are following (or leading!) and we take a wrong turning and end up in some place where they cannot find us. Such contact and the ability to be in a state of awareness of it is directly proportional to the desire of the heart and soul for there to be that contact.

To the Lord and the heavenly hosts we are never lost, in any sense of the term. Assuredly, the contact is not even dependent upon the establishment of a physical sanctuary of prayer and communion, although there is no doubt that such a place, set aside from the hustle and bustle – and all too often, clamour – of horizontal, or outward, earthly, activities and distractions, is highly conducive to such awareness. When a place is reserved for prayer, spiritual attunement and contemplation, a refined, uplifting and spiritually empowered psychic energy is created, and builds there. A place set aside for sacred purpose deters other, less refined energies from infiltrating and diluting or dampening-down those exalted vibrations. This can then be used by those in the Earth life who are of one heart and one mind with those vibrations, to establish a greater degree of attunement with souls of like desire in the Heaven realms, including, and especially, the Lord Jesus.

"It is our heart, the 'seat' of the soul, which is the meeting place with the Creator Spirit, The Holy One, God."

But in reality it is not the location, prayer table or physical structure that is the sanctuary of communion with the Lord specifically, or the Realms of Light in general. It is our heart, the 'seat' of the soul, which is the meeting place with the Creator Spirit, The Holy One, God, or whatever name we are comfortable with in our communing activity. It is the sincerity of our heart which determines the clarity of the lines of communication between us and our heavenly Father, the Source of All. The Bible makes this clear throughout. Sadly, this message is sparsely received in today's world. Two thousand years ago Jesus spoke of the people of his time as a 'faithless and perverse generation', and in that, very little has *outwardly* changed, though we shall see, as we read on, that this is in the advanced stages of a complete transformation.

Meanwhile ego's maxim is 'seeing is believing' or 'I'm from Missouri, *show* me'. Yet, again, the Bible is full of calls for people *first* to believe and *then* they will see. Jesus illustrates this with his repeated statements to those healed from their various infirmities by his responding to their supplications, **"Your *faith* has made you whole"** (Mk. 10:52; Lk. 8:48). When we truly seek after God and earnestly desire the coming of the Kingdom of Heaven on Earth, there is nothing 'physical, tangible' to cause us to have such a desire. It is an inward feeling, and feeling is of the soul, which in reality is our Higher Self, or Christ Mind. To reach, establish communion with, this part of our Being requires faith, trust, belief in and commitment to things which are not of the physical structures of the earthly life. Our five bodily senses are devised solely for perceiving temporal, illusory constructs, and have no capacity for awareness of the things of Eternity. It therefore requires of us *faith* that such a state of Being exists as reality at a higher frequency, which becomes discernible to us when we choose to refine our attunement to awareness of that exalted, elevated wavelength.

By faith, trust, believing and earnestly *desiring* the Kingdom of Heaven on Earth, we create a tiny, yet spiritually radiant and powerful microcosm of that reality – Heaven – here, in our earthly lives. The Kingdom of Heaven, whether on Earth or in the spirit realms, is not a structure; it is a state of awareness of a reality which becomes *our* reality when we make the conscious choice to live in harmony, at one, with the qualities that make the Kingdom of Heaven what it is: a way of living and being in which souls radiate who they *really* are, brothers in the Sonship of God. *"Beloved,* now *are we the sons of God . . ."* (1Jn. 3:2).

The Kingdom of Heaven has nothing whatsoever to do with the practise of a formalised religion in the structured, institutionalised way it has become implemented on Earth, with all its myriad rules and regulations, musts and must-nots. These are of the external world, and not according to the words recorded of Jesus of Nazareth, who counsels us to "Love God and love your neighbour as yourself; on these two commandments hang all the Law and the Prophets." In other words, forget all the rules and commandments (he had plenty to say to the Pharisees about all that, none of which was complimentary) and focus on *Love*. When we come from the place of unconditional, Perfect Love, all the characteristics which are kingdomly will fall into place *naturally*, because, like our Creator, in Whose likeness we are created, this is who we really are, and we won't even have to *think* about any rules and regulations, morals, behaviour standards etc. In Jesus' words, "The Kingdom of Heaven is *within*" (Lk. 17:21).

We all have the seed germ of it within us. It is love, compassion, goodwill; doing unto others as we would have them do unto us; empathy, understanding, a recognition that we are all One in spirit; straightforwardness and transparency; accepting and honouring others and allowing them their differences rather than fearing and hating them (the differences, that is, for if we fear and hate the differences, we will soon come to fear and hate the people exhibiting/expressing those differences); forgiveness (much more on forgiveness and its true meaning later), justice, fairness, generosity of spirit; tolerance, understanding, a deep resonance with and for the *brotherhood* of man. You have the drift; you can add your own perceptions of the facets that contribute to kingdomliness. There is no limit, even as there are no limits with God.

We all exhibit some of these qualities some of the time. When we all exhibit all of them all of the time, we will have the Kingdom of Heaven on Earth, fully and comprehensively. How do we move from some of the qualities some of the time to all of them all the time?

Desire.

How do we truly seek and earnestly desire them?

One step at a time, depending on the underlying strength of our commitment and motivation to this state of desire. If our desire is submerged in fear and other cares of this world that distract us, and dilute our focus on kingdomliness, then our desire is weak, lukewarm; but the Spirit of Creation does not interfere with that because that is our free choice and we are imbued, within the essence of our Being, with the freewill to choose. *Everything.* I say God does not 'interfere', but although a magnet does not 'interfere' with iron filings, it *does* exert a drawing power, by the very fact of its *essential*, magnetic nature. In like manner, the Creator Spirit is inexorably drawing us back to fullness of awareness of, and oneness in, Him, and the end result is as inevitable as iron filings being irresistibly drawn back to the magnet. Ego may describe that as interference, but objectively, it is God simply *being* God, just as the magnet is simply being a magnet. Would we want our heavenly Father to be lukewarm in His love for us?

We will not be punished by an angry, wrathful, vengeful God for choosing freely, any more than a loving parent will angrily, wrathfully, vengefully punish a child for making a choice that is other than the parent's choice. And we are the children, the offspring, the creation of the Creator Spirit. There *are* consequences to our decisions; good consequences when we choose that which is beneficial to all; less desirable consequences when our choices are to the detriment of another person or aspect of creation, but there are *no* punishments, judgements or condemnations from a vexed or capricious god. These are perceptions of people from an earlier phase in the continually evolving, unfolding, progressing Great Rescue Programme, or GRP, for humanity from its illusion of separation from God (more on the GRP later). That programme, or process, has gone forward from there, and new revelations and understandings are now growing, unfolding in the spiritual awareness of humanity about the Creator and our relationship to Him. The perceptions of former times may have been serviceable to the people of those times, but it is not serviceable to mankind today to remain fixed in past perceptions, in an unfolding process that is going irresistibly forward.

As we begin to remember who and what we really are (the offspring, or creation, of the Creator), so do we begin to choose the things of which the Kingdom of Heaven is created, to be our *raison d'etre*, our motivating purpose in life. As we begin to experience the palpable benefit of this choosing, in terms of fear fading and inner peace growing in us, so does such become a commitment, a driving force for us, just as it was with Jesus. Why else would he have *deliberately* planned to have himself so brutally executed if it was not because of his unconditional love for us all and his commitment to his great desire for us all: our awakening to the fullness of remembrance of our oneness in the Sonship of God, and that the Kingdom of Heaven is within us?

The Kingdom of Heaven (on Earth *or* in Heaven) is not a state of solemnity, of outward piety and religious display; neither is it the holding of judgemental attitudes toward ourselves and our fellows. Rather, it is a state of joyful remembrance and awareness by each of us, that 'I and my Father are One'; that we are all indivisibly connected to, one within, the Spirit of Creation, the very life force which keeps us upright, functioning and alive. The joyfulness which comes from that awareness is not something we can adopt at will, as if selecting an item of apparel from a shop. It is an inward state of Being, our awareness of which *grows* in us as we remember, one step at a time, our true, eternal nature, heritage and destiny. Who, indeed, could not be joyful as the impact of such remembering comes filtering through the illusory conditioning we have all adopted over the years – and indeed, the lifetimes – and gradually transforms those illusory perceptions into the true Light of the New Dawn for mankind; the Kingdom Age? As this new awareness, remembrance of who we really are, grows within us and we become more loving, understanding and forgiving, so, conversely, do we gradually leave behind our burdens of guilt, fear and Earth-mind contrariness, which is the split-off, ego-dominated, judgemental, upside-down, wrong-thinking part of our mind.

*   *   *

In 1981, Theresa and I took the children to Vancouver for a visit. It was eleven years since we had left there, and I was curious to know how our feelings about the place would be, returning after settling back into life in England. I was also very eager to see Olga again; she who had been my spiritual mentor and 'got me hooked-up with Jesus'.

It was a pleasant experience being back in our old stamping ground again. My memories of the almost-seven-years spent there in the 1960s were fond, and had been crucial in terms of the spiritual journey upon which, unknowingly at the time, I was then embarking.

It was a great joy to see Olga again, but of course, eleven years had elapsed, and inevitably, as we grow, the distance between us also grows, (except with a Life-Partner, with whom one becomes 'as one flesh'). It is like trees in the nursery; as they grow, so they need spacing out, otherwise they crowd each other and hamper each other's growth and the natural habit of that growth potential. I had moved on; wife, family, my own path of development to unfold and fulfil. The five or so years of intensive mentoring by her for re-awakening in me my soul's desire for Kingdom awareness and 'citizenship' and getting me hooked-up with Jesus, who would unfailingly lead me back to that state of remembrance, if I was willing to follow, had been the most wonderful, precious, invaluable time. Truly, she was my Godmother in a very real and meaningful way.

Olga was now ninety years old and getting frail, although still very much in possession of all her 'marbles'! We had many belly laughs reminiscing about our former time together and she was wonderful with the girls, aged nine and ten. They held her somewhat in awe because I had spoken of her so often. The Rector had engineered an arrangement whereby Olga's grandson's best friend, Steve, now in his late twenties and qualified in home care for the elderly and infirm, had also become 'hooked' on the words of enlightenment and wisdom she imparted, and he had moved in to look after her. Steve and I had some interesting chats and got to know each other, a wonderful portent of things to come a few years later.

* * *

When I was back on the West Coast again on business in June 1985, I flew up to Vancouver from California for a long-weekend visit. Of course I went to see Olga – now ninety-four – and with Steve and our friend Pauline, we had Communion together. It was the most wonderful, palpably spiritually uplifting experience. There was *Joy of Heaven to Earth come down*.

In December 1985, Olga laid aside her body and in the summer of the following year, Steve came to England for a holiday and stayed with us. We showed him round the beautiful Cotswolds, a timeless, Old-World part of England that visitors from the New World find breathtakingly enchanting, and not without reason. Steve fell in love with England and at the end of his visit he went back to Vancouver, saved up, packed up and moved here.

Steve is very psychic, and his joining Theresa and me for our Communion hour really added power into the experience. He would have awareness of the people – the Master Jesus, the Teacher, the Rector and others in the spirit-world who participated with us, communed with us – describe what he was seeing/hearing/experiencing, and this would help us to pick up the vibes and get attuned to the events. At other times Theresa or I would have an initial awareness, share it with the other two and thus would the three of us 'power-in' on whatever was the 'happening' of the moment. This gave an exponentially greater focus on the process and was much more fulfilling and beneficial for all involved. In not many weeks we were all three operating at a level of dynamic, spiritual at-one-ment we had hardly experienced before.

During one period over a number of weeks I began seeing and feeling a gossamer film, or membrane, rather like a vast sheet of living-light silk, stretching away horizontally in all directions until out of sight. It was floating down from above our heads and over our bodies, as if we were passing through it. The first time I saw/felt it, it went to about our shoulders. Each week it came again and moved from above our heads down, reaching further each time. After several weeks it went down until it was beneath our feet. Although it appeared to be doing the moving – from above down – it felt as if *we* were passing through *it*. I realised

90

this was us actually experiencing 'entering into' the Kingdom of Heaven.

The Kingdom of Heaven is a state of refined, purified vibrations, for those who 'espouse good and eschew evil'. Revelation 21:27 says it this way: "*And there shall in no wise enter into it any thing that defileth, neither whatsoever worketh abomination, or maketh a lie . . .*" What we were experiencing was how this works. That which, at the molecular level, is 'refined' can pass through a semi-permeable membrane, and this gossamer film was a semi-permeable membrane of spirit matter, through which those of one-pointed, committed desire for the Kingdom could pass, but through which souls of unrefined or unpurified desire cannot pass. Not because God is a judgemental, wrathful, condemnatory, partial god, which religious traditions and literal-minded interpretations of scripture would have us believe, but because it is cosmic law. This is described in Jesus' parable of the marriage of the King's son, Matthew 22:11, as a guest at the marriage being found without a wedding garment and not being permitted entry (in those times this was a white, unspotted – clean – garment provided by the host for guests). It is also described a number of times in Revelation as being clothed in white raiment, garment, linen or clothing, symbolising purity of soul, undefiled by '*un*kingdomly' qualities or desires.

Creation works according to laws governing every aspect of its being – the Principles of Life of the Father, or PLFs. Creation is omni-dimensional and can be so because of the cosmic laws that enable it to function as the precision instrument that it is in all its omni-dimensionality, most of which is at a frequency that we, functioning and conscious only through our limited, three-dimensional bodily senses, have no awareness. A precision instrument can only function as such by operating according to precise laws, or regulating procedures or principles.

So, that which is/those who are, spiritually unrefined – *which defileth, worketh abomination or maketh a lie* – cannot enter the Kingdom reality, not because God is playing favourites but because such are unable to pass through the semi-permeable membrane. Put another way, such cannot enter the Kingdom because they simply have no awareness of its existence or its presence, its close, ever-present proximity to wherever they are.

This is because they have chosen to focus their consciousness on another frequency, and if a radio is attuned to one frequency, it does not have focus on another frequency. That does not mean the other frequency does not exist. It simply means that to the *perception* of such a soul it does not exist. In one sense, they are 'a long way from the Kingdom' or 'afar off', but in another equally true sense, none of us is ever far from the Kingdom or from the King because God is never far from us. Indeed, it is impossible for Him so to be because the very life and substance of and in which we have our being *is* God. Nothing is *not* God and how could it be otherwise? As Paul puts it,". . . *he is not far from every one of us: For in him we live, and move, and have our being . . .*" (Acts 17:27-28).

* * *

As the higher-powered psycho-spiritual energies that were created by the three of us participating together in the Communion devotions began to bring us to a higher place of awareness of the events taking place in our midst, and of which we were an integral part, we began to realise that we were entering a new phase of activity. This we came to describe as the Rescue work. It was the beginning of a prolonged phase of activity which was the answer to the desire that had been awakened in me by my encounter with Hugh Dowding, and his book *Lychgate*, in 1967.

"Light generation by elevated desire-thought is cosmic law. It is generated by love, compassion, goodwill; all the qualities that characterise the attributes of the Kingdom of Heaven."

As had been the case with Bobby Kennedy in 1968, the energy generated by the desire-thought expressed in the words of the Communion Service manifests itself in the spirit world as Light. This Light is not photons but is the very Light of Life; there is but one Life and that is the Life of the Creator, and to which Jesus referred when he told us that we are the Light of the world (Mt. 5:14). It was this that had attracted Bobby to us back then. This process of Light generation by elevated desire-thought is cosmic law; it is nothing to do with religious piety. It is generated by love, compassion, goodwill, an attitude of caring and giving toward our fellows; all the qualities that are kingdomly, or characterise the attributes of the Kingdom of Heaven and Its King.

Such qualities stem from an awareness that whatever *appears* to our bodily senses to be the state of spirituality of our brethren, we are, in the truth of Eternity, all one, the pure, innocent Christ; the Son of God. All appearances to the contrary are limited, ego-mind misperceptions. The form of words of the Communion Service, selected mostly from Old and New Testaments, along with hymns, consecration, partaking and offering of unleavened bread and unfermented grape juice – as symbols of the Word of Living Truth and the Love of Heaven as demonstrated by and manifested in Jesus of Nazareth – are all, as an ordered, structured sequence, a mechanism for attuning our mind to the great desire-thought of Jesus for the Kingdom of Heaven on Earth.

When our mind is attuned, operating as one, in harmonised manner, with the Christ Mind – as revealed in Jesus – all with the single purpose of *truly* seeking after God and *earnestly* desiring the Kingdom of Heaven upon the Earth, and *expressing* this desire sincerely through a form of words, hymns and symbolic gestures, we become a great and powerful dynamo, generating *spiritualised* creative psychic power (*psyche* is the Greek word for *soul*) which is visible to those in the spirit realms as Living Light. Further, when we do this in unison with another who is of like mind and desire, here in the earthly life, the power generated is greater than the sum of the parts; and when we do this with two others, a *triangular* spiritualised psychic power-generating unit is created that produces *exponentially* greater spiritualised psychic power than the sum of the parts.

It is worth being aware that at the present state of spiritual wakefulness of most souls in the Earth life, the greater the number of individuals who participate together in such a ritual attunement activity, the greater the chance of such soul emanations being in harmony *de*creases. This is because so few of us are actually, truly, comprehensively of one mind and one heart. Even those of us who truly seek and earnestly desire the Kingdom on Earth are, inevitably, going to have our own individual quirks and foibles at the ego end of our character spectrum, which will create small irregularities in the wavelength, that can distort the receiving and harmonising mechanisms of the ritual attunement (at-one-ment) process. This is why there are, and will always be, schisms in institutionalised religious structures: there are too many ego-distorted perceptions getting in the way of clear understanding of the Principles of Life of the Father. Ego is the separation consciousness and is always working to divide, or separate.

*　*　*

On an occasion in July 1995, when walking the dogs in the hills, with woodland and fields around me, I suddenly saw the Life Force coursing through every tree, leaf, blade of grass, wheat plant in the adjacent field, even the very soil in which all was growing. Everything that is, including the dogs and me, was this Force and It was all One, all connected to Itself as One, all connected *to*, receiving its livingness *from*, having its beingness *in* the Source of All; a Cosmic Umbilicus. Ever since then I have known of and from the certainty that the soul can have only when it has *experienced* such, that that is the reality: we are all One with, or in, the Creator, the Source of Life.

This reality is not dependent for its existence upon beliefs, or doctrines or dogmas or rituals. What, however, will be highly serviceable to *experiencing* that reality, for the purpose of spiritual growth and awakening, is to harmonise our mind and desire/ get attuned with the 'Good Husbandman' ("I am the true vine, and my Father is the *husbandman*" [Jn. 15:1]). This aligns us with the Mind of God, by the agency of the Holy Spirit and/or Jesus, and illumination can and will be given, in *response* to our sincerity, desire and commitment. That illumination becomes a living experience and then we truly *know* the truth, and cannot be diverted from our Path back to God by somebody else telling us *their* truth, because this has come from the Source, through our own within. If we *resonate* with someone else's observations, that can lead to such an experience, but to accept another's statements because they *say* it is true, as a dogma, even though one may not *feel* it is so, will lead to a fading of our innate faculty for receiving direct spiritual inspiration and illumination. Such religious processes then simply become an activity of the intellect, which is ego-mind. This was the yoke to which the scribes, Pharisees and Sadducees had become attached by the time Jesus came upon the scene. It is now the condition in which most of the institutionalised church finds itself today.

Institutionalised religion tells us that we must all believe someone else's perceptions – or lots of other people's (Abraham, Moses, Paul, the Pope, etc.) in the so-called* Christian religion – and those perceptions differ in some key respects from the Eternal Truth to which Jesus came to restore us. Our perceptions are, actually, changing at every moment, but the perceptions of the individuals upon whose life or lives an institutionalised religion is based do not change (according to that religion's perceptions of them) because those perceptions are written down in a holy book and the religion accepts such writings as truth for all time.

It is inevitable that the perceptions and understanding of the *living* Moses, David and Paul (to name but a few) will have changed since their writings and/or experiences in the long ago, which have been adopted by religionists as unchangeable truth, because at the time of their writing *their perceptions were incomplete*. The vision of Jesus was *not* incomplete for those times or for ours because he was *fully* God-realised, living *in* and functioning, operating *from* the eternal awareness, right here in his earthly life. He did not come to start an institutionalised religion and he said so many times and in many ways; for example:

> But thou, when thou prayest, enter into thy closet, and when thou hast shut thy door, pray to thy Father which is in secret; and thy Father which seeth in secret shall reward thee openly (Mt. 6:6).

> Woman, believe me, the hour cometh, when ye shall neither in this mountain, nor yet at Jerusalem, worship the Father. But the hour cometh, and now is, when the true worshippers shall worship the Father in spirit and in truth: for the Father seeketh such to worship him. God is a Spirit: and they that worship him must worship him in spirit and in truth (Jn. 4:21,23,24).

It is therefore highly serviceable for the ritual of spiritual attunement with Jesus and his great desire for the Kingdom of Heaven on Earth to be solitary or near solitary, with preferably two people who are closely attuned to each other, such as man and wife in a strong, spiritually-founded and compatible relationship. The fact that Theresa and I were able to establish such a powerhouse of psycho-spiritual energy for accomplishing so much rescue activity in close harmony with Steve showed exceptional singularity of commitment to the Communion objectives by all three participants. Without that, accomplishments would have been proportionally, or commensurately, fewer.

It can be tempting to think that if two or three can generate much more spirit-power than one, why not get four or five, or twenty, or five hundred together? Jesus knew the importance of this when he said, "For where two or three are gathered together in my name, there am I in the midst of them" (Mt. 18:20). Two or three are about as many as, at this stage in the spiritual awakening of mankind, can truly enter into the closet (the within) together in spiritual harmony at the soul-awareness level and perform a ritual of spiritual attunement that is truly of one mind and one desire. Only when operating in this manner as a harmonised unit can spiritual creative power be generated for accomplishing miraculous, magnificent outcomes to the furtherance of Jesus' Great Rescue Programme for mankind. It takes much commitment and practise for a solitary communicant to achieve this unity, or attunement, or at-one-ment, of mind with the Christ – or Holy Spirit – Mind, and a very high degree of commitment for two or three to achieve it together. It is not in accord with the agenda of the institutionalised church to perceive the words of Jesus as implying a maximum number of people, but that is clearly his intent according to the realities of spiritual, cosmic law.

"If our heart's desire is 'to minister to the sick and fainting spirits of men' then the power we generate will be used for that purpose."

The nature of our desire determines the use to which this desire-generated power is put. If our heart's desire is 'to minister to the sick and fainting spirits of men', (it makes no difference whether such be incarnate or discarnate) then the power we generate will be used for that purpose. It is an automatic process, created by God and put into operation by the Holy Spirit. It works in exactly the way as described in Isaiah 55:11: "So shall my word be that goeth forth out of my mouth: it shall not return unto me void, but it shall accomplish that which I please, and it shall prosper in the thing whereto I sent it."

So, imagine the power for good when not only three like-minded souls in the Earth life join in this activity, but do it in unison with Jesus of Nazareth and all the vast multitude of souls in the Heaven realms who have joined/espoused their lives to his (the 'bride of Christ', see Revelation, chapters 18, 21 and 22) and are all operating in a state of at-one-ment with him. Then, one is *really* cooking on gas! And this is what actually happens and is the purpose for which the Teacher – whom Olga learned, toward the end of her incarnation, was/is one and the same man as John, the seer of Patmos, 'the disciple whom Jesus loved', the author of the Fourth Gospel, the author of the book of Revelation, the disciple who outran Peter to Jesus' tomb – put together the tapestry of fragments that is the Service of Mystical Communion with Christ as an instrument of attunement with the living Jesus on the Christ-desire wavelength.

It has been my observation over the decades since I first committed my life into the care, guidance and protection of Jesus, back in the early 1960s, that the so-called Christian church of Earth-life, in all its schismatic manifestations, is not consciously, actively definitive in its 'mission statement' that it is earnestly desirous of, and committedly working for, in espoused relationship with the *living* Jesus Christ of Nazareth, and in 'communion with the saints', the Kingdom of Heaven *on Earth*.

In fact, during my time as an active member of the Anglican Church, other than rote recital of the Lord's Prayer, I never heard anyone in or connected to the church make any reference whatsoever to, or activate discussion about, the pivotal desire of Jesus, and therefore the pivotal importance to those who profess to be his followers (in these times), for the Kingdom of Heaven, let alone the Kingdom of Heaven *on Earth*.

It seems fairly obvious that the Kingdom of Heaven already is fully established and operational *in Heaven*; after all, two thousand years ago Jesus said he was going to prepare a place for us so that he could come back to receive us into that place. Any follower of Jesus who feels that Jesus, who is recorded as stating "All power is given unto me in Heaven and in Earth" (Mt. 28:18), would not yet have accomplished that objective (the Kingdom of Heaven *in Heaven*) by now is surely not a serious follower of or believer in the power and authority of Jesus, who states "Thy kingdom come, Thy will be done **in Earth**, as it is in Heaven" (Mt. 6:10) and this therefore is clearly his great desire.

The Kingdom of Heaven on Earth is actually only a *staging post*, or stepping stone, because we cannot return to our true Home *in Heaven*, or Eternity, permanently, until our apparently separated, individual, split-off-from-Truth minds have been fully restored to the unified state of Christ-Mindedness. That is what we are here on Earth to do. It has to be done here in time and place, so that we can be released from belief in separation from God and the oneness that is the Sonship, and leave illusion behind, to return to our true Home in the reality of Eternity. That is why we have to keep coming back here, because we have not yet achieved that state of fully awakened, re-unified Christ-Mindedness. When we have achieved that state, our *true* state of remembrance, we will be able to leave the illusory universe of time and place behind.

Without the help of Jesus and/or the Holy Spirit we may never be able to get there. With Their help we can save an indeterminate number of incarnations, but we can only ascend into the eternal reality of Heaven when we have returned to full remembrance, while we are here, in 'egoland', because it is only here that relationships between/within the Sonship appear to be broken. So it is to 'here' that we must keep returning, incarnation after incarnation, until we remember *why* we are here, and work to restore the broken relationships to wholeness.

Wholeness is oneness, not of body – because bodies are not what we are in eternal reality – but of *Mind*; Christ Mind. That is our spiritual birthright, heritage and destiny. With Their help we can get there immeasurably quicker. According to *A Course in Miracles* (ACIM) the healing process is possible only by a mechanism that Jesus calls 'true forgiveness', which is described in this writing at the end of chapter 11.

Just as with the prodigal son, who, only when he had 'come to himself' (awakened to the remembrance of who he really was),

was ready (able) to return to his father's house, so is it with us. When we have 'come to our Self', and *only* then, will we be ready to leave behind us this 'far country' and return Home forever. That is why we should pray, attune our lives with and work for the Kingdom of Heaven on Earth – so that we can, having arrived at that place, leave the Earth and all the *apparently* physical universe behind us and return to the Kingdom of Heaven *in Heaven*. Since this process has already been completed by he who incarnated as Jesus of Nazareth, he is eminently qualified to help us, his brethren in the Sonship of the Father, to return to that Place.

Of course the ego does not want this to happen, so tries to persuade us that Jesus is not going to help us; *he has gone away*. Ego, through its construct, the institutionalised church, which has so misrepresented the real Jesus, has persuaded most of us that Jesus, as he is perceived through the false image made of him by Laodicean, ego-religion, is too confusing to follow, other than round and round in ever-decreasing circles.

The real Jesus is so different from the false image of him known around the world that if people actually knew him they would follow him joyously, without a moment's hesitation. He is to be found in the *within* of each and every one of us. When we start to *truly* seek after God and *earnestly* desire the Kingdom of Heaven on Earth, Jesus, who stands at the door of our inner life and knocks, will be heard by us. And if we open our door and invite him in, he will enter and will fellowship with us, bringing joy, peace and love far beyond all the treasures of Earth. He will also bring spiritual enlightenment of which the world has no awareness. This will lead to our awakening and our readiness to ascend to the eternity of Heaven *as one* with him and all our brethren in the Sonship.

The Mystical Communion with Christ, in which Olga was instructed during out of body visits to the Realms of Light, is an attunement mechanism by which contact with the life and fully enlightened Christ-Mind of Jesus becomes meaningfully possible.

In Luke 12:49 he says, "I am come to kindle fire on the Earth; and how I wish it were already kindled." That, assuredly, states how great is his desire for the Kingdom *on Earth*. Logic clearly indicates that it is the 'on Earth' part of the Lord's Prayer that is the crucial part of the statement, since one can construe that our heavenly Father's will is already (being) done in Heaven, because Jesus says as much in the same sentence. If the words 'on Earth' were not the crucial part of his great desire, why would he have gone to the trouble of incarnating and deliberately submitting himself to the brutal torture and execution as described in the Gospel accounts? He could have simply saved himself the trouble and waited in Heaven until each soul departed the Earth life and greeted and escorted them to the *heavenly* Kingdom.

But it is here, in the illusory world, and its etheric counterpart, that we appear to be stuck, and it is *here* that we need his help. So he had to come here and establish that link with us in the illusion that is this world, so that he could work with us while we seem to be here, to awaken us from the *belief* that we are here in time and place. This is because, until we have awakened from this dream world, we will keep alternating between Earth and its etheric counterpart – which is not the *eternity* of Heaven but simply the other side of the same, illusory, coin. So, however much we may have fellowship with Jesus, here in the Earth *or* its etheric counterpart, waking fully from the dream that we are here entails restoring the Sonship to oneness, with our full participation in that process, by the act, or practise, of true forgiveness.

"In the midst of the Earth ariseth my city after the fashion of the Heavenly"

It may seem that this issue is heavily laboured here, but this is because it is central to the life and purpose of Jesus, and therefore it is serviceable to us, his brethren, in these, as in all, times to be consciously focused on this matter. I do not see this as being the case in the leadership of the institutionalised church in the Earth or in its congregants in these crucial times of the outworking of the Great Rescue Programme. It may serve such better to be more mindful of Jesus' words in Luke's Gospel: "Blessed are those servants, whom the lord when he cometh shall find watching: verily I say unto you, that he shall gird himself, and make them to sit down to meat, and will come forth and serve them. And if he shall come in the second watch, or come in the third watch, and find them so, blessed are those servants" (Lk. 12:37,38). It seems

100

apparent that we are, in these times, entering the 'third watch'. More on the matter of 'three' and 'third' later, when Jesus' parable of the three measures of meal is extensively discussed.

In January 1965 the Master gave the following message to Olga:

"In the midst of the Earth ariseth my city
after the fashion of the heavenly,
Wherein the multitude of them that love me and keep
my words
Minister unceasingly to the sick and fainting spirits of men.
The call goeth out continually, Come, O come ye
to the waters
Everyone that thirsteth. Buy milk and wine without money
and without price,
And nourish your souls, and rejoice in health and joy;
For it is my Father's good pleasure to bestow upon you
the freedom of the city.
Here is freedom from sickness: whosoever will,
let him be free.
Here are riches of wisdom and power: whosoever will,
let him be rich.
Here is knowledge: whosoever will, let him know
the secrets of God
and the power and perfection of His laws.
Here is fulfilment: whosoever will, let him enlarge
his capacity and his influence.
Here is Peace: whosoever will,
let him meditate therein.
Grace be with you."

How poetically and perfectly this message describes the purpose of Jesus and of all who espouse themselves to him and his great desire.

HERE, THEN, WERE THREE SOULS of like mind, *true* and *earnest* in their desire for the Kingdom. How would we be serviceable to this desire? Remember, at the Earth-mind conscious level of awareness, none of us knew the plan, the programme, the power for good into which we were tapping and which is, in reality, *within* us, just as the Life Force, the Creator Spirit is within us all because it is one and the same force as – and indivisible from – our own life.

---

*"There is no demarcation between our own life
and the Universal Life Force."*

There is no demarcation between our own life and the Universal Life Force. Like most of us in the Earth life, this truth was rather fuzzy in our minds. But we had *desired* to get on the path to remembering clearly who we are, and had chosen to follow him who had remembered who he is and was manifesting that Beingness: Jesus of Nazareth, the Anointed Messenger of the Holy One. So, anything was possible! As Jesus puts it, "With men this is impossible; but (in our oneness) with God all things are possible" (Mt. 19:26); and, "If thou canst believe, all things are possible to him that believeth" (Mk. 9:23).

The students were ready and The Teacher had come; we were not alone, not without help and guidance. These words of the Master were given to Olga Park for the encouragement of *all* who, of sincere heart and seeking mind, earnestly desire to know, or remember, Spiritual Truth:

> "Do not fear to tread the path I have marked out for you. Do you think it was only to men of old that I have shown myself? Have I not said that if any man open to me I will come in and sup with him, and he with me?
>
> "For I seek such and knock upon the doors of their hearts that they may open and receive me and know of a surety that I live. Blessed is he that hears my knocking; thrice blessed is he that opens to me.
>
> "I am the guide of many. Let no man confuse you saying, 'He is high and lifted up and cannot manifest to the children of men.' For though I speak through the mouth of an angel, and though I write through the hand of a messenger, it is I; for I also am of your brethren of Earth, and it is the will of the Father that all shall know me, from the least unto the greatest.

"Come unto me, all you Little Ones, and you that labour, and I will refresh you with the joy of Heaven which I had with the Father before the time in which I dwelt with men.

"Do not be discouraged that the revelation is imperfect in the beginning. Great things shall you do if your faith in me holds fast. These things have I spoken that you may know of a surety that I am the Messenger of the Holy One.

"Peace be with you!"

On the path of progress back to whence we have all come – eternal joy, in oneness with the Father Creator – we are led, taught, reminded, shown the Way by example and by *experiencing*; not by being *told*, as in a schoolroom. The Master has said to me many times over the decades that the path along which he has been leading me has been agreed 'aforetime', which is his way of explaining that before we incarnate, the purpose of our incarnating is agreed/decided by us; and for those who have chosen a high calling – such as in the service of others and for the greater good of mankind – that deciding will always have been in close consultation with those who will be our spiritual guide(s) during our earthly sojourn.

If we choose a path of Earth-life service or commitment that is at one with the great desire-thought of Jesus, then it is logical that it is likely to be Jesus – or at least, one (or more) from the Realms of Light acting under his authority, and the wisdom and spiritual empowerment that imparts – with whom we will desire to consult and agree aforetime as to what our particular mission will be and how it will unfold as our Earth life progresses.

The choice is always and entirely ours; no-one else *ever* decides for us. That is cosmic law. We have free will, *always*. There are no press-gangs in Heaven! Each step we take is of our own choosing and the overall direction of our life journey is influenced, nay, determined, by the desire of our heart, which is the seat of our soul in the Earth life. This remains with us throughout each incarnation, albeit most often as a 'seed memory', subliminal to our Earth-conscious recollection, but always there at the soul level of awareness. Our higher-Mind, or 'Big Self', will call into our Earth-life presence circumstances or opportunities for this aforetime-choosing to be brought back to the surface of our remembering so that we can then make free-will choices to travel in that direction.

This, by way of example, is what happened to me with the circumstances that brought me into contact with Olga's book and also with Hugh Dowding's book. This isn't to suggest that a book will always be such a device for reminding us of our chosen path of experience, but it does suggest that a book – a recounting of someone else's experiences – can be highly serviceable to such a process. If one strongly resonates with such recorded events it is very likely that one will desire to proceed in like manner. That is because the seed memory of one's pre-incarnation choice has been triggered, 'germinated', by the process, and begins to grow in the Earth-life part of our being.

---

*'So-called' because the church as it is and as it has been structured for many centuries, is in so many respects, not acting according to the life-example and teaching of the One they claim to be following. If they were, the pews would be full and the Kingdom would be here, fully manifested in our midst, in all its love, joy and glory.

8: The Rescue Work Shifts Up a Gear

Although there had been several rescue events over the years, such as Bobby Kennedy in 1968 and Rachel, the Dutch Jewess in 1969, now that Steve was sharing our Communion practice and we were so much on the same wavelength, it was time for the desire of my heart, for the rescue and release of 'all sorts and conditions of men', trapped in a time-warp of terror, or even if not terror but aimlessness, hopelessness, to move into a higher gear of fulfilment. This began in the late 1980s and progressed into the early 1990s, for a period spanning about five years.

One night in December 1991, I awoke in the small hours of Sunday morning with backache. As I lay there brooding upon the significance of why this had been part of my life experience since the age of ten (as a result of a gymnastics accident) and what to 'do' about it, it dawned on me that there are untold numbers of souls, in this life and the next, who are experiencing immeasurably worse situations than am I. This moved me to start praying that I might be serviceable to the help of such souls.

As I did this, I became aware that all parts of my body were becoming 'electrified' – charged with spiritual energy. I could see it, like blue lightning, and feel it acting upon and filling the various parts of my body, including my back, up to the top of my head, arms to finger-tips, legs to toe-tips, with tingling, uplifting, healing peace. The aches and stiffness were washed away and within not many moments I was deeply asleep again.

During the Communion Service later that same morning, as I made the offering of the bread 'for all those in need, sorrow, sickness or any adversity', I was suddenly in the dual consciousness, where one wall of the bedroom in which our sanctuary was situated disappeared and gave an open view of the staircase, which was now two or three times as wide as its physical counterpart. Up the wide stairway toward us was proceeding a host of Vietnamese people – men, women and children of all ages. It was not possible to count them, but my guess is that there must have been about three hundred souls. They at first came with diffidence, but I welcomed them sincerely and lovingly and bade them enter in to join the banquet feast to celebrate the marriage (union) of Heaven with Earth, as per the great desire of Jesus of Nazareth. This union is not of bodies, that, in marriage become 'of one flesh', but of one *mind* – Christ Mind.

I immediately realised this event had been orchestrated by John, Theresa's brother, who had made five tours of duty in Vietnam with the US Marines during the 1960s and early 1970s and had laid aside his body in 1979, aged thirty-five, from a heart attack. Indeed, there he was, at the top of the stairs, welcoming these new arrivals with a smile and a heart brimming with love and joy, and, along with many other Inner Plane servers, was helping to set them at ease by creating a loving and convivial atmosphere.

John said to me, "Brian, you and Theresa are right; it is Carl (*a friend of Theresa's who was in the US Navy and had been killed in Vietnam*) and I, along with a number of buddies from 'Nam days who have been working on this for a while. Our time there brought us a deep and abiding love of these people and their gentleness, and we could not turn our backs on their plight. Paul teaches us we are all one blood – one life – and brothers in Christ Jesus. That is to say by his love and enlightenment we become brothers, and differences of culture and skin colour are nothing. Indeed, it is soul colour, not skin colour that counts in the greater scheme of things. We thank you for your help in creating the bridge to enable us to go in and get our new and old friends out. The celebration is great today."

It was a deeply moving, inspiring, rewarding and joyous occasion.

Up to that time I had never heard the word *bridge* used to describe the process of an Earth-incarnate person acting as an intermediary between those from the Realms of Light and those who are in some dark and fearful place in the afterlife, having been dispatched there by traumatic means such as was the case innumerable times during the tragedy called the Vietnam War.

As I have deliberated this since that occasion it has become clear to me that the term 'bridge' is interchangeable with link, agent, helper, intermediary or any other word to describe a person or situation which can be serviceable as *go-between* in bringing about a rescue, or change of awareness, perception, understanding or circumstance for a soul or souls.

'Bridge' is perhaps more meaningful, in that a bridge is something which is able to give support to those who are passing over a gap or chasm from one place of being or perception to another. Hugh Dowding used the term 'Lychgate' in his book of the same name, because for him a lychgate is a place through which one passes as one moves from one place into another (from the world at large into a place of prayer, contemplation and spiritual awareness).

John has been a true stalwart for bringing help, peace, freedom and grace to many souls in this life and the next over the years since 1979. On one occasion back in the late 1980s, when my parents were getting toward the end of their sojourn here, Theresa and I were driving down the motorway to spend a weekend with them, to give love and support in their enfeebled condition. I suddenly became aware of John being with us. He was driving a team of six horses from the front of a wagon, the type depicted in Western films about wagon-trains of migrants crossing the American continent.

He was having a wonderful time of this, standing, with reins in one hand, urging the horses to go faster, waving his hat in the other hand, hootin' and hollerin' to beat the band, a grin as wide as the Grand Canyon splitting his face. Then, as I became more attuned to this unlikely scene, I became aware that he was not alone! There were dozens of wagons accompanying him, each, as his, loaded with 'victuals' for Ma and Pop. The victuals were not food or other provisions in the physical sense, but love, goodwill, good cheer, tenderness and giving from the heart and soul from John and his associates toward my parents.

To my astonishment all the wagons were not following in single file, one behind the other, as depicted in the movies, but side by side, stretching out many times wider than the physical motorway, and about the height of our car above the surface of the ground. All the souls in the other wagons were having just as

107

much fun as was John. This was an act of selfless giving, grace and tender mercy toward my parents which welled me up with gratitude toward all these dear souls.

"Why are you doing this?" I asked John in amazement. "Ma and Pop are not your family."

He dismissed this instantly with the light-hearted rejoinder, "Nonsense. *You* are family and your family are my family. We are all family together; God's children one and all."

Clearly, he was not to be deterred, and I was not about to try to put him off this mission.

Theresa and I had a wonderful weekend, as did Ma and Pop, who, it was evident, were greatly uplifted in their spirits and restored to fullness of heart by the time we spent together. There was no doubt in my mind that even though they had no awareness of John and his wagon-train of love, that great infusion palpably contributed to the raising of their flagging spirits.

It is events such as this that make the fellowship of Heaven, experienced here in one's earthly life, so indescribably enriching, uplifting, encouraging, reassuring and affirming of the inherent, fundamental goodness of Creation, the Creator and indeed, of all living things. With that as an accepted, adopted understanding of Universal Principle, it then becomes possible to look more clearly, meaningfully and constructively at any situation in life which appears to be in contrast to that Absolute Truth and see how such apparent contradictions could be so.

For example, a man might be hard on his wife and children, lacking in humour, tenderness, warmth and allowing for sparse quality time with them. This could be readily perceived as the man being 'mean-spirited', and many are often dismissed as such.

For one taking the time to look more carefully, that man may be living in a self-imposed consciousness of fear; fear because he actually loves his wife and family so dearly that he sees it as his responsibility to provide for them an abundance of things of the Earth life – a beautiful home, clothing, food, holidays, toys, the best education etc. – and is driving himself hard and relentlessly to achieve the wherewithal to enable this.

He may not be good enough at his job to actually achieve this; or his boss may have a grudge against him and be holding him back; or there might be threats of job cuts, all and more of which could be causing him fear ... fear of failure to achieve these self-imposed commitments. In reality, his wife may love him so dearly she would much prefer that he be less concerned at how 'successful' he is at work, to be more relaxed and kind to himself (and his health) and be more the fun, carefree soul she married, with time for enjoying their children together.

This, in his heart and soul, is his deep desire, and he is wrecking his health and relationship with those he loves the most trying to get to the place where he can be what he knows himself to be, instead of sitting down with his beloved and opening his heart and soul to her, telling how he really is, how fearful he is of failure. She, perhaps, desires nothing more than for him to do this, but because he is so remote, unapproachable and moody, she is fearful of telling him how she really feels. His children maybe would love to also be able to approach him in a carefree manner, but also are fearful because Dad has been so testy lately, and snaps at them when they try to get his attention.

"People who are uncertain about the benign essence of the Creator, might be persuaded that there is inherent 'evil' lurking in the very foundations of Creation."

And so this artificial scenario is perpetuated and will get worse until health and relationships break down, all because of fear – fear of one of the things most serviceable to humanity: honesty.

This is one tiny illustration of how today's stress-filled society is breaking down at every level. Almost any and every example of dysfunction in society can be a cause for people who are uncertain about the benign essence of the Creator, to be persuaded that inherent evil lurks in the very foundations of Creation. Yet this has nothing to do with the Creator, but is the work of the 'uncreator'; the destroyer, the upside-down, insane part of our mind that is operated by, under the control of, ego, the illusory antithesis of the Creator Spirit.

* * *

By early 1996, I had a growing sense of inward desire to know God in a more intimate sense than as *God, Father, Holy One,*

Creator Spirit, or some such rather remote, formal term. Jesus is recorded as calling the Father 'Abba', a Syriac word, denoting filial affection and tenderness (*Barnes' Notes on the New Testament*). I was half inclined to borrow Jesus' word and tried this for a while but somehow it didn't sit well with me; this was *his* term and I felt it was presumptuous to use what was personal between him and his Father.

At the time Theresa and I were soon to become grandparents and had been discussing by what names we would each wish to be called in this new status. We had referred to my dad as Pop and his father had been known as Poppa. I did not wish to be known as *Pop* because to me, this was my dad, but I liked the idea of *Poppa* because it had a family tradition about it but was far enough removed from my own experience (Poppa had passed away on my second birthday, so I didn't really have much sense of intimate connection with him, as I did with Pop, even though I have enjoyed wonderful, personal, loving, fun contact with him in recent decades). So we agreed that for our grandchildren-to-be, Theresa would be known as Granny and I would be known as Poppa. It had a warm, close, familial feel about it for our family circumstances and I resonated well with it as a term of endearment.

This desire for a term of equal endearment for my relationship with the Holy One grew and in February I asked Him for a suitable name by which I could show the personal love, honour and respect I have for Him. His instant response was, "Papa." It was immediately apparent that there was a subtle but distinct difference in pronunciation between Papa and Poppa and yet the two are sufficiently close as to have an obvious connection. Indeed, the North American pronunciation of the two words would be indistinguishable. How characteristic of our loving, caring, heavenly Father to have selected a name which He knew would have such a close and personal meaning for me, in response to the desire of my heart. So, henceforward God the Father was for me, by His invitation, Papa.

* * *

During our Sunday morning Communion Service on May 5, 1996, I was feeling very frustrated that after decades of faithfully following the Master Jesus, I seemed to still have many more questions, unknowns, than answers. I felt as if I was walking a treadmill; taking the steps but not getting anywhere, and I was fed up with the lack of apparent progress.

I said to Papa, "Beloved Papa, heavenly Father, Creator Spirit: there is so much I don't understand about You, the nature of Life, consciousness, peace and on and on."

As I formed these words in my mind I saw Him, appearing as a 'Fatherly figure'. He put His hands on His hips, threw back His head and roared with laughter.

"My son, the Keys to the Kingdom lie not in answers but in faith, trust, commitment, obedience to My Word. Because you are My children I love you, and you are responding, making yourself available by faith and obedience, to be drawn by My love.

"I make the rules – you don't; indeed you cannot because by your own acknowledgement you don't understand. All I require of you is commitment to Me and I will fulfil your heart's desire for righteousness, justice, goodwill; let not your desire, which I know is an unquenchable flame within you, ensnare you into the belief that you must accomplish it. I will accomplish it for you because of your desire and your commitment. And answers shall be the result, not the cause, of your fulfilment, of your desire.

"This is cosmic, universal law; My law. It is perfect; your lack of understanding does not alter this one iota. Therefore, be at peace, relax and be glad that I am in charge and that I am able to accomplish all that I have ordained.

"You are learning, slowly, to accept that My timing is not your timing. Continue in this way. Meanwhile, occupy according to that which is needful and My revelation shall be placed upon you as you are able to receive it. All is well. Rejoice and have no anxiety."

* * *

In the summer of 1999, as I walked with Susie, our little rescued Lhasa Apso dog, in the woodlands of the Cotswold Hills, suddenly a dump truck upended a load of bricks right in front of me. There must have been twenty tonnes of them. This was, of course, not a physical event but in the dual consciousness. The bricks were black and shiny, as are the bricks used in the damp-proof course of older houses. This load was obstructing the path in front of me. My initial reaction was, 'Oh, no, another obstacle to progress along the path of spiritual growth.'

"Do not fear adversity, for it is the very stuff of which opportunity is made, and without adversity there can be no opportunity. Rather, welcome it and give thanks for it."

"Why these adversities when all I seek is to be serviceable to the Kingdom?" I asked Papa.

Immediately He spoke:

"Do not fear adversity, for it is the very stuff of which opportunity is made, and without adversity there can be no opportunity. Rather, welcome it and give thanks for it. Each such encounter is an opportunity to transform adversity into fulfilment and create some magnificent new structure to the glory of God and man reunited in the Kingdom of Heaven on Earth. In truth We are a 'Desire and Construct' partnership, working together in creative unison. You may perceive Me as the Great Architect and you as 'merely' the bricklayer, but I say to you, how can the architect realise the grandeur of his greatest designs without the bricklayer to bring them into the fullness of their manifestation?"

"There is perfection in everything, everyone and every situation. When we fail to see the perfection and see only adversity, we are not looking closely enough."

Another example of the 'adversity into opportunity' principle shown to me was the dunghill. This is an unsavoury phenomenon in the perception of most people; a thing to be avoided as full of disease, unpleasant smells, waste material. Yet, by spreading this onto and cultivating into the soil, it is transformed, out of view in a secret place, into nourishment for the crop, enabling the new life to bring forth a rich and fruitful harvest. In the natural order, without the dunghill, such would not be possible.

There is perfection in everything, everyone and every situation. When we fail to see the perfection and see only adversity, we are not looking closely enough.

Most people would perceive being flogged nearly to death as being adversity of the worst kind, but for Jesus, about to be nailed to a wooden cross and left to die what the executioners expected to be a slow and agonising death, the scourging by the Roman soldiers was the perfect thing because it so weakened him – surely as robust and healthy a soul as one would ever be likely to encounter – that it foreshortened his time on the cross by a great many hours. It is made clear in *A Course in Miracles* that pain does not exist in the presence of purity and innocence, making it evident that Jesus did not experience pain from either the scourging or the crucifixion, a blessing beyond human imagining. Nevertheless, the scourging would have brought a collapsing of the time required on the cross before he was ready to depart from his body; a highly desirable thing.

If/when we are prepared to accept that adversity is an illusion, then we can view it correctly as actually the perfect thing at the perfect moment. It then provides us with opportunity, the very raw material, the stuff, to demonstrate, to experience, our true, eternal, spiritual nature by transforming it into fulfilment. This is some 'bountiful harvest'. Then, truly have we taken a major step toward being 'like unto the Son of Man' (Christ man – *Homo Dei Spiritui* – fulfilled man; man who has arrived at his spiritual destiny: Oneness with the Father Creator).

* * *

On another occasion, during Communion on Christmas Eve 1995, as I stood making the offering, suddenly I heard John's voice behind my right shoulder. He was singing that soul-stirring hymn known as the *Battle Hymn of the Republic*, which starts 'Mine eyes have seen the glory of the coming of the Lord . . .' This startled me; it was not in the order of service at all! As I realised what he was doing I also became aware that he was not the only one singing this hymn. In front of me unfolded a scene from the nineteenth century in the American west. There was a group of about five or six U.S. Cavalrymen at their frontier outpost. They were standing before the flagpole, performing a ceremony of raising or lowering the flag. They looked battle-weary; their dark-blue uniforms were dust covered and ragged. The impression I had was that they perceived themselves as the only 'survivors' of some recent encounter with the indigenous people, although clearly they had not survived bodily, but were unaware of this. The vibration indicated fear and uncertainty. The ranking officer was a sergeant. They also were singing this same hymn. John was in perfect time with them although they had absolutely no awareness of him and his singing.

Suddenly one of the men noticed me and fell back a pace or two, raising his arm in front of his face, partly as if to shield his vision from what he had seen, and partly pointing at me as, with a fear-filled, almost disbelieving voice he stuttered-out the words, "L-l-look – an angel!" I realised that from their perspective, I was certainly an 'apparition' from nowhere – a different time and place. Having no understanding of such 'supernatural' events, along with their seeing my etheric body rather than my physical, it would seem a reasonable conclusion for this hapless soldier to reach.

I immediately said to him and his colleagues, "I am not an angel but I *am* a friend, an incarnate soul from another time and place. I have been brought to you to explain your situation and make you aware that help is at hand. You are what you would understand as 'dead' and have not realised it. You are stuck in the circumstances which you *believe* you are in, vainly awaiting help from your fellow soldiers back at base camp. I have here with me a friend who, like you, is in spirit. He has come to help you. His name is John and he also was a soldier in his earthly life. You cannot see him just now but if you are able to accept what I am saying you will become aware of his presence and then he will be able to help you and take you to a place where you will be at peace and can be restored to your loved ones."

"He radiated peace, love and goodwill. This put these lost and frightened men at ease."

At this, John stepped forward and I could tell they now

were suddenly able to see him. He radiated peace, love and goodwill. This put these lost and frightened men at ease. John walked toward them, arms outstretched in amity and greeting, introducing himself, smiling in friendship and speaking words of encouragement. They crowded round him, and stood listening to him for a few moments. Beckoning them to follow him, he turned around and walked back toward me, the men following a few paces behind him, with a look of hope and anticipation on their faces and the beginning of a renewed spring in their heels. As he got alongside me he held up his hand for a high-five and gave me a huge, theatrical wink, his eyes sparkling in love, joy and satisfaction at yet another co-operative rescue mission successfully completed. *Glory be!*

The amount of this type of rescue work that is continually taking place is mind boggling; assuredly the need for it is beyond the comprehension of most people in the Earth life, yet it is entirely and wonderfully in accord with the Master's words to Olga Park in January 1965:

> *"In the midst of the Earth ariseth my city*
> *after the fashion of the heavenly,*
> *Wherein the multitude of them that love me and keep*
> *my words*
> *Minister unceasingly to the sick and fainting spirits of men . . ."*

(see chapter 7) and is entirely in harmony with the loving, caring, compassionate Jesus of the Gospel accounts of his life on Earth.

Most people today are at the place of awareness which says 'I feel bad/awful/terrible about all those being killed, brutalised, terrorised in wars, torture, natural disasters, famine, genocide etc., but what can I do?' And there, sadly – and unnecessarily – it is so often left. It does not have to be that way. All of us *are* able to help, in some way, even if we are not aware that our help is being beneficially received. All it takes is a compassionate heart and a *desire* to help. Desire is the beginning of all things and without it, nothing happens. If there is a single shred of compassion and desire to help those in distress – in the Earthly life or its etheric counterpart – a simple blessing, *sincerely felt*, from the heart and mind in unison, toward those in distress does, *always*, palpably help. There are, and can be, no exceptions to this. It is not necessary to *see* the help or be sensorily aware of the benefit provided. What makes the difference is faith – an absolute certainty beyond all doubt that the blessing, *sincerely sent*, does facilitate the help. The stronger the faith, the greater the help.

On one occasion during the early 1990s, when John was in my thoughts, suddenly there he was, a few paces in front of me, radiating his joy out toward me and into the universe at large. As soon as I saw him I spontaneously said, "God bless you." As the words were formed I saw a globule of what looked like golden syrup leave me and fly toward him. It was about the size of a gymnasium medicine ball, and moved through the air at about the same speed as if I had thrown such to him. It caught him amidships and he staggered back under the weight and force of it, almost as if winded by its impact. I was taken completely by surprise at this, but it was a graphic demonstration to me of the actuality, the *substantial*, palpable nature of the blessing. I feel confident that its size and impact upon John did not hurt him; rather, my impression was that he responded as he did to demonstrate to me the very solid reality of blessing.

I had seen this golden syrup-like spirit substance before. I was walking our dog in the local, city greenspace, communing with the Creator and getting onto His wavelength of love, and there, in front of me appeared a wall of it about twenty feet/ six metres high. It was moving slowly forward, like lava from a volcano, enveloping everything it encountered. As soon as it met resistance from anything or anyone unwilling to be enveloped, it stopped and waited until the resistance ceased, then it moved forward again. The vibration of this substance was – is – love; agapé, cosmic, eternal, *unconditional,* all-encompassing, Perfect Love.

I had, and still have, no doubt that this is the love of God, the Creator Spirit, which constantly, ceaselessly seeks all created beings, passionately longing to bring love, blessing and nurture; to embrace and enfold all within Itself. Yet, It will *never* force Itself upon those who are unwilling to receive It. Hence, It waits, endlessly, eternally, infinitely patient, until recalcitrance, fear, hate, guilt, judgement, antipathy – or whatever other ego-induced conditions are keeping the individual separate from his Creator

– runs out of steam and subsides, leaving the soul who bore such misperceptions exhausted, bereft and unresisting.

Then It starts rolling forward again, enveloping and embracing, loving, restoring, uplifting, even when the recipient has no discernment of Its presence. It is this very Essence of Creation, the Stuff of Life, the Breath of God, which heals all: a broken bone, a broken heart, a dejected or fearful spirit. Acceptance of this unseen truth, and thanksgiving for it, hastens such repair work. This is why Jesus gave thanks for all the miraculous outcomes wrought through his presence and intercession.

So, when I said to John, "God bless you," the globule of golden syrup that emanated from me and flew to him was the love of Papa within me, hastening to bestow Its blessing upon this, His beloved son, John.

The reasons it looks and behaves like golden syrup are: being spirit substance, it is translucent; the love of God is Golden, pure, refined, unsullied; it sticks to us and will never leave us if we are willing to receive it; it is adaptable, flexible, malleable, serviceable to all our moods and all our needs; it is solid enough to have substance, yet pliable enough to shape itself to every circumstance; it will envelop and embrace us but will never overwhelm us. Hence its waiting, with infinite patience, until we are ready to receive it, yet always there, *available*. It has two additional, distinguishing qualities of appearance that are not possessed of golden syrup: it is *alive* and it emits living *light* from within itself.

No wonder Jesus said "Bless them that curse you" (Mt. 5:44) and Paul writes to the Romans: "Bless them which persecute you: bless, and curse not" (Rom. 12:14). Indeed, the scriptures are full of counsel to bless, at every opportunity. How greatly today's world, at family, community, national and international levels, could tangibly benefit if only there was the faith and belief in the value and meaningfulness of such admonition.

9: Friendship, Angels and Revelations

This was a period during which we were not just involved in rescue work; it was a period in which our understanding and awareness of the close links and relationship between us and the Inner Plane Servers, our friends, loved ones, guides – all acting in unison of purpose and life with, and under the power, authority and leadership of Jesus – was growing. My earlier perception, for many years, was that this was all the most wonderful blessing; that I had somehow, in spite of my assumed 'unworthiness', been chosen by the Spiritual Lord of mankind for some special, kingdomly service. I had hardly been able to believe that all this was really happening to me. And even if it was, would it *continue*? Surely, my luck would run out at any time and I would be back to reality with a wallop?

The implication, somewhere deep in my unconscious mind, was that what I had been experiencing was 'a privilege'. The legacy of ego-constructed religionist doctrines and dogmas deeply ingrained into the cultural psyche of Western civilisation over centuries was, part of me believed, that I should be grovelling in servile gratitude, accepting any and every 'crumb from the Master's table' without question, and blindly worshipping a deity that had graciously deigned not to destroy me with a thunderbolt for stepping out of line! None of that perception was supported by the evidence of my own experiences, but rationale seems to have little effect on ego-inculcated, cultural conditioning and mind-contorting.

* * *

In 1993, Steve and I spent a few days visiting the Lake District and other scenic and historical parts of the north of England. We set off from Gloucester in my car (Theresa was 'holding the fort' at home and in the office) and arrived at the Lakes late morning. There is an energy there that I have never encountered anywhere else on Earth (not that I have been everywhere else!) and it evokes joy from the heart which radiates from there and uplifts the spirit. After an initial stop to admire some views and let Steve gain a 'flavour' of the experience that is the Lake District, we realised it was lunch time. Heading off down a country lane we arrived at a pub nestled in the hillside, far from the madding crowd. How could we resist?

As we sat there enjoying our home-cooked meal and glass of traditional English ale, we became aware of John, Theresa's brother. He was pacing around on the flagstone floor in the bar area; up and down, round and round, agitated with what was clearly a degree of excitement that was almost too much for him to bear. Eventually he sat down at our table on the bench next to Steve, put his hands on the table, palms down and banged his head slowly on his hands, up and down three or four times. It was an act of someone so excited he did not know where to put himself. He knew something we did not; but we were very soon to find out! Moments later the Master Jesus came in the door to my right, at the far end of the bar, some six or seven paces from where we sat. I was on a bench one side of the table, facing Steve, who was seated on a settle against the wall.

The Master walked towards us with an expression on his face that was barely concealing his joy and puckish mood. He was dressed as a head waiter in a black tailcoat with a stiff collar and bow tie. His hair was present-day, short back and sides, but there was no mistaking his vibration, bearing, demeanour; his very *Being*. It isn't what one perceives with eyes, or other bodily senses; it is what one has inner-awareness of with the light of one's spiritual discernment that tells us the truth about a brother. Over his left forearm was draped a starched white linen napkin, such as waiters use in expensive restaurants (this was a no-frills country pub, for Heaven's sake!). He walked up beside me and bowed slightly, in a deferential manner befitting waiters, to speak to us. "Is everything all right?" he enquired solicitously, in as serious a tone as he could muster in the circumstances. Then, after a slight pause, during which he was trying, but failing by this point, to maintain his straight face, he burst out with the words, "Are you *HAPPY*!!!?" Steve and I were deeply and profoundly overwhelmed by this light-hearted demonstration of the joy and fun that being in good fellowship with Jesus and all the hosts of Heaven actually is.

The purpose of this exercise, I realise, was several fold: to bring spiritual, heavenly joy to our already uplifted, holiday-mood spirits; to demonstrate that the fellowship of the Kingdom is a very *non*-pious experience, and full of lightness of heart and joy of living and being; to fulfil the words recorded of him in Luke's Gospel: "Blessed are those servants, whom the lord when he cometh shall find watching: verily I say unto you, that he shall gird himself, and make them to sit down to meat, and will come forth and serve them" (Lk. 12:37).

The reality of this *experience* was that this and all my encounters with Jesus and the 'hosts of Heaven' had been on the basis that they loved, honoured and respected me just as much as I loved, honoured and respected them. And further, that they were just as grateful to me for my one-pointed commitment and loyalty to them as I was grateful to them for their stalwart, unwavering, always-accessible love, help, encouragement, reassurance, illumination, inspiration, guidance and protection. Rather than being an inferior, subordinate, second-class 'go-for' to these Beings of the Light in the realms of Heaven, they saw me as equal with them in this wonderful, co-operative partnership between this group of Citizens of the Kingdom of Heaven, of which they were domiciled in the 'Heaven' part of the Kingdom and I was domiciled in the 'Earth' part of the same Kingdom. Above all, they desire us in the Earth life to lighten up in our approach to matters eternal and spiritual! So many of us are so po-faced in our demeanour toward religious activities and commitment, even singing hymns of joy and thanksgiving as if they were a dirge. Jesus said, "I am come that they might have LIFE, and that they might have it more abundantly" (Jn. 10:10). Not the religion of guilt, fear and unworthiness rammed down their throats ad nauseam!

During our time in the north of England there were several other happenings that were also greatly uplifting to our inner being.

Steve and I visited and walked along a stretch of Hadrian's Wall, built across northern England by the Roman Emperor Hadrian in the second century CE. As we walked along the top of the wall, soaking up the atmosphere of the place and its history, we became aware of a number of Roman legionnaires trapped in a time warp of the early part of the first millennium CE, still patrolling the wall. By our speaking with them, and with the help of Jesus and Theresa's brother, John, and no doubt many others also, they were freed from being stuck in that era. There were about twenty legionnaires that we were aware of. After much rejoicing and celebrating at their release from their predicament, most went their way, but one in particular, who we came to know as Claudius, remained with us. He and John struck up an immediate rapport, and when Steve and I got in the car to drive to a nearby pub for lunch, he and John sat in the back exchanging military anecdotes and experiences from two very different periods.

"There was a giant cross of living-gold sunlight about four or five metres high with its base implanted in me."

The following day we visited a place called High Force, a waterfall high up on the River Tees in County Durham. This is set in a well-maintained, wooded parkland area. After admiring the view from the lower end of the waterfall we climbed up the steep steps at its side to explore the top area. Steve and I sat on rocks beside the top of the waterfall admiring the view in glorious, late spring sunshine. Suddenly my focus of attention was switched from the horizontal, Earth consciousness to the vertical, soul awareness, and something made me look up. To my awe and astonishment there was a giant cross of living-gold sunlight about four or five metres high with its base implanted in me. It was as if I was its earthly base or foundation.

At Communion not many days later I wrote:
At the symbol of the lights, the Master appeared to my left as he showed himself to John of Patmos (Rev. 1:12-16), in the seven branch candlestick, or menorah. To my right, slightly in front, was the giant cross of gold light that I had seen embedded in me

at High Force. Then the Master moved from my left, in front of me, to my right, where he merged with the cross of gold light, and they became one. I knew that the cross represented the Father, and was a two-dimensional portrayal, or symbol, of intersecting Life lines not just in three dimensions or multi dimensions but *omni* dimensions, representing His omni-Presence.

Whilst in County Durham we also visited the Bowes Museum, near Barnard Castle. It was built in the 1800s by Sir John and Lady Josephine Bowes, in the style of a French chateau. It houses an astounding array of artefacts, collected by Josephine from all over Europe at truly staggering cost; indeed, sufficient to nearly bankrupt Sir John. All these treasures are displayed over three floors. Across the hall from the main entrance were larger-than-life, full-length portraits of the couple. As Steve stood admiring the likeness of Sir John, suddenly he was aware of him standing there beside the portrait, looking quite sombre. Steve immediately said, quietly, under his breath, "God bless you." This instantly caught Sir John's attention and broke his muse. Turning to Steve and smiling, he said, "Why, thank you, sir."

We duly began our exploration of this vast collection, and as we ascended a wide staircase to the next floor I became aware that we were being followed by someone from the spirit world. I had been aware of her speaking for some while but had not been focused on what was being said. On the stairs it came into focus, and to my amazement she was saying just one word, over and over, in a distressed, hopeless monotone: '*Trinkets*'. That's all she said. As the impact of this lodged in my mind, suddenly it all became clear who and what this was about.

It was Lady Josephine. She had devoted many, many years to amassing this collection; it had been her life's work. The intention was to display these priceless artefacts – paintings, furniture, sculptures, jewellery, clothing, ceramics and much, much more – for the edification of the poor and uneducated masses, to uplift their awareness and understanding of the wider world.

Of course, as soon as she departed this life for the next she realised that this had been a massive folly; the poor and starving masses would have benefited much more by help with employment, healthcare, nutrition, education, sanitation and the like. They saw her endeavours as the excesses of the super-rich class, and contempt was much more likely their reaction than gratitude.

As all this sank in I became filled with compassion for this dear, lost and deluded soul, who had, she clearly now felt, spent her sojourn in time in pursuit of something purely to indulge her own misperceptions regarding the important things in life. She now realised she could have done something truly philanthropic for her less materially fortunate fellows. She was wandering aimlessly in this place that had now become her prison, bereft of hope for herself, and filled with sorrow at being unable to undo her 'burdensome' error. As she followed us despondently about, repeating the word *trinkets* endlessly, she wrung her hands in despair. As I shared this with Steve he now became aware that Sir John also was with us and he was anxious for whatever help we might be able to give to his hapless wife, who was quite unaware of his presence. He stood there with a look on his face that betrayed a whit of hope amidst his otherwise joyless countenance. Steve and I both spoke silently to Josephine, assuring her that there was no longer any requirement for her to remain in this place or this state of mind; that hers was a well-intentioned error and that no harm was done by it; that the poor would, as Jesus reminded us, be always with us; that she could ask for help and release from this by Jesus and would be instantly re-united with her beloved spouse and restored to joy, inner peace and love.

The utterances of *'trinkets'* ceased. Steve and I looked at each other and suddenly we had no heart for more of this place, though we had barely scratched the surface of all it proffered. We headed out into the sunshine, and as we walked around the chateau to the car park at the rear, there were John and Josephine, hand in hand, countenances radiant with life, love and joy. They waved exuberantly to us as they skipped like teenagers across the immaculate lawns, calling out their heartfelt thanks for our help.

No doubt Josephine has now consulted the Master Jesus for more serviceable ways to help her distressed fellow travellers on the Path Home to Eternity, ably aided and abetted by a delighted John.

* * *

A week or two prior to the short break with Steve in the north of England, I had been to Poland on business. On the plane back from Warsaw to London on a Sunday morning there was terrific turbulence that tossed the plane about in all directions. I saw two angels, one each side of the plane. They held it in what looked like a giant 'cat's cradle', which was supporting the plane and allowing it to move with the turbulence, whilst keeping it totally safe. The angels were having a wonderful time, laughing and rejoicing, helping to reduce the effect of the turbulence on the plane by manipulating the cradle with their hands, rather like a puppeteer manipulates a puppet on a string. It was clear that the plane was so well within their protective care that there was absolutely no need for any concern whatsoever!

Soon the turbulence eased and being Sunday morning I decided to hold the Communion Service 'in my head'. In my dual-conscious awareness the plane was full of Christ communicants occupying the seats, in place of the 'ordinary' passengers.

At the offering I saw the Master Jesus as a steward, walking up the aisle between the seats, handing out the eternal life bread and Christ-love wine to all the communicant passengers. At the end of the service a rousing "Three cheers for Jesus of Nazareth" was given. He smiled shyly and modestly at this. He then walked up the aisle to where I was standing – in the dual consciousness – as officiant and put his arm around my shoulder, declaring of me to the communicants, "My beloved brother." His love overwhelmed me and I fell spontaneously to my knees at his feet. He reached forward and put something on me. It appeared to be a combination of an enveloping, etheric cloak and also a loop of ribbon with a cross of the most gleaming gold, about six inches/ fifteen centimetres high. It seemed to be at one moment a simple cross of horizontal and vertical intersecting bars with the vertical bar slightly longer than the horizontal bar, and at another moment a 'cross potent' or equilateral cross in a circle. The ribbon and the cloak were of red, purple and blue. I interpret this as a symbol of being *in* the Earth (red), *of* Heaven (blue) and achieving balance between the two (purple).

The Master said, "I give you this badge of office." I interpret this to mean as officiant of SMCC Communion.

I said, "Of myself I cannot do this, but by your love, grace and power so shall it be possible."

I have since come to believe the *real* badge of office is the giant cross with its base in me, and that which the Master put around my neck is a symbol.

I HAD BEEN AWARE for some years that the Kingdom of Heaven on Earth programme may well take a quantum jump in terms of some future event that will bring it more universally – or at least, extensively – into the awareness of the Earth's inhabitants, which I now realise are the *seemingly* separated, divided, fragmented Sonship of God. But a number of experiences and messages about kingdomly issues had left me in no doubt at all that the Kingdom of Heaven is *within* us (all!) (Lk. 17:21) and that we don't have to wait for any future, outer event to experience that truth as reality in our earthly lives, here and now, at any and every next moment.

"The Creator Spirit withholds nothing from his children, in spite of Earth-life ingrained perceptions to the contrary"

It is, according to the words of he who assuredly knows, Jesus of Nazareth, *at hand* (Mt. 4:17) and always has been. Jesus, as Anointed Messenger (that's what the title 'Christ' or 'Messiah' means), came to remind us of this, to call this fact to our attention and give multiple tips, hints, indicators and helps as to how we might become aware of its reality. All this as part of his being the Chief Executive Officer of his Great Rescue Programme for us all, to restore us to the eternal reality of Heaven, our true and only Home, forever. All that is required in order to experience this is to *believe*, and to be willing to receive and accept it unto our selves; to re-attune our minds to the wavelength upon which it exists, by *truly* seeking and *earnestly* desiring it. The Creator Spirit withholds *nothing* from His beloved Son, in spite of Earth-mind ego-ingrained perceptions to the contrary: "Fear not, little flock; for it is your Father's **good pleasure** to give you the kingdom" (Lk. 12:32).

If it is the Father's good pleasure to give us the Kingdom, assuredly it is the good pleasure of all who love the Father – whether in this life or the next – to also have this 'Kingdom-giving' ethos. There has never been a whiff of an indication that the Lord Jesus or any of the Christ-servers in the Realms of Light had any sort of 'withholding agenda'. Quite the reverse has been my awareness, based on experience of loving contact with and from them, over many years. But it is clearly a principle, on which all enlightened souls work, that they do not push information at seekers other than in response to questing; "*Ask*, and it shall be given you; *Seek*, and ye shall find; *Knock*, and it shall be opened unto you" (Mt. 7:7).

In today's world there is a demanding attitude widely prevailing that the answer to a question should be given immediately, verbally, literally, definitively. Such an attitude is not founded in spiritual humility. The approach of the Lord and the Christ-servers is more to inspire, encourage, gently point the seeker in the right direction and assist him to find the answer for himself. This, it is evident, is because when a person finds an answer for himself (with or without conscious awareness of help), the answer is much more meaningful and likely to stay with the seeker than if given, like a hand-out, from an external source. There is a great sense of *accomplishment* rather than of being 'spoon-fed'.

One Sunday morning in January, 1991, during a contemplative time before beginning our Communion, I was studying the order of the service and noticed particularly that a significant part of it consisted of extracts from the books of *Psalms*, *John's Gospel* and *Revelation*. At the very moment this awareness lodged in my consciousness, the Teacher (whom Olga had come to understand in her latter years, from clues given her by him, was John, the seer of Patmos, who wrote John's Gospel and Revelation*) burst, or more realistically, exploded, into my understanding the certain, absolute *knowing* that he was also one and the same as King David, of Old Testament renown. This was not spoken as a statement, but given, placed in, revealed to my soul 'knowingness', which is not in any way an intellectual process. It is illumination, revelation; like a curtain being opened and instantly the reality is there, complete, and no step-by-step logical thought processes are used – or necessary – to bring one to that place of knowing.

The experience was so staggering – albeit, not in any negative sense but simply because it had been so sudden, unexpected and explosive – that I felt as if I was in shock and needed to grab hold of something to steady myself from falling off my seat. Although he had given me this information 'unsought' in one sense, it was in response to my seeking, questing into the origins and reasons for things being as they were in the order of the service.

During the Silence in the Communion later that morning the Teacher explained that he had used this opportunity to bring this revelation because it would be serviceable in the future for me to have this awareness; it would help to tie together what would otherwise later be seen as loose ends.

In 1996, I decided to read the Bible through from beginning to end, which I had never succeeded in doing before. Several changes in my perspective came about as a result of this. I had heard many theologians and other sincere seekers after spiritual truth state that they saw the God of the Old Testament as a God of wrath, vengeance and judgement; somewhat of a contrast to Jesus of Nazareth – frequently referred to by Christians as the *King of Love* and the *Prince of Peace,* not to mention 'the *Son* of God'. Keep in mind that this same Jesus said, "I and my Father are one," and "If you have seen me, you have seen the Father."

Contrary to that perception of the Old Testament God, the overriding impression left with me from my reading was that the God of the Old Testament wished to be perceived by the people He had delivered from centuries of enslavement in Egypt as a loving, caring, solicitous, protecting, patient, forgiving, concerned Father (Deut. 32, esp. verse 6; Jer. 7:23; Prov. 3:11,12) and that if the people lived a dissolute life, turning away from the guidance He had given, there would be inevitable *consequences,* which are entirely different from *judgement, condemnation, punishment* or *retribution.* Sounds like the average, concerned parent in today's society, doesn't it? He warned the people countless times and kept on sending His messengers to admonish them, and by and large they paid no heed. Sounds like today's generation, doesn't it?

Prior to reading the whole Bible through I had assumed it was Jesus who introduced the concept of God as heavenly *Father,* but in fact the first reference to this is by Moses (Deut. 32:6). Further on in the Old Testament, in a message to Nathan for King David, referring to the distant-future Messiah – Jesus of Nazareth, born about a thousand years later, a direct descendant, according to

Scripture, of David – the God of the Old Testament, of the Israel people, said, "And when thy days be fulfilled, and thou shalt sleep with thy fathers, I will set up thy seed after thee, which shall proceed out of thy body, and I will establish his kingdom. He shall build an house for my name, † and I will stablish the throne of his kingdom for ever. **I will be his father, and he shall be my son.** If he commit iniquity, I will chasten him with the rod of men, and with the stripes of the children of men: But my mercy shall not depart away from him . . . " (2 Sam. 7:12-15).

Now, with the awareness that David was one and the same soul as John, the seer of Patmos, I realised that it was no wonder that he (John) was 'the disciple whom Jesus loved' and that Jesus used the term *Father* to describe the Creator Spirit. From Jesus' place of Oneness in Papa and spiritual awareness of those around him, he would immediately have known that John was one and the same as his 'father' or direct ancestor, David, who had been so crucial in securing the safety of the Israel people into which he, Jesus, would incarnate and establish his great God-mission for all mankind: the *Kingdom of Heaven on Earth*. Without David's mission a thousand years earlier this would not have been possible. How those words from 2 Samuel 7:12-15 must have resonated for Jesus when he read them, as assuredly he will have done, since he was clearly very well versed not only in the scriptures of his people but also of *their arcane and esoteric meanings*, which those lacking the light of spiritual discernment – such as the Pharisees – would have failed to see or understand.

* * *

During this time of reading the Bible from cover to cover, inevitably I came to the well-known story of Daniel's three friends, Shadrach, Meshach and Abednego, who are thrown into the fiery furnace (Dan. chapter 3). Reading this again caused me great distress.

"Here am I," I said to Papa, "feeling satisfied that I am strong in my faith, trust, obedience and commitment, having trodden the Path for thirty-odd years, and suddenly I am reminded of what faith, trust and obedience are *really* all about. Where does this leave me? I definitely do not feel that I am anywhere near ready to be thrown into a fiery furnace for my faith."

I felt grossly inadequate, leaving much to be desired, wanting.

He was clearly aware of all this and in characteristic manner was instantly there with the perfect answer.

"You are not called to be tossed into a fiery furnace."

The reassurance and relief I felt at that was enormous, but He hadn't finished. After a pregnant pause to allow the impact of this first sentence of His response to sink in, He said, "You are called . . ." pausing again to allow the drama of the moment to build, and although I did not *see* Him in the conventional sense of the word, I was *aware* of His smile and the humour in His intonation . . ."to be **patient**, that My purposes in you might be fulfilled."

That had indeed seemed to be the story of my life! From the time of first encountering the living Lord Jesus in a basement room in Vancouver in January 1967, a fire of zeal for him and his mission was kindled that burned unquenchably in me. From that day, I had a desire to share with my fellows the good – nay, *magnificent* – news of his living reality. Not as presented by the institutionalised church, which is so embroiled in petty politics, rules, regulations, details of mundane matters, such as: should women be ordained (never mind whether the ordained person was passionately committed to preaching the gospel – literally, Good News – of the Kingdom of Heaven on Earth. The gender of the person seeking to be ordained was somehow, ludicrously, made the central issue). And, should practising homosexuals – presumably of either gender in order not to be 'sexist' about this – be accepted into its fabric? This has raised what is, for the church, the fundamental issue of whether those professing to be followers of Jesus and the scriptures they esteem as holy, should maintain allegiance as to the *absolute* accuracy and origin of the Word of those scriptures or move into a new place of *selective* allegiance, in accordance with the changing morality of society, thus, surely placing, for a person making such an allegiance-shift, a question mark against the authenticity and authority of any other part of those scriptures.

All my fire for 'spreading the good news of the real, *living* Jesus' was to find very little outlet into the world around me. Indeed, this was in accord with the counsel of the Master Jesus himself, throughout the decades since my fist encounter with his livingness.

In March 1968, a few days after I had moved into my own flat, there was a knock at the door. I answered it, thinking it would be for the previous tenants, since nobody knew I was there yet. When I opened the door a man and a woman were standing there, but said nothing. I interpreted this as surprise on their part to find me there when expecting to be greeted by the previous occupants. Still they said nothing. Then the penny dropped. They were proselytisers, most likely Jehovah's Witnesses. My assumption proved correct, and they began their routine. However, I was bursting with zeal for my own good news. Needless to say, they were not listening to *my* news and I had no interest in *theirs!* I had heard it before and it did not resonate with my own *experience*, which I was so eager to share with any and all comers.

It was a salutary lesson for me, and the Master spoke immediately the door was closed at their departure. "Do not go out looking for people to speak with and share your message; rather, I will bring them to you. For I know the hearts and minds of all, and will bring only those who are ready to hear your speaking, and will inspire you and give you the words to speak to their hearts." Strictly speaking, I had, of course, not gone out looking for them; they had indeed come (or been brought – I was not able to tell which at the first instance) to me, but the message of the Master was not to be construed in that most literal of ways. What he was saying is, *observe*, and if a person whose path crosses yours gives some indication to you (it may be unwitting from them but discernible by you as a sign, *if you are watchful*) that they are ready to hear of the esoteric realities, then, and only then, speak more openly of them to the person. Further, if that person is ready, the Spirit of Truth will put the words into your mouth that will resonate strongly with the inner being of that person.

Later, when I recounted this experience to Olga, she shared with me a message given to her by the Teacher in 1948: "Guard thy tongue: especially to strangers to this way of life and the knowledge and wisdom of the spirit. Give place to the views of others, even though you know them to be in error. Send forth a prayer for such, that they may come to the fuller knowledge and the clearer sight."

On another occasion, the Teacher said to Olga, "Your heart outruns your head. You may stand at the cross-roads of life and offer your good things to them that inquire, but run not down every alley pressing them upon the halt, the maimed and the blind; for think you that your treasures will, as if by some magic, create in them a new set of values? You know within yourself that it is not possible, for it is contrary to spiritual law. As the Master taught, so we know – to him that hath shall be added."

Then, in the autumn of 1970, not many weeks before Theresa and I were due to sail back to England, one Saturday afternoon when Theresa was out and I was busy making a bread pudding (old family recipe!), it was as if a bell had rung in my head, to switch the focus of my attention from where it was lodged in the physical world, concentrating on my culinary endeavours, to the spirit realms, and the Master Jesus said, "My son, I would speak with you." I immediately washed my hands to remove the cooking ingredients, went to the sanctuary, lit the votive candle (fire or flame is a symbol of the Realms of Light in the spirit world and a candle flame helps to focus the awareness on/attune to those realms), picked up my pen and opened my notebook.

He told me that when we returned to the land of our birth we would not find kingdomly fellowship there to the degree we had enjoyed it with Olga; that fellowship there *would* be, sporadically, but not at the level to which we aspired. We were not to be dispirited by this, but rather to turn more purposefully to the Heaven world *within* for fellowship at this rarefied level, and *there* we would always find food and drink for the soul to satisfy our hungering and thirsting.

Needless to say, I was surprised, somewhat disappointed, at this, although appreciative of the forewarning. With the benefit of hindsight I now see that my time with my mentor, Olga, had run its course, that she had, indeed got me hooked-up with Jesus and that it was time now to branch-out on the path of my own forward, spiritual progress and life-purpose, or birth vision.

Fellowship, in matters concerning the eternal and invisible, there *has* been since 1970 and our return to the land of our birth but, as predicted by Jesus, not, until several years after the turn of the century, at the level shared with Olga. For fellowship at a level satisfying to the zeal for the Kingdom that burned *within* me it was necessary to go within, to the contact with the Realms of Light, where dwelt Jesus and all our loved ones in spirit who were fellow servers of the Christ purpose. This was the perfect thing, for it was discipline without which I would not have been focused, one-pointed, able to grow in the facility for attunement with the *source* of my inspiration and guiding.

For all those intervening years it was my longing to be 'out there, doing something, spreading the *magnificent* news'. But that was not to be in any substantial manner. I was limited to one-on-one, occasional encounters with those who were 'brought to me' – usually as one of those 'chance' encounters – as the Master had told me would be the case in 1968. Most of those who were brought to me were only ready to receive a *few* morsels from the banquet table the Lord was preparing for me – for 'all who will'. The lesson of patience was a hard one for me to learn, such was my eagerness for the Kingdom on Earth. The Rector reminded me, in 1976, of the importance of achieving and maintaining a balance between 'doing' and 'being'; that inward, spiritual peace is a state of *being*, not doing.

It is not easy to get the whole picture when it is a decades-long process and one is being led in blind 'faith'. Only since the commencement of the new millennium has the whole purpose of this life-path of patience become clear to me, as the Master promised repeatedly that it would when the time was right. Now I am clear that it was agreed 'aforetime' that multitudes of experiences of the reality of the Heaven world and its proximity *to* ('the Kingdom of Heaven is *at hand*'), its indivisibility *from*, its oneness *with* the Earth life, was my life path and purpose. This, to enable me to share them with my fellows in the Earth life – who are not at that place of awareness but are ready to begin the awakening process – from a position of authority born of experience.

There is no authority like experience, and I have experienced the *living reality* of the Kingdom of Heaven, here, in the Earth life, on many, many occasions over the decades. When one has had the experience, one does not *believe* it; one *knows* it, at the soul level of knowingness, which brings a certainty of knowing that is beyond all doubt. Any who have not had such experience of knowing can only imagine what such certainty is like. It is not a process of the intellect, which is an ego device, engendered to foment argument, debate, doubt and confusion. No-one can take it away or argue from a textbook position, or from religious doctrine or dogma, that it is not so. My life has been a process of creating a vast tapestry of experience fragments that have now been lovingly, diligently and expertly sewn together to form a huge, synchronistic, *cohesive*, picture of that reality, thanks to the unwavering guiding, inspiring and revealing leadership of my life by Jesus.

That could not have been possible if I had known from the beginning what was to be the path, the process, the plan of campaign. My Earth mind, in its limited understanding of the path of spiritual growth, would have got in the way of the spontaneity of the unfolding pattern of life, living always in anticipation or expectation. As it is, all the experiences of the tapestry have been *un*expected, *un*anticipated, and that meant that my Earth mind had nothing to do with the forming or manifesting of each experience. I can say, with no hint of false modesty, that my Earth mind is nowhere near as creative as to be able to fabricate the wondrous experiences with which I have been so blessed!

---

* There are those who say that it is highly unlikely that the author of the fourth gospel and the book of Revelation are one and the same person; that their writing styles, vocabulary, etc., are entirely different. I had not made that observation about it (it seems to me that both documents present an esoteric perspective, which I believe is significant, whereas the other three gospels do not) but am willing to give place to the opinions of much more scholarly commentators than I. However, to that I would add several observations. Revelation was likely written decades after the fourth gospel. He had undergone a massive expansion of spiritual awareness in that time, and that could lead to a different style of expression, especially as the experiences and encounters of Revelation are of such a fundamentally different nature from the gospel. This person is, as stated above, also the same who incarnated as King David. His manner of communication and expression to me, here, as 'The Teacher', has undergone an evolution over nearly forty years. That is substantially due to the evolution of my receptive capability in that time. Also significant is the great array of evidence that the church has interfered with the original manuscripts at various stages of its history.

† It is worth also keeping in mind that when Moses asked the God who appeared to him in a 'burning bush' for His Name, the reply recorded (and therefore, it could be said, is 'straight from the horse's mouth') is: "I AM THAT I AM: and he said, Thus shalt thou say unto the children of Israel, I AM hath sent me" (Ex. 3:14).

10: Tapestry Fragments

During the mid 1990s, four 'tapestry fragment' events occurred, all of which I now see were synchronistic, but which on each occasion appeared to be isolated, unconnected events.

In the first event, June 1995, as I was getting ready for bed one night, emptying the loose change and other oddments out of my pockets and placing them on the chest of drawers, I saw a young man walking toward me, from behind, slightly to my right. It should be explained that in the soul awareness, one's field of vision is 360 degrees. There are no limitations such as presented to the physical, where the field is restricted to the front and the sides; soul vision is 'all-round vision'.

"As he got within a few paces he stopped and said,
'I want you to enter the Holy of Holies.' "

This young man looked about twenty-five years old; he was of average height or slightly more, and of slim build. His hair was light brown, short back and sides but a bit longer at the front, inclined to flop slightly and be of the type that would require occasional pushing back from the forehead. He was wearing a navy blue blazer and grey slacks. His whole demeanour was entirely relaxed and casual. There was no doubt in my mind that he was English. As he got within a few paces he stopped and said to me, *I want you to enter the Holy of Holies.* He spoke these words in such a matter-of-fact way that he might have been saying, 'I want you to go and buy some milk', or any other such mundane, throw-away line.

As you might imagine, I was flabbergasted at the words and the incongruity of who had spoken them. I had never seen this young man before and had no idea who he was, or indeed if he was an actual person. It seemed to me that only God – Papa – (or Jesus of Nazareth) should have the authority to speak words such as these using the first person singular pronoun, but to hear them spoken by this relatively callow youth in a way that – although casual in tone and manner – indicated that he clearly had the authority to speak them, seemed inappropriate, to say the least. I have wondered about this over the years since it happened and had no idea who he was or who he represents. More recently I have come to understand that who he is, is of no relevance at all because he was a *messenger*, delivering a Message from the One Who wants/wanted me (just as He wants all His children in the Sonship) to enter the Holy of Holies.

The Cosmic Process, it seems, is established in such a way as to require that when an important person or event is about to arrive or take place, a herald, messenger or harbinger is sent ahead to announce the imminent arrival. The most well known of these is, of course, John the Baptist. But this principle applies even in 'lesser' events, such as Jesus appearing as a waiter in the Lake District pub. Then, John (not the Baptist!) had been the harbinger, announcing to Steve and me by his actions and body language, rather than by words, that a significant event was about to take place.

One might readily wonder why such is necessary, but clearly, an important event or person will be better received if those to whom such a visitation is about to be made are aware beforehand that something of great significance is going to happen. They can be ready for it and therefore appreciate the importance of it more greatly. If Papa had manifested from 'on High', with such a momentous statement, I feel sure it would have caused me trepidation to some degree or another. After all, to me at that time, the Holy of Holies was in the Jerusalem Temple of Biblical times, into which only an elect priest of Israel was permitted once a year and nobody else at all, under pain of death. This was the place where, according to the Bible, the power of the Almighty had its seat in the Earth, in Old Testament times. Any 'ordinary' person approaching would be 'blown away' by the awesomeness of that power. It was a place, for those not so authorised, to be held in fear and trembling, to be considered only from a safe distance. This is well documented by Ezekiel in the Old Testament and elsewhere. I had no aspirations to enter into such a disquieting place because it did not resonate with any of my experiences with Jesus of Nazareth or the Papa who was drawing me closer to Himself by Unconditional *Love*, gentleness, tenderness, intimate solicitousness.

"Suddenly I saw 'me' walking across the grass toward me, starting from about fifty or sixty paces away."

In the second event I was taking my daily walk with our dog in the nearby city greenspace, enjoying the sunshine and birdsong. Suddenly I saw 'me' walking across the grass toward me, starting from about fifty or sixty paces away. This was an etheric-substance, non-physical, manifestation of my exact, identical likeness. Nothing like this had ever happened before, and I stood there watching in wonderment, eagerly waiting to see what would happen next. This apparition walked right up to me, round behind me and merged with me. The Voice of the Holy One spoke: "Behold, I come quickly."

I had experienced overshadowing by discarnate souls on numerous occasions, including Jesus. On every occasion I was aware of another soul-identity moving into my soul-space, or aura. In such an experience one has full awareness that the other soul is 'not oneself' but another, different person. There is no sense of a 'perfect fit' between one's own soul form, or vibration, and theirs. In this instance, I had a very definite awareness that here was an absolutely *perfect fit*, perfect match, in every sense with which one could have any such awareness.

What could this possibly mean? But, even as I found myself asking this question, I knew within exactly what it meant. There is only one 'being' that could manifest in this manner and that is He who created me: Papa. This was He who had manifested to Moses in the burning bush. Since He is the Source *of* All, *in* all, there is a very real sense that He and I are one. When Jesus said *I and my Father are One,* he was making a true statement about himself as he had full awareness of it at the time he spoke those words, and also about all the rest of humanity, even though most of the rest of humanity still does not have the awareness, the experience, of

136

it being so. His statement could therefore be inferred as prophetic about the rest of mankind.

I believe most churchgoing Christians have a perception that for any of us 'mortal' souls to claim we are 'sons of God' is a blasphemy of the first magnitude because, for them, Jesus is the one and only, for all time, Son of God. Yet this perception is not supported by the Scriptures, which state directly to the contrary on several occasions, of which the most notable are:

Jn. 1:12: *But as many as received him, to them gave he power to become the sons of God, even to them that believe on his name.*

Rom. 8:14: *For as many as are led by the Spirit of God, they are the sons of God.*

1Jn. 3:2: *Beloved, now are we the sons of God, and it doth not yet appear what we shall be: but we know that, when he shall appear, we shall be like him; for we shall see him as he is.*

What I was experiencing was a demonstration of the truth of this statement by Jesus – *I and my Father are One* – in its application for me. If we are made in the likeness of God, then we all, in some esoteric – not biological, physical – way, have the likeness of God. This is true for each and every one of us, including, one hardly need say, Jesus ("He that hath seen me hath seen the Father" [Jn. 14:9]). So, if this was a fulfilment of the words of Jesus, "If a man love me, he will keep my words: and my Father will love him and we will come unto him, **and make our abode with him**" (Jn. 14:23), with whose identical appearance, or likeness, might I have expected Papa to come in terms of His taking up his abode with/ in me? The milkman? My neighbour? At such time as the milkman or my neighbour choose to love Jesus and keep his words, Papa will, assuredly, come unto them and make His abode with them – in response to their earnestly desiring it. No doubt, at such time He will make His appearance to them as identical to them.

For decades I had passionately loved His Son, Jesus, followed him, truly sought after Him and earnestly, passionately shared his great desire for the Kingdom of Heaven on Earth. Papa had decided that now was the time for making His abode with me and so He appeared, to my awareness, as identical to *me*. The logic is hard to ignore, and importantly, it is supported by the Scriptures. Further, why would He not appear in every detail as identical to me if He was about to make His abode with me? If He was not identical to me the fit would not be perfect and there would therefore be part of me in which He had not made his abode. Since the God of Creation – the Creator Spirit – occupies every part and aspect of His Creation, how could there be a part of me in which He would not make His abode?

"As I lay there with the light extinguished, I suddenly became aware that there was the figure of a man standing at the foot of the bed."

In the third tapestry fragment event, I had got into bed and was settling down for sleep. As I lay there with the light extinguished I suddenly became aware that there was the figure of a man standing at the foot of the bed. This startled and somewhat unnerved me because the figure was in silhouette form and was totally black. There was absolutely no light at all, of any kind, emanating from this form. It was like a black hole in a way, utterly bereft of any indication of the Light of Life. In my experience, this signalled a presence from the realms of darkness, and I was not eager for an encounter of that ilk. This form was very tall; I would say at least six feet six inches (two metres). As I took in this apparition, a voice which I knew to be Papa spoke from what I assumed at the immediate moment was where the mouth of the apparition would be, but realised, as I considered this later, was actually above and behind the head of the form.

The words spoken were, "Man, the Temple of God." Nothing else. There seemed to be many contradictions to this experience. I realised that the apparition was not an *actual* human but a representation of one, rather like a cardboard cut-out or a mannequin; utterly lifeless. If this form was intended to be a representation of man as the temple of God (1Cor 3:16: *"Know ye not that ye are the temple of God, and that the Spirit of God dwelleth in you?"*), it did not seem like the kind of representation I would have anticipated. Where was the light; where was the animation, the life, the livingness? This was devoid of all. This left me feeling distinctly unsettled and uneasy. Was this some sort of intrusion from the realms of darkness, trying to confuse me? Yet, at the same time, I knew of an absolute certainty that the voice that had spoken was Papa. Something did not add up.

As I lay there considering this, suddenly Papa spoke again, this time from beside the bed, to my left, about at my waist level but at the height of a standing person. This time He said, "*The Lord whom ye seek shall suddenly come to his temple.*" (Mal. 3:1: Behold, I will send my messenger, and he shall prepare the way before me: and the Lord, whom ye seek, shall suddenly come to his temple, even the messenger of the covenant, whom ye delight in: behold, he shall come, saith the LORD of hosts.)

This time, there was no sense of darkness and nothing unsettling. On the contrary, this left me feeling completely comfortable and at peace, and at the same time with a sense of excitement because I *knew*, at the soul-knowing level, that there was going to be a third message, creating a trilogy which would bring meaning to the whole experience. I waited in eager anticipation. Nothing happened. Anticipation began to turn into something closely resembling anxiety! I waited some more, and after maybe two or three minutes – a very long time when waiting in a situation like this – He spoke for the third time, "I will come unto him and will make My abode with him" (Jn. 14:23: Jesus answered and said unto him, "If a man love me, he will keep my words: and my Father will love him, *and we will come unto him, and make our abode with him.*")

Needless to say, I was not able to piece all this together and create a complete picture of it straight away. Also needless to say, I cogitated this very carefully, and my conclusion about it from the advantage of minute examination over time is that the black form was a representation of the temple without the presence of Him with Whose occupancy it would ultimately be filled. It was a symbolic representation of the temple vacated by its rightful occupant, the Son of God, who believes he has separated himself from his Father Creator – an upside-down perception if ever there was one! Without the Life, the Light of the Creator, there would be, there can only be, emptiness, nothingness, darkness, an absence of anything, including, and especially, light because light and life are synonymous. If one can envision any part of God's Creation from which the Creator Spirit is (or could be) absent, assuredly this form was it. Nothingness. Only a 'black hole' in the *form* of man but utterly devoid of Beingness. A form, one might say, awaiting re-occupation by the Source of All, the very spirit, or essence, of Life Itself; all-knowingness; perfect Love; creativity in all its boundlessness.

Here was a demonstration of the truth revealed in *A Course in Miracles* that the world, the physical universe, our bodies, and indeed, all that is of time and place – and is therefore destined to pass away – are not created by God, the Creator Spirit; that all that is of time and place is a dream of separation from Him, and that Jesus is, by his Great Rescue Programme, leading us back to Papa. When we have been 'made ready', or prepared – by the retraining and correcting of our misperceptions of our true reality, so long held by the apparently split-off-from-Truth, separated part of our mind, or ego, and restored to our true, Christ-Minded, thinking and knowledge – we will be re-unified to the oneness of the Sonship in the Father Creator.

Now, the words from Malachi; the next stage in a progressive sequence of events. First there must be a temple, otherwise there is nowhere for the Lord to come *to*. His is a promise as much as a prophecy. A promise and a prophecy at two levels of experience; first about Jesus of Nazareth, which was fulfilled about four hundred years after Malachi wrote those words, and ultimately about all of mankind – Jesus' beloved brethren in the Sonship of the Father. The first coming to the temple – Jesus – is now an historical event; the second is an event, a work, in progress at this time of writing. At one level of perception, God is already in His temple or temples – all seven billion of them, in the sense that the Life of the Creator Spirit is the same life which keeps us upright and mobile. Most of the seven billion of us are not consciously aware of that truth, but that does not render the statement untrue; it simply means there is no awareness of it because we are focused at the Earth-mind (ego-mind), or little-self level, whereas our true reality is our Christ Mind, or Big Self awareness. When an individual becomes ready to *experience* the 'Lord, coming to His Temple' – it will only happen as a result of *sincere and committed* seeking – then such will be the case. But it will not be of his own,

Earth-mind, determination, and indeed, it certainly was not of mine.

---

*"He has already appeared to those who have heard his knocking at the door of their lives and invited him in. **Such are already seeing him as he really is and** are becoming like him."*

The third message, from Jesus' words to the disciples at the Last Supper, rounds off the promise and has already been specifically fulfilled in those whose lives are an enactment of Jesus' words from that verse in John's gospel: *Jesus answered and said unto him, "If a man love me, he will keep my words: and my Father will love him, and we will come unto him, and make our abode with him"* (Jn. 14:23). In a broader sense it is fulfilled for all mankind already because the very life which keeps our earthly body upright is the life of the Creator Spirit. Most of mankind are simply not yet aware of that reality and are living in a state of blindness to, or forgetfulness of, that ultimate truth. It is like our good friend, John, the beloved disciple, reminds us: *"Beloved, now are we the sons of God, and it doth not yet appear what we shall be: but we know that, when he shall appear, we shall be like him; for we shall see him as he is"* (1Jn. 3:2). He has already appeared to those who have heard his knocking at the door of their lives and invited him in. **Such are already seeing him as he really is and *are* becoming like him.** This is both true and inevitable because the Purpose of God in man (His offspring) goes forward, ceaselessly, inexorably, infallibly and unstoppably.

This verse from John's epistle clearly states that we are *already* the sons of God (even if most of us are not yet actually living in harmony with, or focused upon, that reality; not yet manifesting it in *our* reality) but that when we attune our lives with the Life Source, or raise the vibratory rate of our thinking to the Kingdom – which happens automatically, one step at a time, when we *earnestly* desire It, believe in Its reality and are willing to co-operate with the process – then will that reality appear and manifest itself in and through us, just as it did in Jesus.

How can glory, love, joy, peace, radiant Light of Life,

empowerment over 'death', empowerment with eternity and all that is the Spirit of Creation, become manifest in that which is attuned to badger baiting, placing profit motive and expediency, self-serving, greed for the treasures of Earth which perish and moth and rust corrupts (Mt. 6:19) in preference to following the admonition of Jesus, "... seek ye first the kingdom of God, and his righteousness . . ." (Mt. 6:33, but the entire chapter is in fact a perfect blueprint for 'it' – our Sonship of God – to appear)?

It is noteworthy that Jesus counsels us to seek first the Kingdom of God. Not second, or anywhere else. *First*. Why would anyone choose to seek that which is *unconditionally loving, peaceful, life-enriching, life-fulfilling, free from sickness, all-compassionate, magnificent, glorious, beautiful*, other than first, when it – the Kingdom of Heaven – is available to each and every one of us, right here, right *now*? It is always our free choice and we are never coerced, for we are created in the likeness of the Creator, with free will to *choose* the Kingdom or to be like the prodigal son and waste our substance with riotous living (Lk. 15:13) (or whatever distraction temporarily sidetracks us from our journey on the path back to eternal, joyous, fulfilling, creative Love).

The fourth tapestry event was presented during sleep, as a dream. In this I was walking with Jesus along a gently winding, gravelled pathway through what appeared to be at first open countryside, with woodland, and then gradually, as we progressed on our journey together, becoming landscaped areas with lawns and shrubs. It was a warm and pleasant day, with sunshine and fresh air invigorating to body and soul. He was walking on my right, no more than a hand's breadth in front. This signified to me that he was at the same time leading and walking *with* me, beside me; not ten or twenty paces in front, as I had seen him so many times over the decades, during which he looked back over his shoulder from time to time and said, "I lead; do thou follow."

Now, he was *beside* me as in companionship, fellowship, but sufficiently ahead to indicate that he knew where we were going – which I certainly did not! We were engaged in warm, companionable, easy conversation, just as do two close, loving, trusting friends of longstanding acquaintance, but I had a sense that there was a definite purpose about our journey, with a specific destination to be reached, somewhere ahead. It was detectable in his stride, even though we were unhurried in our pace. I was totally at peace and enwrapped in the embrace of comfortableness, joy and upliftment of spirit. My state of being was in noticeable contrast to that when I was in his presence at the 1968 tea party with him, Olga and Theresa!

After a few minutes we rounded one of the gentle bends in the path and I could see before us, across a more expansive, undulating lawned area, a building. It was all white – pure, alabaster white – cube-shaped, about four or five metres high. It was constructed from stone blocks, perfectly cut and fitted and had neither windows nor doors. The stone blocks were *alive* and radiating living light.

We progressed toward this structure, and as we got about fifteen or twenty paces from it the Master began to rise from the ground, moving more rapidly ahead of me toward the building until up against the wall facing us. During this progress he had begun to morph from his human form until, by the time he reached the wall, he had transformed into an opening in the wall. He *became* the opening, the entrance, where previously there was none. The opening, which <u>was</u> Jesus, morphed, finished as a door frame; there was no door, just the frame. It was about two metres square and made from solid, living, radiant gold. It is not possible to find words to describe this adequately, yet still I must try. He moved toward the building, not walking but *gliding* through the air above the ground, morphing as he progressed, so that the entire move from beside me to when he became the entranceway was a seamless process. At the same time the very movement was, without a word being spoken, an *invitation* for me to enter into the building though the Golden Portal that he had become. ("I know thy works: behold, *I have set before thee an open door, and no man can shut it:* for thou hast a little strength, and hast kept my word, and hast not denied my name" [Rev. 3:8]).

> "His countenance was filled with indescribable joy
> and His smile radiated that joy and love toward me.
> His joy was so great that He could not speak."

With awe and curiosity I moved toward the Living Portal

until I was standing within it, able to see inside. It appeared to be a single room; all the walls were white, as on the outside. However, it was not the structure that caught my attention but the occupant. It was Papa. His appearance was just as I had seen Him when He told me the Keys to the Kingdom lie not in answers but in faith, trust, obedience and commitment (May 5, 1996). Since it is part of Western, Judaeo-Christian culture that God is our heavenly Father, how else might one expect to see Him but as a Fatherly figure? This is not to say that this is the only way, or form, or manner in which He is capable of presenting Himself for any, or all, of the fragments of His beloved Son to 'see'. He stood about two or three paces into the room from the entranceway. His countenance was filled with indescribable, ineffable joy, and His smile radiated that joy and love toward me. His joy was so great that He could not speak. Instead, with body movements He welcomed me, bade me enter, by a slight bowing, a gesture of the arms and taking a small step backwards. I felt that His joy was as the joy of the father in Jesus' parable of the prodigal son, who watched every day for his son and when he saw him returning 'a great way off', ran to meet him and 'fell on his neck and kissed him . . .'

I entered, as He had invited. The room was only lightly furnished, in a manner characteristic of an Edwardian English parlour. To my left was a polished wood dining table. Beside that was a chair facing sideways-on to the table and slightly away from it, so that one could sit down beside the table without having to move the chair. It was a ladder-back dining chair of the same, rich, dark wood as the table, with a padded seat covered with striped cream and light-brown satin. To the right, toward the back wall, behind and to the side of Papa was a multi-tiered, fluted-edge, circular table, also of the same polished wood as the main table. It was laden with plates of good things to eat, such as one might find in a characteristically English Sunday-afternoon tea. Behind Papa was a large wing-back easy chair that seemed to be His favourite seat. Those were the only furnishings that particularly caught my attention, but I had no sense of sparseness about the room. It all seemed very homey, inviting and entirely comfortable to my soul. (*Now, years later, with the benefit of long-term consideration of that room, I find myself inspired to add that any sense of incompleteness there may have been could only be rectified by the awaited presence of Papa's Son.)*

There, my awareness, or recall, of the experience ended, but the inference was clear: that Papa had invited me – representative, or symbolic, of his one beloved Son – to 'enter in' to His presence, into a place of 'Togetherness'. Jesus, the Anointed Messenger of the Holy One, was the conveyor of the invitation, and had taken me, led me, over half a lifetime of leading, to the place where the invitation would be meaningful for me. (What is the point of inviting a kindergarten child into a science museum? Better to bring the child, one step at a time, by the process of year-by-year education, to the place where he will be able to appreciate the wonders of the place, and *then* take him there.)

So, the big question is, what was this place? It was absolutely clear to me that this is the Holy of Holies – or more meaningfully, a symbolic representation of it. Although this information was never given to me verbally or in any other definitive way at the time, the previous tapestry events and the path I had been treading, with Jesus leading, over the years, and then accompanying me on this specific walk, meant no such further statement was required; the affirmation was in the *experience*.

What, then, IS the Holy of Holies? According to the Old Testament, it is the place of God's manifestation on Earth, the meeting place between God and man. The Old Testament descriptions of the meeting of God and man are places and events of fear and trepidation for man, whether in the Holy of Holies of the Jerusalem Temple, of the Wilderness Tabernacle which was its precursor, of the Ark of the Covenant or at Mount Sinai, where Moses met with God for the issuing of the 'Law' and the Ten Commandments. The Old Testament Holy of Holies, or Most Holy Place, was the innermost sanctum of the Jerusalem Temple, the design for which was given to King David by God through the mechanism of automatic writing (1 Chron. 28:19). It was a cube, separated from the Holy Place, (also a cube, of similar dimensions to the Holy of Holies) by a thick curtain, or veil, woven in red, blue and purple cloth. At the moment of departure of Jesus' spirit from his body on the cross the record states that this veil was torn completely in half, thus ending forever, so the record indicates, the perceived inaccessibility of God to man, because Jesus had bridged that gap. If that is not a cause for joyous celebration by humankind, assuredly, there cannot be one!

In all the years – decades – during which I have been blessed by experience of the intimate, loving, tender, patient, understanding, gentle, fun, relaxed nature of Jesus of Nazareth, there has never, *ever* been a moment in which anything he said or did was cause for me to be fearful of him. Yes, in the early days of my journey with him, I was hesitant, uncertain how to 'be' in his company, but it was always he who put me at ease, winning my absolute confidence, trust and relaxation in his presence. In the fewer years that I have been blessed in intimate relationship and communion with Papa, there has never been a single moment in which anything He did or said was cause for me to be fearful of Him either. On the contrary, all the encounters with Jesus and Papa have been reassuring to me of the *unconditional*, non-condemnatory acceptance (of me and all the fragments of the Sonship, *as I am/we are*) and love for me (and all of us) by God, Jesus and all of Heaven.

According to the place on the path of spiritual evolution that the Israel people of Old Testament times were, the Holy of Holies was of a single, specific material design and shape and purpose, and it was a place accessible only to the most holy of holy men. But the purpose of the Great Rescue Programme is not a static event; it is an ever growing, unfolding, outworking plan. It is a process whereby mankind, 'separated' from God, is being grown (spiritually) by the Good Husbandman, drawn *back* to God by the Spirit of Truth, and that Spirit is LOVE. Love *only*, perfect, unconditional; not judgemental. Jesus, the Messiah (Anointed *Messenger* of the Holy One) came to remind us of that and to demonstrate it ("I have not come to judge the world, I have come to save the world" [Jn. 12:47]). His saving is not from eternal hell-fire and damnation by an angry, wrathful, jealous, vengeful God, but from our own misperceptions – of God, of ourselves and of Creation – which are causing so much dysfunction in this world.

This unfolding process of redemption, or Great Rescue Programme – restoration to Oneness with the Creator Spirit – is an ages-long process, and is described by one of Jesus' least understood, least-referred-to parables; the parable of the leaven, or yeast. In this, Jesus states, "The kingdom of Heaven is like unto leaven, which a woman took, and hid in *three* measures of meal, till the whole was leavened" (Mt. 13:33). The lack of spiritual discernment of the scriptures by modern-day translators has caused them to change the wording to omit the reference to three measures: *"The kingdom of Heaven is like yeast that a woman took and mixed into a large amount of flour until it worked all through the dough."* (Mt. 13:33 NIV). Here is a good example of change for change's sake not always being serviceable.

The three measures refers to three, two-thousand-year-long eras in this six-thousand-year-long programme by the all-empowered-by-the-Father Jesus of Galilee for leading, drawing his brethren-in-the-Sonship – us – back into the Oneness, into the Kingdom of Heaven on Earth or, by an alternative perspective, the Holy of Holies. What could be Holier than the Kingdom of Heaven, whether in Heaven or on Earth, where the Good Husbandman is cultivating, growing us, so that we might bear much (spiritual) fruit? ". . . every branch that beareth fruit, he purgeth [i.e., prunes] it, that it may bring forth much fruit" (Jn. 15:2). It is worth keeping in mind here that Holy has nothing to do with religious piety but is to do with attunement – at-one-ment – with the Source of all Life, the Creator Spirit, and this is a joyous, natural, spontaneous, *non-fearful* state of being.

The first measure of meal refers to the two-thousand-year period from Abraham to Jesus (the Arian age within the context of the precession of the equinoxes). The second measure of meal refers to the two-thousand-year period between Jesus' time on Earth and now (the Piscean age within the context of the precession of the equinoxes) – the cross-over from the end of the second millennium to the beginning of the third millennium CE. And the third measure of meal refers to the period from now forward for the next two thousand years (the Aquarian age within the context of the precession of the equinoxes). During this last period the *'whole* will be leavened' and the Kingdom of Heaven will be *fully* established and operational on Earth. In reality, the Kingdom is here already and has always been for those who are in a state of at-one-ment with it, such as was Jesus. No-one, not God or Jesus, nor anyone else, is withholding the Kingdom from us; we are, by our own (ego) *self-imposed* blindness, perversity and 'stiff-necked-ness', excluding ourselves from what has always been there for us, if we are willing to *freely* receive it, . . . *without money and without price* (Is. 55:1). Jesus said, two thousand years ago, "The time is fulfilled and the Kingdom of God is at hand" (Mk. 1:15). If it was at hand two thousand years ago, where, one might readily enquire, is it now, since neither Jesus nor the Father, the *King*, have removed or hidden it from us?

"In the time now with us and immediately ahead,
the outpouring of the Spirit of God is taking place upon
the consciousness of the fragmented Sonship"

In the time now with us and immediately ahead, the outpouring of the Spirit of God is taking place upon the consciousness of the fragmented Sonship, and those who desire and are ready to awaken to it are becoming aware of it. This is already apparent – and will become increasingly the case as the leavening continues – in many enlightened individuals and groups and in many thousands of books already in print, as well as websites on the Internet, setting out plainly their Spirit-inspired awareness of kingdomly ways of being, of living, here on Earth, *now*. Why wait? *It is the Father's* **good pleasure** *to give us the Kingdom!*

The programme may seem like a long time – six thousand years – to those of us here, now, seeing the world moving, by the perverse and stiff-necked actions of those who have assumed authority over the people of the various countries and cultures and religious persuasions of Earth, into such dangerous and desperate times. The fact is, it is a blink of the eye in *eternity*, and that is where we – all of us – are from.

The first measure of meal, The Abraham Measure, had to be set in place to create the conditions into which One *empowered* to organise and preside over this whole six-thousand-year programme could incarnate; ("All power is given unto me in Heaven and in Earth" [Mt. 28:18]). It may seem to the casual observer as if the historical events were simply happenings in the Earth by (or to) people in the Earth, and that it was merely 'chance' that brought about the events in the life of Abraham and those who followed after him. A closer look reveals that we are all citizens of eternity, sojourning in time, and that the *real* nature of our being is spiritual, operating *through* a body. It is the *Spirit* of man, in its inextricably-linked relationship with the One Spirit, the Creator Spirit, (even though, with our Earth-mind consciousness most of us have no discernment of this *spiritual* relationship) that is *actually* directing the overall, big picture of the unfolding Great Rescue Programme events on Earth, and always has been and always will be, until the end of time, and *the whole is leavened*. This truly is *cosmic* synchronicity, for goodness' sake. The spirit of man is in a 'desire and construct' partnership, or relationship, with the One Spirit – from and in Which (or Whom) we have our origin and our being – functioning in the Earth life through the physical bodies that are our instruments of manifesting and expressing whilst sojourning here.

Abraham was the progenitor of a race of people who, often kicking and screaming, were the agency by which the all-empowered Anointed Messenger could come, to take the leaven from the first measure of meal, which was proving (using the terminology of bread making) during this period and carry it though into the second measure of meal. This would then start the proving, *spiritual* leavening, process of the second two-thousand-year period; 'The Jesus Measure'. The second measure has now proved and is being carried through (by the Holy Spirit, Who is the leavening power) to leaven the third measure – 'The Kingdom Measure' – . . . *'till the whole was leavened.*

It may appear to many, who have looked to the Christian Church over the last two thousand years, that that measure of meal has *not* been leavened and has instead, gone very flat, crushed by all the unserviceable-to-the-Kingdom, un-Christ-like ideas, events and activities perpetrated, or encouraged, by it (the institution known as the church) in the name of Jesus. He knew what would be the events during these past two millennia at the time he manifested to John of Patmos in the first century CE, and as allegorically described by John in the book of Revelation. So the activities of the church claiming to be his followers and his representatives on Earth – and which have, in so many ways, been about as polar-opposite from his life, example and teaching as possible – have been of no surprise to him.

"His empowerment is easily adequate to compensate for the lack of any such spiritual power or discernment by those who claim to be his followers on Earth but in reality are not."

However, that in no way negates the desire, purpose and activities initiated by him by his incarnation, life, crucifixion, resurrection, ascension and the work upon which he has ceaselessly been engaged since, about which the church of Earth and most people on Earth have no awareness or understanding. That lack of awareness is of none-effect on any part of his programme. His all-empowerment is easily adequate to compensate for the lack of any such spiritual power or discernment by those who claim to be his followers and/or representatives on Earth but in reality are not. Jesus himself says it all: "Not every one that saith unto me, Lord, Lord, shall enter into the kingdom of heaven; but he that doeth the will of my Father which is in heaven" (Mt. 7:21).

The mechanism for the transfer of the leavening agent (the Holy Spirit) from the second, or Jesus measure to the third, Kingdom measure, is the reincarnating of millions of souls who, throughout the Jesus measure, have grown to love him and to espouse him and his great God-mission for all mankind. That love and espousing has been engendered in such by the example he brought with his life on Earth, which they came to love, honour, revere and desire to emulate during *their* earthly lives, but has been rendered immeasurably more substantial during their life in the spirit realms after a life – or indeed, multiple lives – of Christ-commitment (as distinct from church commitment) on Earth. This is because, once a soul has laid aside his earthly body and returned to his rightful place in the spirit realms, he will have actual, substantive fellowship with the real, living Jesus in those realms.

With the exponentially greater understanding such fellowship will provide of the real purpose and plan of Jesus, such love, commitment and espousal to him and his mission will become commensurately greater. That mission is the raising (leavening) of the consciousness of humanity to the fully spiritually awake level of awareness, whereby we will all remember our Oneness with, or in, the Source of All, just as did Jesus two thousand years ago. Then, truly will we all be aware of our empowerment, from our own within, which is the place of contact with Papa, the Creator Spirit, for the fulfilment of Jesus' words, ". . . the works that I do shall he (who believes) do also, and greater works than these shall he do . . ." (Jn. 14:12).

This has nothing to do with ego – the mechanism employed by most of those who believe themselves to be 'running the planet' at the present moment, and which is the upside-down, split-off-from-Truth part of our mind – but is unconditional love; loving our neighbour as our self.

Our neighbour is not just the family living next door, but also round the other side of the planet, with a different skin colour, a different culture, a different belief system. And all the other creatures that inhabit planet Earth with us. We will no longer see them as so much 'commodity value', (or, indeed, 'nuisance value' if they are in the way of our wish to grub-out their habitat for our own requirements, without a concern for their wellbeing, or even survival) for converting into cash by abusing them and depriving them of their own natural dignity, feeding them on their own excrement, the brains and offal of other creatures, prophylactic incorporation of antibiotics and growth hormones into their diet, all for profit motive.

Those souls who have grown to love Jesus and espoused themselves to him and his mission are incarnating now, in these times, and the generations ahead, by the millions – after all, how many have come to that place of love, commitment and espousal in *two thousand years?* – each with his or her own mission for the Kingdom, agreed aforetime in consultation with Jesus or with some other enlightened soul from the Realms of Light, authorised by him for such consultative work (Jesus is not afraid to delegate!). Such souls are described as Indigo or Crystal (Christ-all) Children. There are a number of websites about them, which any internet search engine will quickly find.

Many of these souls will be unaware of their espousal to him and his great mission in their Earth-life consciousness. Mikhail Gorbachev is just such a soul. It seems doubtful that he, in his Earth-mind awareness, had a conscious commitment to Jesus and his Programme, yet he was instrumental in dismantling the

Soviet empire, moving hundreds of millions of people out from under the yoke of a repressive system of government, and thus enabling their moving significant steps toward freedom to enter the state of being described herein as the Kingdom of Heaven on Earth. These souls are being/will be activated by their own seed-memory from their various Jesus-measure incarnations. Truly, the Kingdom of Heaven is *within* us, thus ensuring that no ego-dominated, Earth-structured institution will be able to subvert the process. Thus will they carry-over the leavening agent from that second measure into the third measure *until the whole is leavened.*

"This is now a time, the time, for returning home to the Father, who unconditionally loves us and rejoices so greatly that we are accepting His invitation to enter into the Holy of Holies, the Kingdom of Heaven."

The Holy of Holies is not a place in – or of – which to be fearful. God is not wrathful, judgemental, condemning; He is unconditional, Perfect Love. He is as described by Jesus in his parable of the prodigal son, in which the father looked out for his errant son every day and when he saw him 'afar off', he ran to him, embraced him and welcomed him *unconditionally* back into his home, rejoicing. That was a time for celebrating, for leaving behind all fear and doubt, and it was the father's unconditional love for his straying son, returning to the fold, that removed any and all doubt. This is now, similarly, a time for rejoicing and celebrating because it is a time, *the* time, for returning home to the Father, Who unconditionally loves us and does not judge us but rejoices so greatly that we are accepting His invitation to enter into the Holy of Holies, the Kingdom of Heaven. Thus – working in fully aware, deliberate, co-operative partnership with the Architect of the desire-and-construct plan, or programme, and His Anointed Messenger – we can and will, if we are sincere in our desire, by co-operating with the Holy Spirit within us, bring the blueprint of the Kingdom from its *desire* stage into the *construct* stage, *here, in the Earth.*

152

11: The End of the Beginning

When one is on a journey, it is serviceable to have a vehicle to facilitate that journey. When the journey has been completed and the destination reached, the vehicle has served its purpose and can be dispensed with. Indeed, if the vehicle is not dispensed with and one remains within the vehicle, it can turn from a means of conveyance into a mechanism of restraint and limitation – even imprisonment. This would prevent progress into the next phase of life operations from commencing at the point of completion of that preceding phase. The Way back Home to the Eternity we know as Heaven is a series of journeys, opportunities or stepping-stones, each having its beginning as its predecessor comes to its natural conclusion, having completed its cycle. For all in the illusory, manifest universe operates in cycles, from birth or germination, through the growth, flowering, fruiting and eventually seeding stages. This is a process that operates at every level, from single-cell life units to solar systems and galaxies.

The Service of Mystical Communion with Christ – as assembled by our beloved friend the Teacher (David, son of Jesse/John, 'the disciple Jesus loved', the seer of Patmos) and brought into the Earth life by the agency of Olga Park – has been such a vehicle for me. It has been a magnificent, all-sufficient vehicle, with Jesus of Nazareth as driver and guide, along with innumerable other fellow travelling companions from the Realms of Light whose lives are resonant with Jesus' great desire for the Kingdom of Heaven on Earth. These diverse travelling companions, including and particularly Jesus himself, have made this journey one of love, joy, peace, protection, enlightenment, blessed good fellowship and continual wonderment at what (and *who*!) might lie around every next corner.

It has been for me an exquisite journey which, one could say, began with my meeting Olga Park in 1965 and concluded when Jesus walked with me up the beautiful, landscaped pathway toward the white cube structure, morphed into its golden portal through which I passed into the joyous, welcoming presence of Papa, our heavenly Father, into the Holy of Holies, the *Place of Togetherness in/from which is taken the next and final, completing step back into the Oneness* from Which we have come.

Thus were fulfilled the words of Jesus to me in 1996, "My job is to lead you back to God." He had accomplished the task he took on when I asked him to be the spiritual Lord and Guide of my life. In reality, of course, he had taken it on long before I asked him, because he knew well before I did (in my Earth-mind consciousness) that this was to be ("And it shall come to pass, that before they call, I will answer; and while they are yet speaking, I will hear" [Isa. 65:24]) because it had been agreed between him and me aforetime.

When the tutor completes his undertaking to teach the pupil – the student of the Mysteries – and the student graduates, the relationship between the two undergoes a fundamental change. At the start, the student is *down* here and the tutor is *up* there in terms of the student's perception of the relationship between them, and of the Mysteries. If the tutor does a good job (and I can vouch that there is no better tutor than Jesus of Nazareth – "For there is nothing covered, that shall not be revealed; neither hid, that shall not be known" [Lk.12: 22]) then the time will assuredly come when that graduation will occur. The tutor then welcomes the graduate and bids him (or her) to 'come up higher', knowing that his graduate student has been well prepared to go on and do great things, to fulfil the potential with which he began his studies, his journey.

"The student will see that he also has been grown by the Good Husbandman into a place of greater spiritual awareness and empowerment."

The student instinctively, intuitively, becomes aware of the change in the relationship and the growth in his own stature. He who was revered from afar, perceived as being so much loftier as to be in an almost unreachable place, is now seen from a much uplifted vantage point; still as being all-wise, unconditionally loving, all-sufficient. But the student will see that he also has been grown by the Good Husbandman into a place of greater spiritual awareness and empowerment. *This in no way dishonours or diminishes the tutor from his true and rightful station. On the contrary, it honours him and affirms his place as the great teacher that he truly is. The mark of a good Master is not how many students he has but how many he brings to graduation.*

The former student is then ready for the next journey, having graduated from being a *seeker* of the light to a *bringer* of the light ("**Ye are the light of the world** . . . Let your light so shine before men, that they may see your good works, and glorify your Father which is in Heaven" [Mt. 5:14,16]). This is not to say that the student has, at this juncture, arrived at his final destination; the place of restoration, or awakening, to *full* God-Self-realisation. Jesus teaches us in *A Course in Miracles* that we learn as we teach. In other words we grow in our spiritual discernment as we share with, or impart to, our brothers, our awakening awareness of the Truth of Eternity as they journey Home with us. I can attest to this being so, because as Theresa and I surrender ourselves into the guiding Light of the Spirit of Truth, or Self, for the prayerful, contemplative study of *A Course in Miracles* – and other sources of spiritual truth or wisdom – we find new enlightenment and understanding comes to us spontaneously at appropriate moments. Such enlightenment is freely available to all the fragments of the Sonship, because all-knowing was given us at our creation, and is an integral aspect of the Truth of our Being. We chose to dispense with it, or forget it, at the imaginary separation, but we are freely restored to awareness of it as we awaken, *in response to our asking.*

This has also become very palpably the case with the writing of the weekly *Messages of Encouragement* (MoEs) that I was prompted to begin in 2005, and evolved into a regular event in 2006 (posted on the Honest2Goodness website). Often I would – and still do – commence the writing with a particular line of consideration intended, but a new thought would spontaneously come into my mind, which it was clear the Holy Spirit meant for inclusion. This then leads to awareness of reality of which I had no previous understanding, and the MoE ends up being on a totally different subject matter, of which I had no prior conscious knowledge or remembrance.

It has been evident throughout my journey with Jesus that our peace of mind, comfort and wellbeing is of paramount importance to him, to Papa, the Holy Spirit and to all in the Realms of Light. They know that sudden and dramatic changes of experience or awareness can be deeply disturbing to our equilibrium, and They always introduce significant expansion of our perspective as gently as possible, to prevent us receiving too big a jolt. This principle was applied to my entry to the Holy of Holies, and it was presented to my mind as being an environment in which Papa knew I would be comfortable. Hence Its furnishings having the appearance of an Edwardian English parlour. Such was an environment with which I was familiar and which engendered pleasant, happy feelings because it reminded me of my grandparents' home, which evoked similar feelings, helped greatly by the presence of good things to eat, during childhood visits.

After the transcendent, unforgettable experience of entering the Holy of Holies parlour for afternoon tea with Papa, I was not sure where I went from there, and contemplated this very carefully for some time. Although I knew this event was the entering in to the Holy of Holies, the question was: *What happens then?* And the answer at which I have arrived is that the Holy of Holies is, in a greater sense, not just a place but a state of being wherein we are restored to our rightful estate: Citizenship of the Kingdom of Heaven. I realised that entering into the Holy of Holies is, initially, entering into *the togetherness* with the Creator Spirit.

After this preliminary entry process and the period of adjustment that follows such a magnificent, wondrous event, one's awareness emerges into a further state of being, which is that even more than being in *togetherness*, one is indivisibly within *the Oneness* ("I and my Father are One"). This can be experienced on a temporary basis, and will become permanent when we have been prepared, grown, made ready and purified. This then becomes the final part of the returning-home, Great Rescue Programme process, and our own, Earth-mind-conscious self-will (ego), action or determination plays no part in it. It is *in response* to the desire of our heart and soul that we are drawn by the Creator Spirit, one step at a time, at a pace with which we are comfortable, able to assimilate the meaning of the process and remain in a state of peace, harmony and balance within it.

* * *

One night, during the mid 1990s, in bed after extinguishing the light, I lay on my back ('facing heavenward') and began attuning, communing, with Papa. After a few moments of switching off from the distractions of time and place, I began to feel the peace of Heaven enveloping me. Then I became aware of Papa, above me, looking down upon me with incomparable, all-encompassing love. The sense of togetherness with Him was exquisite; a moment to capture and hold onto forever; a treasure of inestimable value – calm, still, acceptance, tranquillity, love and joy.

After this long moment had totally enthralled me in its tender embrace, Papa's smile of perfect, ineffable love seemed to grow. He moved closer, and at the same moment, drew me upwards, into Himself. 'I' merged completely into Him, became one with Him. This was not a stifling experience; not a loss of a sense of Being, but of emerging from all sense of time and place, limitation and restriction, into the freedom and limitlessness of Eternity. Apart from the Love, which was breathless in its majesty, utterly beyond words, beyond imagining, the absolute feeling of completion held me in its stillness. I didn't want to move, to do anything, because there was nothing *to* do.

All was completed; now, I was simply, sublimely, *Being*. The sense of completeness brought with it an awareness of the total lack of wanting, of scarcity, of fear, or inadequacy. How could there be a sense of lack when everything was mine, because it is Papa's, and I am now one in Him?

Any attempt at describing this experience falls hopelessly short of the mark, for words are but symbols, mostly devised to describe unreality, so cannot serve adequately to portray *reality*.

After timeless moments in the Oneness, in the unutterable Completeness, the experience began to fade. I tried with all my heart, mind and being, to hold onto it. The prospect of losing this – all of which, somewhere in my mind, I knew, had always known, was my destiny, my inheritance, my creation-right – was beyond contemplation. I tried to recall the pattern, the process, the procedure, the mechanism by which this wondrous event had taken place, *determined* to repeat it, and learn how to regain its preciousness at will. But it was all to no avail and to this day it has recurred only on a greatly diminished level.

Yet it was not long – a few days, a few weeks – before I realised plainly that this was not of my doing, or my separated will, and of myself it was unattainable. This is Papa's Will, and is re-attainable only by the complete alignment of our will – the will of each of us who desires it – with His. He knew the desire of my heart, and out of His love, His *Perfect* Love, He had given me this taster, this promise, of all that awaits me; awaits His one, beloved Son, to whom He has given everything. I know of a certainty beyond all doubt that this is the only, true reality that awaits us all.

To *know* the Light fully, we must *welcome* it fully. We may think we welcome it fully, but unless we are totally sure of this, it is not, yet, apparent to us. But desiring it will bring the *fulfilment* of our desire, accomplished for us by our unlimited Self, the Spirit of Truth, Who is all-empowered by God for this, His one and only task. When we desire it sufficiently, we will be willing to co-operate with Him in this.

Being in the Oneness is a totally *knowing* awareness that there is no difference, no distance, no separateness between oneself and the universal, omnipresent, eternal Creator Spirit; that His Mind is our Mind, indivisibly *One*. One has access to It at *all* times, *is* It, and there is none of It which one's Self is not; none of It is withheld from one's Self because one *is* the One-Self.

"There is no reason or cause for fear at this process of awakening into the Oneness; it is not about becoming less *but about becoming* more."

Yet, even more amazing and difficult to find words to describe is the absolute awareness that this does not bring an end to the Being that is Self. Self becomes fully restored, reunified to Its rightful place as the unlimited, complete *One* Son of the Father Creator; a state of being that is immeasurably greater and more magnificent than one's former, *apparently* separated, 'little self', with all its finiteness and limitations. That will never for a moment be missed or yearned for again, because one has moved from the Adamic consciousness, 'Red Earth' (ego) end of the spiritual spectrum to the 'Blue Heaven' (Self-realised or God-filled) end. There is no reason or cause for fear at this process of awakening into the Oneness; it is not about diminishing but increasing; not about becoming *less* but about becoming *more*. Much, much more. Immeasurably more. *Everything,* in fact. Who amongst us would not, in his *right* mind, be willing – *eagerly* willing – to exchange his littleness, his limitations, his mortality, for Everything; eternally?

This is who we *are*. Each and every living soul, incarnate or discarnate. So when Jesus said, "I and my Father are one" (Jn. 10:30), it was entirely true for him, but it is also true for *all of us*. Jesus remembered this truth, but most of the rest of us have forgotten it. He was fully God-filled, having travelled the path back to remembrance of Oneness. Most of us are some way behind on that same path, in a state of varying degrees of forgetfulness about who we really are (*"Beloved, now are we the sons of God, and it doth not yet appear what we shall be"* [1Jn. 3:2]). Jesus came to remind us. Will we choose remembrance or will we choose to remain clothed, or even bound, in conditioning that denies us our reality by stating that we are all separate from God because we are all 'sinners' and have fallen short of the mark in the sight of God?

That is like saying a young child has been naughty and therefore must be thrown out of its parents' house and banished forever, no longer worthy of its parents' love and acceptance. Is this proper parental behaviour? How much more will our heavenly Father continue to love us *unconditionally* regardless of our mistakes, or misperceptions? "If a son shall ask bread of any of you that is a father, will he give him a stone? or if he ask a fish, will he for a fish give him a serpent? Or if he shall ask an egg, will he offer him a scorpion? If ye then, being evil, know how to give good gifts unto your children: how much more shall your heavenly Father give the Holy Spirit to them that ask him?" (Lk. 11:11-13).

IT IS MADE TOTALLY and unequivocally clear in *A Course in Miracles* that the ego is the upside-down part of our mind that eventuated as a result of a momentary, delusional attempt to separate our self from our heavenly Father. Of course it is impossible to be separate from God because He is the Essence, the Source, the Origin of Life, Love, Creativity, knowledge and awareness that occupies every part of Creation.

According to *A Course in Miracles*, God established what is referred to as the Atonement (At-onement) *principle* before the apparent separation. This is rather like designing a fire-escape into a building before its construction. One does not use, or have any need for, the fire escape unless or until there is a fire, but it is eminent good sense to have it in case the need arises. Well, the 'fire' started, or the need for the fire escape arose, when Papa's one, beloved, perfect, eternal, invulnerable Son – Christ – had a momentary thought, a tiny, mad idea, wondering what it would be like to be what he is not; separate from his Father, in Whose likeness he was created.

Of course he could not *actually* separate from his Father Creator, because, as Jesus also reminds us in *A Course in Miracles*, an idea never leaves its Source. Papa's Son was/is a 'Thought of God', an idea, created in His Mind and *extended* therefrom, but never *leaving* his Home in Papa's Mind, just as, when we send out love to a brother, that love does not leave its source in our heart-mind, but extends, radiates from it.

But he could *pretend*, or dream, that this had happened, and within this dream of separation, a part of his mind split off from his *fully-awake-and-one-in-Papa* mind, appearing to separate from the eternity of Heaven and enter what seems to be the opposite thereof: time and place. This apparent separation into a fantasy state of upside-down perception seemed to take place, at what cosmologists or quantum physicists dub the *Big Bang*, about fourteen billion years ago (so say they!), in linear-time measurement.

For the fantasy to have the semblance of reality, and thus be a believable experience, this split-off part of his mind had to undergo a state of forgetfulness of his one, *true* Identity. Because the Mind of God's Son is imbued with all the creative power of his Father Creator, it was possible to fabricate a state of perception that could seem to be believable, *but only if this voluntary, self-imposed state of forgetfulness of his true Being was entered into.* As

160

soon as remembrance of Self returns, the illusion will be seen for what it is and will be over. In the reality of Eternity, or Heaven, it is already over because in truth it never happened. Only within the time and place dream experience does it appear still to be happening.

Because *within the dream* Papa's Holy Son has forgotten who he is, and believes unreality to be reality, and therefore perceives and experiences it as such, it would be, at least in theory, impossible to be restored to wakefulness, or remembrance of his true, eternal, safe, free, all-loving, invulnerable Being. This is where the 'fire escape' comes into its own.

The instant the apparent separation came about, Papa implemented the Atonement process, switching it from just principle to activated practice. At that moment, He created the *Holy Spirit*, the *Spirit of Truth*, the *Voice for God* to be inextricably with His Son – within him, in fact – and accompany him as he journeyed into 'a far country', a world of make-believe, where everything appears to be real, but is not, and cannot be because everything is constantly changing, decaying, degrading, including the bodies we adopt as our false, separated, individual, limited identity. If we believe such is, or could ever be, a creation of God, we are mistaking illusion for reality.

So, the Atonement process has been operational since the separation appeared to begin. That seems like a very, very long time ago, and ego would raise the question, 'If God exists, and has this *fail-safe* plan for the rescue of His Son from time and place, and restoration to Eternity with Him, why has He taken so long? Fourteen billion years is a vast, unfathomable length of time; if He is so almighty, why didn't He just snap his fingers and have it all over immediately?'

There are two ways of looking at the answer to this question. The first is, *it never happened in the first place*; His Son never left Home, and is still There, safe and sound, as he always has been, always will be and could never not be. Not seeing it or being aware of this does not make it untrue. It *is* true, and Jesus came into the illusion bringing the reality, the Light, the Truth of Eternity with him, and demonstrated it right here for us, in the dream; showing us – *being* for us – the Way Home. If Jesus hadn't come we, the fragmented Sonship – one, appearing as many –

would, assuredly, find it immeasurably harder to be able to grasp the Truth of Eternity from this upside-down place of perception.

The second way of looking at this question is: time, as we perceive it in its *apparently* linear format, does not exist in *reality* – Eternity – and Eternity is where Papa *is*, so time does not exist for Him. If it does not exist for Him, we can be assured it does not exist. Period. The split-off part of the mind of the Son made it up as a ruse to *appear* to be separate, *in a far country*. Because Papa gave His Son free will at his creation, He would not – could not, because His Will is inviolable, including by Himself – interfere or set boundaries for him.

So, when His Son had his moment of wondering what it would be like to not be as – or *Where* – he really is, Papa did not stop him, because He knew that: a) separation is, in reality, impossible; b) the free will He had given was inviolable; and, c) He had established the failsafe principle (the 'fire escape') of the Atonement.

Time is part of the illusion of separation from Eternity, and only *appears* to progress in a linear fashion, so fourteen billion years or fourteen micro-seconds are all the same – nothing – other than in the perception of a confused, fragmented, upside-down, split-off-from-reality part of the mind of Papa's Son. Linear time does not exist for God. For Him, and for His Son – when he is in his right mind – there is only the eternal moment of NOW, which is *perfect* Love, joy, peace and the sublime ecstasy of oneness in the Heart of God.

That state of Being is unchangeable, eternal, forever. And who, in his right mind, would want to change that state of Being; to throw it all away in exchange for fear, uncertainty, confusion, doubt, guilt, death?

The instant the separation – the Big Bang as it is perceived (though not understood) by cosmologists and quantum physicists – began, the Atonement process came into operation, and the Voice for God started calling Papa's Son back Home to Him. That process, that Call, is like a magnet to iron filings, exerting its influence on the split-off, confused, separated part of the mind of Papa's Son, though that part has been – and still largely is – unaware of the Calling. Nevertheless, during the whole time that appears to have elapsed since the separation, the Call has never ceased.

Eventually, one, whom we now know as Jesus, heard the Call and chose to follow It. It was always certain that there would be a first fragment to actually follow the lead of the Voice for God, because It spoke the Truth of Eternity, and, regardless of appearances to the contrary, that is the 'language' of Papa's Son, just as it is his Father's. There was only one place following such a lead would take him, and that was Home, to full wakefulness and remembrance of his true Identity as Christ.

That restoration to oneness in the Heart-Mind of God would inevitably have caused him to realise that all the other fragments are one, with him, in the Sonship, and that not only he, but Papa also, could not be complete without *all* the fragments being gathered together and restored to oneness of Christ Mind remembrance. That restoration to oneness would have brought back to Jesus' awareness, his total certainty of knowing, experiencing, *being*, that, like his Father, he is Perfect Love – Love for, or of, his Self, Papa and all the rest of his fragmented Self, or 'brothers'.

Perfect Love, the state of Being to which Jesus was restored, gives *everything* in absolute, unswerving, total commitment to rescuing those who have forgotten that this is Who they, also, eternally Are, and instead perceive themselves as broken, lonely, lost, confused, fearful, unworthy, guilty, limited, mortal . . .

And, having remembered and been restored to wholeness, he was empowered with all power in Heaven and Earth, to complete his all-consuming desire for, and commitment to, rescuing his brothers and restoring them to full awareness and experience of their oneness with him in the Sonship of He Who Is the *Source* of Perfect Love – God. Thus, under continuing guidance, inspiration from Papa's Voice and His ongoing Atonement process, Jesus implemented, and is leading, the Great Rescue Programme. Holy Spirit knew this would be the case, for He knew the end from the beginning.

The Great Rescue Programme is the final phase of the Atonement, and will be its completion. The Atonement may appear to be a fourteen billion-year process, and its final phase, the Great Rescue Programme, a six thousand-year process, but all that is literally *nothing* – because time does not exist, and the only moment is the eternal moment, the Holy Instant, which is, forever, *now* – and when we are all *lovingly* wakened to Heaven's reality, we will forget time and place, with all its limitations, just as we forget an insignificant, nonsensical dream when we have wakened from a night's sleep.

The separation is, therefore, an illusion, but very *real-seeming* to those of us in the Earth life who see the physical universe – including our own bodies – as *the* reality, *the* truth, *the* actuality for them.

According to *A Course in Miracles*, the upside-down part of our mind (not brain) is the antithesis of all that characterises the Creator Spirit (unconditional Love) and manifests in our Earth-life as negative, divisive, accusatory, judgemental, capricious, comparative, critical, spiteful, attacking, fearful, manipulative, self-serving, guilty and the like. This is 'Satan' as characterised in religious mythology. Until humanity is willing to metamorphose from its self-perception as a crawling 'caterpillar' into a soaring 'butterfly', all these unkingdomly qualities will continue to manifest in the Earth-dimension of human consciousness.

Ego-mind is very powerful, deceiving, guileful, and release from its insidious, possessive hold over us is possible only, first, by desiring it and second, by accepting the help of Papa God, the Holy Spirit and the first 'butterfly' – Jesus – (all three of Whom act in unison, as One Mind, One Being). That requires a shift of perception from the 'I will' of ego-mind self-determination to the 'I AM' awareness – which is the absolute certainty of all-knowing – of Eternity.

This is no more possible for the human intellect than it is for the intellect of a caterpillar to effect its own metamorphosis into a butterfly. It is nothing to do with intellect (which is a device of ego-mind to prolong our illusory state) but is of the Life Force, which is the Spirit of the living, eternal Creator. The caterpillar, led by the drawing power (which is Love) of the Life Force (God), withdraws from its previous, Earth-crawling activity and is dissolved, at a cellular, molecular level, then recreated in its true state of being as the butterfly it always truly was, is and will be.

This allegory is equally true, at a metaphysical, mystical, spiritual, esoteric level (the true, eternal reality) for God's seemingly fragmented Son, Who is the Christ: us.

We have to be *willing* (that is, *desire*) to allow Him to lead us in this process, accomplish this *for* us, because He has endowed us with free will, and He never withdraws that free will and imposes upon us what we are unwilling, or unready, to receive.

This is the only real challenge facing humanity today, and all the other perceived challenges stem from failure to recognise this one challenge – actually, *opportunity* – and embrace it, totally.

Fortunately for us, Jesus *does* recognise this and for this reason has implemented the Great Rescue Programme – which, as explained in Chapter 10, is described by Jesus in his parable of the three measures of meal, the third of which is now leavening – for us all, (including those of us who have no awareness of it, or refuse, through ego-mind fear, contrariness and perversity, to recognise it) and he is empowered for this by the Source of All, our heavenly Father. Resisting it is, as ego-mind humanity is experiencing, noticeably less comfortable and noticeably more fearful, painful and destructive. Co-operating with him (and/or, the Holy Spirit, the Spirit of Truth, the Holy Breath, our true and eternal, undivided Self) and the Great Rescue Programme will enable its accomplishment more quickly and more comfortably for us all. We are at free choice, every moment.

The Great Rescue Programme, or final phase of the Atonement, is centred in the recognition that the physical universe and all that is in it is not God's creation but is a projection of ego-mind. None of it, including us, is *really* here; this is nothing more than a dream. We are all One in the Sonship of God in Eternity (Heaven) – always have been and always will be. Therefore none of what *appear* to be events taking place here has *actually* happened and therefore we are not, and cannot be, guilty of the 'sins' of this illusory world. The only way to break free of ego's hold that keeps us coming back here in vain attempts to outwork and resolve the karma accrued from one incarnation to the next is to recognise this and release our self and our fellows who appear to be here with us by enacting a procedure Jesus calls *true* forgiveness, as distinct from *false* forgiveness.

The difference between true and false forgiveness is:

False forgiveness is when the 'sin' is *acknowledged* and then forgiven. However, the flaw here is that by acknowledging the 'sin', we give it reality. This is a ploy of ego mind, which wants us to be, and remain, bogged down in a false world of sin.

True forgiveness . . . here, the words of Jesus from *A Course in Miracles* are the most serviceable to our forming a clear and uncluttered understanding:

> "[True] **Forgiveness recognises that what you** *thought* **your brother did to you has not** [actually] **occurred.** It does not pardon sins and [therefore] make them real. It sees [instead, that] there *was* no sin. And in that view are all *your* sins forgiven. *What is sin except a false idea about God's Son?* [True] **Forgiveness merely sees its falsity, and therefore** <u>lets it go</u>. *What then is free to take its place is now the Will of God."* *

*   *   *

I cannot let the relating of my blessed, precious encounters with the real, living Jesus and what they have taught me about his Great Rescue Programme for us all – his perfectly-loved, perfectly-innocent brethren in the Sonship of God – draw to a close without including what he, himself, tells us about the Second Coming of Christ:†

"What is the Second Coming?

"Christ's Second Coming, which is sure as God, is merely the correction of mistakes [i.e., mistaken perceptions] and the return of sanity. It is a part of the condition which restores the never-lost, and re-establishes what is forever and forever true. It is the invitation to God's Word to take illusion's place; *the willingness to let forgiveness rest upon all things without exception and without reserve.*

"It is the all-inclusive nature of Christ's Second Coming that permits it to embrace the world, and hold you safe within its gentle advent which encompasses all living things with you. There is no end to the release the Second Coming brings, as God's creation must be limitless. **Forgiveness lights the Second Coming's way because it shines on everyone as one.**

"The Second Coming ends the lessons which the Holy Spirit teaches, making way for the Last Judgement, in which learning ends in one last summary that will extend beyond itself, and reaches up to God. The Second Coming is the time in which all minds are given to the hands of Christ, to be returned to Spirit in the Name of true creation and the Will of God.

"The Second Coming is the one event in time which time itself can not affect. For every one who ever came to die, or yet will come or who is present now, is equally released from what he made. In this equality is Christ restored as one Identity, in Which **all Sons of God acknowledge that they all are one.** And God the Father smiles upon His Son, His one creation and His only joy.

"Pray that this Second Coming will be soon, but do not rest with that. **It needs your eyes and ears and hands and feet. It needs your voice. And most of all it needs your willingness.** Let us rejoice that we can do God's Will, and join together in Its holy light. Behold, the Son of God is one in us, and we can reach our Father's Love through Him."

And this, the final paragraph from page 455 of the "Workbook For Students"** entitled **"What is the Last Judgment?"**:

"This is God's Final Judgment: 'You are still My holy Son, forever innocent, forever loving and forever loved, as limitless as your Creator, and completely changeless and forever pure. Therefore awaken and return to Me. I am your Father and you are My Son.' "

Amen!

"Workbook For Students" Part II, *A Course in Miracles,* Second Edition:
* "1. What is Forgiveness?" p. 401.
† "9. What is the Second Coming?" p. 449.
** "10. What is The Last Judgment?" p. 455.

PART TWO

Vignettes*

* Vignette: a brief, evocative description, account or episode.

There have been many experiences and awarenesses over the years that do not necessarily fit the narrative in any either chronological or other sequential manner in Part One yet do augment and complement it. They are offered here to provide further insight into and understanding of the Universal, Loving, Creative Intelligent Force called Life, Love, God, Papa – or whatever resonates for you – and the process of our emerging remembrance of the truth of our eternal, spiritual reality. May these vignettes be beneficial in assisting our restoration to Oneness in the Creator for all Eternity – our true and only Home, which we know as Heaven.

There are twenty-seven Vignettes, as follows:

1.	"Stand in the Holy Place; Stand in the Lowly Place"	171
2.	Hal/Sitting Bull	174
3.	Buffalo Bill	179
4.	First Encounter with the Holy Spirit	180
5.	The Free Gift of Forgiveness	183
6.	Goddess Theresa	186
7.	Broken Ankle at Crickley	191
8.	*Seeds of Redemption*; Charles	196
9.	Fleas; "Don't give up!"	200
10.	An Open Letter	206
11.	The Crucifixion: "I did it to get your attention."	224

12. The False Doctrine of Sacrifice as the
    Path to Salvation   231

13. A Mass Rescue and Healing   238

14. "There is no light of discernment."   243

15. Animals and Eternity   246

16. Peter: "I came to clear the way for her."   249

17. Religious Mythology   251

18. The Not-So-Distant Shore   252

19. Ted's Passing, Rescue and Going Forward   256

20. From Breaking Rocks to Breaking Bread   267

21. Laser: Amplifying the Light for the Kingdom   272

22. Jim, Ship's Doctor   279

23. Exorcising Possessing Spirits   283

24. Religious Misperceptions of Duty   292

25. The Gathering of the Clans   294

26. Tyndale the Translator   297

27. Jesus in Bedrock Hell Fastening the
    Escape Ladder to the Floor   300

1. "Stand in the Holy Place; Stand in the Lowly Place"

In the early hours one night in October 1997, I had awareness of Papa; how beneficial it is to our spiritual growth to focus, focus, focus on Him, honour Him, love Him, give thanks to Him, rejoice in Him, TRUST Him, immerse ourselves in, give ourselves to, Him, allow this focus to be the Light. Or rather, be *aware* that this activity amplifies the Light which fills us, stimulates the radiance within us until we cannot contain it any more and it bursts forth in/as a mighty laser beam upon the world (of un-God-aware humanity) around us. This brings blessing, transformation, God Power to make new, whether by uplifting or disintegrating and re-creating (as in the metamorphosis of caterpillar into butterfly).

Papa spoke in the midst of all this: "Stand in the Holy Place." Then I was suddenly aware of myself, as it were, in the form of a lowly invertebrate, like an inchworm, down on the ground, crawling across the debris of a woodland floor, in the darkness of the night, but illuminated by a full moon. As I wondered why I was experiencing this, Papa spoke again: "I AM in this (and all such lowly creatures). Do thou stand in the Lowly Place."

This was the end of the experience, but while the first admonition had no meaning for me on its own (other than the obvious), when both statements are considered in relation to each other, the implications were exponentially greater.

The fact that this scene was at night symbolises spiritual darkness, or absence of the light of spiritual discernment for humanity in the time and place consciousness. The inchworm symbolises the low level of existence to which the Son of God is subjecting himself in his self-inflicted game of seeming separation from his Father. And the moonlight symbolises the psychic consciousness, as distinct from spiritual awareness and knowledge, which always, without the fire of spirit to empower, uplift and direct it toward the Light of Eternal Truth, follows the path of least resistance, and sinks lower and lower, or further and further from the Light.

Nevertheless, the perfect love of Papa is boundless, and reaches down to us in the lowly place, irrespective of whether we have conscious awareness of it, and however low we allow our self to fall.

"By being disdainful *(or fearful) of what we perceive as the lowly place, we* make *ourselves lowly (spiritually). Conversely, our willingness to stand in the lowly place, in spiritual humility (as Jesus did) immediately restores us to holiness."*

For many years I had been trying to reconcile in my mind that on the one hand we are taught to perceive God, the Most High, as pure, unsullied by anything 'unclean'; to wear our best suit to church; to avoid the things one did not discuss in 'polite company', whilst on the other hand, that nature (which from the dawn of human consciousness has been seen as God in diversity) includes slugs, excrement, bacteria, malaria-carrying mosquitoes, thistles, vultures, stinging nettles, rattlesnakes, animals eating each other alive, parasites, famines, and untold other aspects that are not the 'Sunday best' face of God. If God is Life, and that Life is everywhere, indeed, in every*thing*, He must be in the Life that is in all the 'unsavoury' parts also, even when there is no awareness of His Presence.

What I immediately realised Papa was telling me by this message is that He is *the All-Knowingness* in all these things; that it is the All-Knowingness in all these things that is Holy, and that standing in the *lowly* place in *perfect, unconditional love, blessing, acceptance, joy, thanksgiving* – all the characteristics that we can readily identify as being Godly – is the humility that is an indivisible aspect of the Holy One, and that transforms a lowly place into a *Holy* Place. This experience was reminding me that by being *disdainful* (or fearful) of what we perceive as the lowly place, we *make* ourselves lowly (spiritually). Conversely, our willingness to stand in the lowly place, in spiritual humility (as Jesus did) immediately restores us to holiness. Jesus demonstrated this by words *and* actions:

Take my yoke upon you, and learn of me; for I am meek and lowly in heart: and ye shall find rest unto your souls (Mt. 11:29).

When thou art bidden of any man to a wedding, sit not down in the highest room; lest a more honourable man than thou be bidden of him; And he that bade thee and him come and say to thee, Give this man place; and thou begin with shame to take the lowest room. But when thou art bidden, go and sit down in the lowest room; that when he that bade thee cometh, he may say unto thee, Friend, go up higher: then shalt thou have worship (honour, respect) in the presence of them that sit at meat with thee. For whosoever exalteth himself shall be abased; and he that humbleth himself shall be exalted (Lk. 14:8-11).

He riseth from supper, and laid aside his garments; and took a towel, and girded himself. After that he poureth water into a bason, and began to wash the disciples' feet, and to wipe them with the towel wherewith he was girded. Then cometh he to Simon Peter: and Peter saith unto him, Lord, dost thou wash my feet? Jesus answered and said unto him, What I do thou knowest not now; but thou shalt know hereafter. Peter saith unto him, Thou shalt never wash my feet. Jesus answered him, If I wash thee not, thou hast no part with me (Jn. 13:4-8).

2. Hal/Sitting Bull

In a 1990 Communion, as I held the bread aloft during the consecration, Steve said he could see it shining as bright as a magnesium flare and that he had become aware of a group of Native American chieftains, sitting in a tepee around a fire. At the same moment that Steve had seen the shining bread, so had it equally attracted their attention. Steve realised that one of these was Sitting Bull, who was deeply bewildered by this sudden awareness. We explained to him and his friends what was happening, that there was nothing to fear and that he was welcome to join us if he desired.

Clearly, he did desire and we have had many encounters with him over the years. In one such, Steve and I were having a pub lunch after he had helped me clear out our old offices when we moved the business back to the house. As Steve and I sat in the pub enjoying the convivial atmosphere and I lit a post-prandial cigar, Sitting Bull suddenly stuck his head over a room-divider screen right beside us and, beaming genially said, "I will smoke the pipe of peace with you!"

* * *

In November 1996, I was brought into the presence of Henry VIII. He had been stuck in a time warp for about four hundred and fifty years in Earth timing. He was wandering the wood-panelled corridors at Penshurst Place, still dressed as he did in the sixteenth century, with a glowering look on his face. He emitted a vibration of sullenness, rather like a petulant schoolboy. I asked him why he was so unhappy. He said he was sick of being surrounded by fawning, toadying sycophants, who he knew did not respect or like him and were afraid of him, when all he really wanted was a true friend, who would speak as he found. He said that his entourage were yes-men but did not do as he really wished.

I told him I was not afraid of him, would speak as I found and would be a true friend if he so wished. He was noticeably surprised at my candour but even so, this did not satisfy him because he was disgruntled that I did not show him all the appropriate courtly respect that he felt he should be accorded as King. Nevertheless, it was obvious that he secretly and begrudgingly was glad to be spoken to in such a forthright manner, which he never got from those around him. He also indicated that he felt trapped in this place. I told him that it was his negative attitude that was actually entrapping him.

Although our discussion had discernibly made an impact upon him, he was not ready to outwardly budge from his obdurate posture and I realised it would be best to leave him to reflect upon our encounter and visit with him again later.

When we met the next time, a few days later, it was clear he was pleased to see me, and his demeanour had lightened significantly. He was still rooted in his earlier opinions of his courtiers and the lack of real freedom and power, to which he felt he was entitled as King. We chatted, and I debated with him the unserviceableness of his attitude. By the end of that meeting he was less rigid than at the beginning in his adopted stance on how life had dealt him a poor hand, but it was nevertheless clear that he was not yet ready to go forward into the Light of spiritual freedom, so I decided to leave him to consider these things in his own time again.

At a third meeting, just before the start of a Communion Service, we had a long heart to heart. He was now truly oscillating between wanting to let go of, and being rigidly stuck in, his long-held views, of which he had been so certain he was right, and therefore, why should he change? After all, he was the King (*damnit!*). But here was this stranger who actually spoke to him *straight – the impudent whelp!* – and made a lot of sense, and to whom he was drawn as someone he could trust, and, in spite of himself, he actually could not help liking; and by unequivocal talking was causing him to perceive things in a way that for centuries he had been unable, but more, unwilling, to see. Yet every time he came within a whisker of relenting and giving up his four-hundred-and-fifty-year old charade, he drew back again.

"I am the King!" he proclaimed. "I *will* be respected and why should I give up my rightful position?"

Nevertheless, he accepted me as a true (not sycophantic) friend now, and I told him he is no longer King. He said if he gave up all this he would have nothing; he was fearful at this. I told him that outwardly, Jesus had nothing in this life but he was the only true King of this world. I told him we must be prepared to give up everything, in accord with the Lord's teaching. I invited him to stay for our service. At that moment I became aware of the Master Jesus and Sir Thomas More being with us, although Hal (as Henry VIII is widely and affectionately known) had no such awareness at that moment. Thomas spoke to Hal through me.

"Hal, there is only one true King and that is Jesus of Nazareth. Until you can acknowledge him not just as '*the* Lord' but Lord of *your* life, in all sincerity, you cannot go forward."

As the impact of these words sunk in, Hal suddenly became aware of the Master and immediately, spontaneously, fell to his knees and bowed his head in allegiance.

"My liege," he said, in *deep* humility.

The Master, radiating joy, peace and love, stepped forward and reached out his arms to Hal, saying, "Arise, Sir Hal." He took the Master's proffered hands and stood. As he did so his raiment was transformed to a simple white robe, except he still had on his hat.

"Hal," I said, "you still have on your old hat!"

He became aware of it, and pulling it off his head he threw it over his shoulder.

"I don't need *that* any more!" he exclaimed in a loud voice, filled with great joy.

At last he has gone forward and accepted the Lord's reality, and perhaps even more important, his own true reality.

* * *

At a subsequent Communion after the rescue of Hal, he and Sitting Bull encountered each other. They stood face to face, a little less than an arm's length apart in the middle of the floor, where there was a clearing about the size of a boxing ring, with everyone else seated around them. It was a very dramatic moment. The atmosphere was charged with anticipation.

They looked deeply into each other's eyes for several minutes. Both are big men, well over six feet tall, and both, in their different ways, very impressive figures, with a natural nobility emanating from them. During this time, not a word was spoken, but the exchange of information that took place between them, through their eyes, into their minds, was that of centuries of each other's peoples' histories, and how European Man, represented here by Hal, had so dreadfully impacted upon the lives of the Native American peoples, represented here by Sitting Bull. This mind-to-mind exchange of information was like two computers downloading data to each other, and was happening at least at the same rate as today's high-speed microprocessors work.

"The issues between them could not rest, nor could forgiveness and reconciliation be established until their relationship was brought back into fair and equitable balance."

I could sense, if not actually hear, the exchange taking place. Sitting Bull was imparting to Hal the actual *experience* of the events that had taken place – how his people had been so ill-used by European colonists – and how this situation clearly called for redress. The issues between them could not rest, nor could reconciliation and fair and equitable balance be restored and established in their relationship without full understanding and true forgiveness; for to understand all is to forgive all. Only then could both races move forward *together*, freely, unencumbered, into the light of the third – fulfilment – measure of meal, the Kingdom Age, now dawning on planet Earth.

For his part, Hal would have had no awareness of the genocide that had taken place west of the Atlantic Ocean – after the end of his incarnation, by colonists from Europe – and this was therefore an update for his record. At the soul level these two men and the peoples they represented are One, as are we all.

Culture, skin colour and any other illusory, outward differences are things to be accepted and honoured rather than feared and attacked. All these things and the implications of them for their respective peoples and what to do about them, to bring about that redress and restore peace, harmony and balance between these two races, so long at odds with each other, were exchanged between them.

There was no enmity, no animosity between these men. They were simply being provided, at last, with an opportunity to come to a place of meeting on equal terms, to exchange information, views and commitments to each other, on behalf of their respective peoples.

After their information exchange was completed, there was a sudden change of mood. Each turned slightly to his left and, still without a single word being spoken, they raised and linked their right hands at eye level, with inner wrists touching, and performed an on-the-spot, rotating ritual dance, eyes interlocked, gaze never breaking. It was a curious dance, with only legs moving, slightly reminiscent of Irish dancing, but with a very different style of leg movement. In Irish dancing only the legs move, from the hips down; in this dance, the only parts of their bodies that moved were their feet, from the ankles, and for much of it they were on their toes, almost like ballet.

It seemed incongruous for two such big, noble-looking, powerful men to be moving so easily in this unusual manner; bodies and heads remained in a fixed position in relation to each other, simply rotating as their feet moved. After several clockwise turns they stopped, switched hands and reversed the dance, anticlockwise. This was done several times. They moved in perfect synchrony even though there was no rehearsal and nothing spoken. I knew this was an act, a symbol of reconciliation between them and their peoples and the sealing of their respective commitment to work together for the establishing of a kingdomly relationship between those they represent.

Truly, we had been witness to as momentous an occasion of healing and restoration of relationships as anyone might be blessed to see. I give thanks that this Communion ritual was the instrument by which it was able to be brought about. What is now the significant issue is how each individual member of these races, incarnate and discarnate, desires, chooses, implements such a state in his own heart, mind, soul and actions toward his fellows of that other race (and indeed, all other races).

At a later encounter with Sitting Bull I said to him, only half joking, "I now wish to know you as 'Standing Bull', because you have increased in stature by such a quantum leap that I can only envision you as standing, tall and proud." He was greatly appreciative of these words of commendation.

3. Buffalo Bill

Not long after the experience with Hal and Sitting Bull, one Sunday morning before Communion, as I got into the shower, I suddenly saw William F. Cody (Buffalo Bill). His face was at an angle to me and I could tell he had no awareness of me. It was like a life-size cameo image of his head and shoulders. He was looking away into the distance. I knew who it was immediately because I had been an avid reader of the Buffalo Bill annuals as a boy, and also visited the Buffalo Bill Museum at Boulder, Colorado in 1967. Further, when he had toured the UK with his Wild West Show in 1904 he had given a scouting knife to my grandmother (then nineteen years old), who immigrated to Canada approximately eight years later. I still have that knife today.

Having recently been considering the awful acts against the Native Americans by European colonists and the role of W.F. Cody in those events, I blurted out, before thinking about it, *"How could you have done that?"* Instantly he was gone, blown away by my indignant outburst. Although he had not seen me, the force of psychic energy directed at him had severed the connection. I believe that if I had thought more carefully and been empathetic, accepting and non-judgemental, a link could have been established that could have created huge opportunities for further progress in the reconciliation process between the Native American and European races.

Nevertheless, with the resourcefulness of the Lord and all the other Beings of Light working with him for the Kingdom of Heaven on Earth – to which such reconciliation, along with reconciliations between all the other broken relationships that cover planet Earth, will contribute so greatly and so invaluably – other opportunities will, assuredly, abound.

4. First Encounter with the Holy Spirit

By the late 1990s, I had been on my journey back to God, with Jesus leading me (how else would I have known the Way!?), for more than thirty years – during this 'act', or incarnation – and by now had also started to become consciously aware of Papa's speaking to me. But so far, the Holy Spirit, to Whom Jesus refers three times in John's Gospel as *the Spirit of Truth* and also *the Comforter*, was still a completely unknown quantity to me.

Yet, Jesus' speaking of 'Him' is highly significant. He said to the disciples at the Last Supper:

> I will pray the Father, and he shall give you another Comforter, that he may abide with you for ever; Even the Spirit of truth; whom the world cannot receive, because it seeth him not, neither knoweth him: but ye know him; for he dwelleth with you, and shall be in you (Jn. 14:16,17).

> But when the Comforter is come, whom I will send unto you from the Father, even the Spirit of truth, which proceedeth from the Father, he shall testify of me (Jn. 15:26).

> I have yet many things to say unto you, but ye cannot bear them now. Howbeit when he, the Spirit of truth, is come, he will guide you into all truth: for he shall not speak of himself; but whatsoever he shall hear, that shall he speak: and he will shew you things to come (Jn. 16:12, 13).

These statements could easily be classified as 'very important', yet as far as I was aware, the world at large knew nothing of Him, and I certainly was completely unable to get a handle on Him, in spite of having a high level of interest in so doing.

However, it was obvious that He knew of my desire, and He made himself known to me for the first time in a very mundane and unlikely situation, as this entry from *Diary of a Christ Communicant* * records shows:

Late October 1997:
Susie (our rescued Lhasa Apso dog) was suffering badly from back trouble, and as I asked Papa's guidance on whether to take her to the vet I became aware of what seemed to be 'Spirit Wind'. I had a sense of it swirling round like a spiralling cloud, with a human-type face, radiating peace, joy and love. It was reminiscent of an illustration in a child's story book of a benign, westerly breeze, blowing in a cloud. There was no sign of physical disturbance – I felt only an absolute stillness and inward tranquillity, serenity, peace; a considerable contrast to the way in which the metaphysical wind appeared to be swirling. I asked what this was and the Voice spoke, from the face in the cloud; it was somehow not Papa or the Master Jesus, yet had Their same authority: "**I AM the Spirit of Truth**," and after a slight pause, "**the Holy Breath**." The rest of the communication was telepathic (or, mind-to-mind communing), explaining that the visitation was to bring a message of positive assurance from Papa, in response to my asking, to leave Susie in His loving hands; not to expect an instant fix but to leave it with Him and be constant in faith; not to be concerned if she didn't eat for a few days.

This experience was, in my heart and the inner discernment of my mind, completely and utterly real, and it gave me a new sensation of awareness, of faith, trust and the ensuing willingness to be obedient to this Inner Awareness.

From that moment, Susie went into the dog's bed under my desk. She never went there before; it had been our previous dog's bed and Susie instinctively honoured that and kept out of it, even after Muffy had come to the end of her sojourn with us. Susie stayed in that bed for four days without moving except to do her business, eat (not much) and come into the house with us at the end of each day.

From that time on, her back gave her no further trouble.

I was reminded afterwards of how the disciples first encountered the Comforter, or Holy Spirit, as described in Acts 2:2: "*suddenly there came a sound from heaven as of a rushing mighty wind, and it filled all the house where they were sitting.*" I can make no claim to there being a 'sound as of a *mighty*, rushing wind', but for just one person, perhaps my attention was easier to attract, and It, or He, was most certainly from Heaven, and appearing as a rushing wind.

What, then, of His words, 'the Holy Breath'?

Let us turn to John's Gospel again, chapter 20, in which it says, on the day of Jesus' resurrection:

> . . . the same day at evening, being the first day of the week, when the doors were shut where the disciples were assembled for fear of the Jews, came Jesus and stood in the midst, and saith unto them, Peace be unto you: And when he had so said, he shewed unto them his hands and his side. Then were the disciples glad, when they saw the Lord: Then said Jesus to them again, Peace be unto you: as my Father hath sent me, even so send I you: And when he had said this, **he breathed on them**, and saith unto them, "Receive ye the Holy Ghost."

Assuredly, this record from John's Gospel affirms the meaning and His Identity in this, my first encounter with Him, the Spirit of Truth. Since then my awakening has progressed to the place of understanding, greatly helped by *A Course in Miracles*, that the Holy Spirit is our connection with Papa and with our true Being while we are in the illusion of time and place. This is confirmed by His explaining to me that that visitation was to bring a message of positive assurance from Papa, *in response to my asking*. *A Course in Miracles* also explains that the Holy Spirit is identical to our true Being, or Self, dwells within our mind, and is the connection with our true, Whole (Holy) Self, or Christ, Papa's Son, until we are restored to remembrance of our true Being.

How characteristic of Papa's Voice to make Himself first known to me in such a mundane, yet close-to-my-heart matter as a wellbeing issue with our beloved, precious Susie.

---

* For details of 'Diary of a Christ Communicant', please visit: www.honest2goodness.org.uk/Diary_post2000.htm

5. The Free Gift of Forgiveness

This event took place during a Communion Service in 1998. The Diary entry for the date describes the event:

Holy Communion September 13, 1998:
As I knelt to make my dedication I felt Papa above and around me. He held me in the stillness and said, "My son, draw closer to Me. Open yourself to receive My love more." I realised that we have been led to believe that we must spend so much time in service to others that we don't allow enough focus on receiving Papa's love and blessing for ourselves, to accept the wholeness that is His eternal free gift to us, and that He longs for us to *receive*. This erroneous belief is 'the lie of Satan'.

"He was holding a bolt of lightning. It was pure living gold, radiant and bright as the sun. He swooped His hand down with it and placed it in my spine."

At the Kingdom prayer, as I spoke the words to Papa '. . . forgive us our debts, as we forgive our debtors . . . ' He jumped in and instantly, emphatically said, "*I forgive you!*" He was holding in His right hand what looked like a bolt of lightning, about sixty centimetres (two feet) long. It was jagged, rather reminiscent of stylised illustrations of such. It was pure living gold, radiant and bright as the sun. He swooped His hand down with it and placed it in my spine. I felt the restorative power with which it filled me.

I realised that forgiveness – and the wholeness into which it releases us – is ours because He has given it to us, and He longs for us to *receive* it. But we cannot receive it until we 'repent'. Forgiveness is integral with repentance, which simply means turning round and being restored to full, loving, eternally-living relationship with Him. Until we 'come to ourselves' and turn around 180 degrees from facing the darkness, and face toward the Light, which is Papa, how can the free gift of forgiveness (and with it the restoration to wholeness and Life) that He constantly proffers be ours until we are willing to gladly receive and accept it unto our self?

I said to Him, "Beloved Papa, truly wholeness, restoration, life itself, is Your gift of the Spirit. It is the Holy Spirit, the Holy Breath, the wondrous Comforter. I thank You for Your revelation today, and joyfully open myself, the door of my life, to receive Your love more. Thank You for giving me Your forgiveness. It is, I now know, the real experience, and does transform our lives from within. I feel freed from the burdens of unforgiveness that have been ebbing and flowing around and within me."

He replied:

"My son, rightfully you say that this is My free gift to all who desire, earnestly, to receive it and hold fast in faith, trust, obedience* and commitment to my Word. It is not possible for you to forgive† others, only to *desire* to forgive others. By so desiring, I give you the gift of forgiveness and then you truly *have* forgiveness. It flows out from you, through you. In Truth, it is not yours to give. All things come of Me and are My free gift to all who will receive freely. Thus can these good gifts not be abused or manipulated by distorted desires.

"Eternal life is My free gift also to all who desire to receive it. Let your desire be pure in all things, My son. I empowered My beloved Firstborn for forgiveness of 'sins' on Earth because it is My gift to give to whomsoever I choose. This was befitting of his status and his mission, so that as many as I gave to him should recognise him as My Anointed Messenger. To you I say, pray for your fellows as many and as often as you are able. So shall the incense rise up to Me as a pleasant aroma and enable the outpouring of My love and wholeness to be received, to enter in whereunto I send it.

"Peace be with you; all is well."

This Communion was seven years before I came to *A Course in Miracles* and the above quote about false forgiveness. When Papa says that it is not possible for me to forgive others, only to *desire* to forgive, but that He had empowered Jesus in this, I interpret this as meaning that all the while the fragmented Sonship perceives sin as real, we are unable, of our limited, persona self, to truly forgive, but when we *desire* to forgive, we begin on the path back to wakefulness, remembrance of our true Being as His one Son, Christ. *Then,* like Jesus, we come to realise that there is no *actual* sin, only a dream of sin, so *true* forgiveness becomes possible for us because, as Jesus states in *A Course in Miracles,* of the "Workbook for Students"***

> "Forgiveness recognizes what you thought your brother did to you has not occurred. It does not pardon sins and [thus] make them real ['false' forgiveness]. It sees there was no sin. And in that view are all your sins forgiven. What is sin, except a false idea about God's Son? Forgiveness merely sees its falsity, and therefore lets it go. What then is free to take its place is now the Will of God."

---

* This means obedience to our own, inner Self, shining the Light of eternal truth into our mind.

† This refers to 'false forgiveness'. As stated on page 638 (4.) of "Part I, Text" of *A Course in Miracles:* "It pardons 'sinners' sometimes, but remains aware that they have sinned. And so they do not merit the forgiveness that it gives. This is the false forgiveness which the world employs to keep the sense of sin alive."

False forgiveness, then, is where the 'sin' is acknowledged and then 'forgiven'. However the flaw in this misperception is that by acknowledging the sin, we give it reality. This is a ploy of ego mind, which wants us to remain bogged-down in a false world of sin.

** "Workbook For Students" Part II "1. What is Forgiveness?" *A Course in Miracles,* Second Edition, p. 401.

6. Goddess Theresa

In a dream experience, I had returned to the house from walking the dog, to find that the kitchen had been stripped of all its fixtures and fittings. The walls and floor were bare, looking as it did when we ripped-out the entire old kitchen a few years before, prior to refitting it. Even some of the rotted flooring was removed. Since I knew this work had been done before, I was considerably puzzled that this had been done again, obviously by Theresa (I 'knew' this was who had done it, though in the physical world she could not have done it by herself). To my surprise I was not upset, just puzzled! As Susie (the dog) and I stood there, metaphorically scratching our heads and wondering what this was all about, I heard Theresa come in the front door. I waited for her to cross the hall and enter the kitchen.

To my amazement and delight, when she entered the room she was absolutely radiant. She was full-figured but not over-weight, beautiful as she had always been, but now looking in her prime of life, the pinnacle of womanhood, again. At the time of this experience she was over fifty, had put on weight from hormone imbalance resulting from menopause and HRT that had been wrongly prescribed, and was experiencing post-viral fatigue syndrome and psoriasis.

"Why have you done this?" I enquired, indicating the shell of a kitchen around us.

She beamed broadly but with a conspiratorial twinkle in her eyes.

"Aaah, that remains to be seen; I have a surprise for you."

She was radiantly beautiful. The awesome attraction to all the senses of the male by all the emanations of the female of the species exuded from every cell and fibre of her being; from her very soul, in fact. After more than thirty years of our Companionship of the Way, I was drawn like a moth to a lamp. The receptiveness that is the essential nature of womanhood invited, awakened, aroused the expressing, giving nature of my maleness. Every aspect and facet of her being impelled me toward her. She was irresistible. We embraced, melded into each other; I the giver, the male, entered into her the receiver, the female and we became merged, yet remained our respective selves, so that the rapture of *experiencing* each other was possible. It was a moment outside time, of experiencing all the energy that is the pure essence of male beingness becoming as one with all the essence that is femaleness. Yin and Yang. Together. Entwined, fitting perfectly together, soul to soul, body to body, life to life.

"It was a moment of sensual ecstasy that at the same time was a mystical, spiritual, soul experience."

I found that if I adjusted the focus of my vision slightly in one direction I had awareness of the soul aspect of her being and the physical ceased to be perceptible to me; if adjusted in the other direction, the physical body came into focus and 'soul Theresa' slipped just out of focus. By careful adjustment of the balance I could have awareness of both. It was somewhat like the special effects of recent sci-fi films where the body of a person is fleetingly shown in computer-graphic representation so that the inside of the person is also visible; only this was a living, dynamic, pulsing experience, and the soul dimension of Theresa was a great deal more than a computer graphic! It was light-energy, not defined by the sharp outline that our physical body presents.

It was a moment of sensual ecstasy that at the same time was a mystical, spiritual, soul experience.

It was in itself a moment to savour, but there was much more to it than that. It was a magnificent reminder to me of who we *really* are. So readily are we persuaded that what we experience with our bodily senses is the only reality, but this is not so at all. For too many centuries we have been told, conditioned, brainwashed that we are conceived, born, live and die in sin and unworthiness; that there is 'no health in us', and this perception has become so ingrained in our psyche that our true, Self-awareness has been blinded by it. In reality we are created in the likeness of the Creator Spirit; His glorious, magnificent, eternal, innocent, perfect Son. Perceptions to the contrary are ego-constructed religious mythology, doctrine and dogma, not remotely supported by my own experiences of and communications from the living Jesus of

Nazareth since 1967 and from Papa, the Creator, since the 1990s.

The blight to our vision, caused by this 'lie of Satan' has inflicted incalculable damage and misery upon God's Children for untold aeons. Because the conditioning of negative self-perception has been passed down from one generation to the next, society continues to reel from the effects, even though the majority of today's generation has seen through the sham and hypocrisy of ego's construct: orthodox, institutionalised, Laodicean religion. This is not to say that every person who attends services conducted by such an institutionalised religion is a sham and a hypocrite, nor that those who lead such services are, either.

Of course vast numbers who attend and lead such events are as sincere as anyone else in what they believe and are doing. It is not the people but the institutions and their constructs, rules, limitations, doctrines, dogmas, exclusivist attitudes that are causing all the sincere, seeking souls to be yoked to unserviceable, negative self-perceptions and to hold such limiting understanding about the Creator, creation, Jesus, themselves and their fellows. It is these mistaken, constricting perceptions that lead to antipathy, rejection, grievance against and judgement of any who do not/will not allow themselves to be thusly limited. These energies escalate one step at a time into superciliousness, hubris and rejection, excommunication, hatred, murder, genocide and many other levels of ungodly, unkingdomly attitudes and behaviours toward those who are not allied to their own unholy relationships, perceptions and beliefs.

Theresa has been a soul subject to such conditioning by the unwitting agency of her parents, and her self-perception was devastatingly distorted by an upbringing punctuated by physical, emotional, psychological and sexual abuse.

For many years we did not know how to deal with this, and it was the cause of much conflict between us. This was because, not having experienced it myself, I had no idea that a soul could have such a negative sense of self worth, such self doubt, especially when I saw Theresa as such a beautiful, giving, caring, compassionate, effulgent soul. She was having perceptions of herself that I could not imagine, and certainly were not part of my reality, and of course she did not verbalise this, so from my perspective all *should* have been well because, *outwardly* in our lives, all *was* well.

Typically what would happen is that I would say something straightforward, hard to be confused about (so I thought), but her perception of what was said would be something very different, usually something unfriendly, negative, demeaning or aggressive. This would lead to her responding as if what I had said was not what I *actually* said, or at least believed I said – it all became so confusing! This would cause me to wonder why her response was not relevant to what I had said and . . . well, you can see that we are already in a tangle.

It would usually get worse from there and I was not the most saintly person when it came to patience. Of course, I did not know she had heard something different from what I had heard myself say, so I was bewildered, frustrated, and after this happening innumerable times and a 'domestic' arising, I began to feel I was walking on eggs and had to think very carefully before saying anything. Theresa, also, was so intimidated by this that she was inhibited about speaking her thoughts too!

But now, in recent years we are moving together through this and she has come to see who she really is. I had *seen* her, *experienced* her as 'Goddess'; female, radiant magnificence. It was a glorious encounter, a prophecy, a foretaste of the emerging, soaring Being of Light that she really is; that we all really are. And gradually Theresa has been moving through a metamorphosis, *remembering* that this is who she really is, and reminding herself (with some help and encouragement from me) that she *is* acceptable – first to herself and then to others. Self-acceptance, self love is the first step toward wholeness and being lovable and acceptable *to*, and accepting *of*, others. The more we crave it, (if we perceive ourselves as not having it), the more we push it – and our fellows – away.

"By looking past the outward, temporal, illusory imperfections to the eternal, magnificent reality of our true Self, then we will become aware of our authentic nature."

When/if we are able/ready to choose a perspective on our

Self that we *are* glorious, by looking past the outward, temporal, illusory imperfections to the eternal, magnificent reality of our true Self, then we will become *aware* of our authentic nature, so that craving will evaporate, because we will realise that we already *are* that which, in our misperceptions, we have craved. We cannot crave that which is already with us. As acceptance that we really are that inner, boundless Self becomes second nature to us, then the outward imperfections that we have previously perceived as being who and what we are will fall away.

The inner Self radiates out from us to our fellow travellers on the Path back to eternal reality, both here in the earthly life and in the etheric realms. This transformation will be gradual and almost imperceptible, just as every moment of every day we shed tiny particles of dead skin until, over time, we have a completely new skin. The difference is that from time to time we will actually become *aware* of changes that have taken place within us and these moments of new awareness will be as milestones, holy instants, on the Way. Ultimately, we will see only the face of who we really are, Christ, the One Son of the Father, reflected in our fellows, and they will see the face of Christ reflected in us.

It is said that when two people are in agreement on a given matter, they are of one mind. When *all* the fragments of the Sonship are in full agreement as to Who we all are, *then* will we be restored to our true, one-minded state of Being: God's one, indivisible, beloved Son. Then will we have the Kingdom of Heaven on Earth.

The kitchen, stripped back to the very shell of itself, is a symbol of Theresa, who for so many years had been encumbered with mistaken, outdated, unserviceable perceptions of herself by the conditioning of her abusive upbringing that her functionality as a 'working kitchen' was severely impaired. She had now arrived at the place where she had been able to remove all those old fixtures and fittings, taking her back to her essential self. From there, a complete 'refit' was now possible, renewing her serviceableness, both to herself and to all who came to her for sustenance and nourishment.

7. Broken Ankle at Crickley

One beautiful sunny day in the summer of 2000, as I walked our dog, Susie, at Crickley Hill Country Park, which straddles the Cotswold escarpment near Gloucester, I turned around to see if she was coming. Momentarily moving backwards, my left foot landed at the rim of a depression in the ground and I came down with all my weight on that foot, causing my ankle to give and my foot to bend in under me.

There was a loud 'crack' and I felt the break happen, right in the middle of the ankle joint. I went down as if pole-axed and instantly experienced agonising pain shooting up my leg and through my body in nauseating waves, bringing me within a whisker of passing out – which I really would not have minded doing at that moment!

A thousand thoughts flew through my mind in a micro-second: how will I get back to the car? How will I be able to get about and continue with all the business of work, gardening, walking Susie . . .? But the immediacy of the pain quickly regained my full attention. I knew I had to focus upon Papa and move into resonance with the wholeness and perfection of Eternity. I had been reminded by Papa that what shows up heavily disguised as adversity is actually opportunity to transform the 'stuff', which we have initially perceived as adversity, into fulfilment. How could I use this understanding to receive healing and restoration to wholeness? I knew it was possible because we have the magnificent example of Jesus and the myriad miracles performed by him. And he reminded us that the things he did, we would do also and greater things than these – if only we can *believe*.

"Faith is everything when it comes to attunement with the Spirit of Life."

When Jesus healed someone he often told them "Your faith has made you whole." *Their* faith, not his. Without their faith in him they could not have *received* the healing, the wholeness that was radiating out from him, freely, unconditionally lovingly, for all who are willing, (by faith) to receive and accept it unto ourselves. Their faith placed them on the same spiritual wavelength as his – or at least on the same waveband. Likewise, we open ourselves to a state of willingness, by faith, to believe, to receive, to be raised up in our spiritual vibratory rate so that wholeness, perfection, is the frequency on which we begin to vibrate until, in due course – which could be a moment, or a lifetime, or however long, according to how earnestly we desire it, and are willing to *accept* what is freely given – we become increasingly resonant and eventually we are completely in attunement (at-one-ment) with the Source and Giver of Eternal Life.

Faith is everything when it comes to attunement with the Spirit of Life. Jesus said of the people of his era, "O faithless and perverse generation, how long shall I be with you?" (Mt. 17:17). Nothing has changed outwardly, but it is now the beginning of the Kingdom Age, and an awakening to oneness is beginning to take place within the hearts and minds of the people of Earth; a readiness for emerging from the chrysalis and beginning a newness of life at a higher level of awareness, drawn by the Universal Spirit of Life, as the Great Rescue Programme moves forward. The wonderful hymn by A. C. Ainger (1841-1919) tells it inspirationally:

God is working his purpose out,
As year succeeds to year:
God is working his purpose out,
And the time is drawing near;

Nearer and nearer and draws the time,
The time that shall surely be,
When the Earth shall be filled
With the glory of God,
As the waters cover the sea.

From utmost East to utmost West,
Where'er Man's foot hath trod,
By the mouth of many messengers

Goes forth the voice of God;
Give ear to me, ye continents
Ye isles give ear to me,
That the Earth may be filled
With the glory of God
As the waters cover the sea.

What can we do to work God's work,
To prosper and increase
The brotherhood of all mankind,
The reign of the Prince of Peace?
What can we do to hasten the time,
The time that shall surely be,
When the Earth shall be filled
With the glory of God
As the waters cover the sea?

All we can do is nothing worth,
Unless God blesses the deed;
Vainly we hope for the harvest-tide
Till God gives life to the seed;
Yet near and nearer draws the time,
The time that shall surely be,
When the Earth shall be filled
With the glory of God
As the waters cover the sea.

The Purpose of God truly moves forward and nothing anybody thinks, says or does can hasten or stop it. However, by truly seeking and earnestly desiring the Kingdom of Heaven on Earth, the individual can and does move into resonance with the Great Rescue Programme and in that sense, he can hasten it – for himself. Then, as he begins to radiate that new state of Kingdomliness from within himself outwardly – not by acts of proselytising but simply by *living* his new, emerging, growing state of beingness – so those around him who are, themselves, ready for a spiritual awakening will be affected by the change of vibration and begin, themselves, to seek. So does the Programme, the Purpose, which is always moving forward, 'working out', draw us into Itself. It is as Jesus explained to me in a January 1995 Communion:

> ". . . In your mind and heart you may wish to be operating at the highest level of aspiration and spiritual awareness. This is understandable when Earth is in darkness and you wish to be one, again, with the Light; and when you are passionate in your desire to shine the Light of spiritual reality in the Earth-life affairs of man, to hasten an awakening.
>
> "You also know, for I have assured you many times, this will not hasten the unfoldment of the programme for raising-up the children of Earth. Your prayers and love and attunement will help you, and will help all for whom you pray, and will add to the transforming Light. **But the season is pre-determined, even as are the seasons of the year. All that you do in my name and with commitment to me and the Kingdom in your heart will contribute sunshine to the days, even though it will not change the seasons;** therefore, keep on with goodwill. Have no fear. Be of good cheer. Relax and enjoy each and every day. All is well. Walk with me. Talk with me. Breathe with me. Live with me. Let the Kingdom envelop and surround and permeate your being. I will expand your influence among the children of Earth. This is possible by your commitment. It is like a dynamo. It generates energy and draws the little ones to the Light as a magnet. Joy be with you all."

As much intuitively as with thought, as I clutched my ankle I said to Papa, "Thank you Papa, thank you Papa, thank you for giving me wholeness and restoration," multiple times, very rapidly, as the waves of nausea and dizziness swept through me, bringing me to the brink of blacking out. After about a minute of this, suddenly, *in an instant*, the pain was gone! Nothing. I stared in wonderment. I waited a few seconds to see if this was a momentary lapse in the pain before it set back in, perhaps at a new level? Still nothing. *Alleluia.* This was an instant healing, just as Jesus had demonstrated innumerable times to the multitudes. Glory be; thanks be; praise be!

Gingerly, I moved my foot. Still nothing. Slowly I got up and put my foot to the ground, gradually increasing the weight to see if there was a point at which the damage done by the fall caused the pain to return. *Still* nothing. I took a step and then another and another and still there was nothing. I could walk just as I had walked five minutes previously. I completed the four-mile walk without a twinge of pain, or even discomfort, and drove home. When I told Theresa and showed her the ankle, there was a barely detectable swelling over the ankle bone and no sign of bruising.

8. *Seeds of Redemption;* Charles

One Friday in February 1995, Theresa and I went to the pub after work for a meal. As we sat at our table with a drink, waiting for our food order to arrive, Theresa hesitantly told me she had had a strange dream earlier in the week. Would I like to hear it? *Of course, go for it!* In this dream she had experienced a whole drama, like watching a film, with characters, places, details all set out.

It is the story of a young woman, Beth, traumatised in childhood by the death of her parents in a plane crash and then starved of love in an uncaring adoptive home. She is sweet-talked into marriage into a brutal family and eventually saved from being beaten nearly to death by her brother-in-law. From there she is taken into hiding by two clerics with a heart for Christian spiritual healing ministry. After prayer counselling by these new, loving friends she is released from the stranglehold of fear, which has dominated her life, and healed by a mystical experience of the Holy Spirit.

There is, of course, much more to the story; indeed, it is a breathtaking drama and Theresa held me spellbound by her telling of it at the pub. When she had finished she diffidently said, "I have been considering writing this story as a book. What do you think?"

Needless to say, I enthusiastically encouraged her and the following week she began. At first she wrote in pencil on a ruled pad, later typing each day's work onto a rather primitive word processor. It was a cumbersome procedure and after a few days I said we would purchase a laptop computer, so that she could write straight into it in a room undisturbed by the phone and other comings and goings. This would take a little while because I knew very little about laptops and wanted to ensure we got a unit serviceable to her requirements. Fortunately, we knew a young man, Tim, who was the IT manager at the county college of agriculture, and we asked him if he could help point us in the right direction.

Some days, maybe a couple of weeks, went by while we were waiting for all these events to unfold, and during this time Theresa told me she had a strong sense of there being someone from spirit with her, helping, inspiring in a consciously co-operative way, with the story, the details, the style and creativity of the writing. Naturally curious, I asked if she had any idea who this might be. She said she had a great sense of what he was like but had no idea who it was. This discussion began to get me in tune with the vibes until I also could sense the presence. Still there was no identity readily coming to light and we wondered about this for several days.

"I believe this man is British," Theresa said to me, "and that he was in the Earth-life until quite recently; certainly during our Earth lifetime; maybe until thirty or forty years ago. If only we could get some initials I feel sure we will be able to work out who it is."

As she said the bit about initials, instantly into my mind flew the initials 'CS.' Of course, there is only one British (I use the term 'British' in the sense of being a citizen of the United Kingdom of Great Britain and Northern Ireland) well-known author with the initials CS and that is, of course, CS Lewis. Suddenly, I 'knew', *instantly*, it was he.

Theresa and I did not know much about CS Lewis, even whether he was still in this world. I had read *The Screwtape Letters* as a boy and we both knew he was a well-respected author. Theresa had been aware of the girls watching TV dramatisations of *The Narnia Chronicles* back in the 1970s and 1980s but had caught only snippets of them because she was always in the kitchen preparing meals when they were on.

We got so excited about this, and wanting to be sure, that I immediately went to the library to look him up. Was I in for a surprise!? Clive Staples Lewis was born in Belfast on the 29th of November, 1898 to Florence Augusta Lewis and Albert Lewis. Most of the action in Theresa's book, *Seeds of Redemption*, is set in Belfast and the mother-in-law to Beth is Clementine Augusta Brady. At the time of Theresa's 'dream' experience – the characters' names had been made known to her as part of the event – she did not know that CS Lewis was 'ghost-writing' (if you will allow the pun) with her. Nor, until my visit to the library several weeks after Theresa began writing the book, did either of us know that he was from Belfast and that his mother had the middle name

197

Augusta.

In the reference book at the library there was a picture of him taken in later years, in which his hair was very sparse. When Tim arrived to help us set-up the new laptop in readiness for use, he sat at the dining table installing the operating system and programming it for us. Theresa and I stood watching him without any idea what he was doing (such was our computer-illiteracy at that time). Suddenly, there was a man from spirit, in the prime of life, with a full head of dark hair, immaculately combed, with a straight parting down the left side of his scalp. He was standing very close to Tim, hands on knees, straining forward to see everything Tim was doing and listening intently to every word he said, his head and eyes moving from the computer to Tim's face every time he spoke. It was so comical I had to bite my tongue to stop from laughing out loud. Tim had no awareness of this other interested party watching and listening to him so raptly! After a few minutes the visitor turned his head sideways to me – still with hands on knees – and said emphatically, "I *like* this young man!"

A few days later I bought a biography of CS Lewis, and lo and behold, there in the middle were some photographs of him at various stages of life, including one of him in early adulthood, with a full head of dark hair, immaculately combed, with a meticulously straight parting down the left side of his scalp. It was *unmistakably* the man I had seen watching Tim with the computer. Here was absolute verification that it was 'CS' who was helping Theresa with this writing.

The interesting thing was that, prior to *knowing* who it was, Theresa had said that she had a feeling she wished to refer to him as 'Charles' and that he was a rather rotund, cuddly, pipe-smoking, 'favourite uncle' type of person – very much how CS was in later life (he laid aside his body in 1963, aged sixty-five). We both still refer to him lovingly as Charles, and on one occasion, when he gave a message of love and encouragement to Theresa, which she wrote by hand as the message came into her mind, at the end he signed off with the name by which we referred to him, capitalising the first and last letters with a flourish, so that it was very obvious that this was Charle<u>S</u>.

The book was finished on November 29, 1995 and Theresa

and I went to the pub to celebrate its completion. Charles was with us in the car on the way there, enjoyed the convivial atmosphere of the pub, and walked arm in arm with us both back to the car as we left at the end of the evening, saying, "This is my best work yet!" As we drove home, we realised that this was the ninety-seventh anniversary of his birth.

9. Fleas; "Don't give up!"

When one has dogs and cats in the home there is always a possibility for those unwelcome little jumping visitors, which can make life miserable for their hosts. Being a person greatly aware of, and concerned about, the impact of man-made molecules on the environment, I have been reluctant to use insecticides to control fleas on our pets. So when they arrived in the home in the early summer of 1999, it didn't take long before they had built up to the point where something drastic was called for to rid us of these little invaders.

I was on the point of succumbing to the use of insecticide when I thought, 'Wait a minute, fleas are so far down the order of life and we, Papa's children, are the culmination of His all-empowered, glorious creation; we have something out of perspective here when we allow ourselves to be placed 'on the back foot' by these creatures.' Jesus would, assuredly, never have even considered using pesticides (were they to have been available during his time on Earth) but equally assuredly he would never have been left in a position of feeling helpless in the face of their onslaught. So, I asked myself, what would he have done? As I reflected on this, the remembrance came back to me that everything that 'turns up' presenting itself disguised as Adversity is really *Opportunity* to Transform Adversity into Fulfilment (OTAF) and that this can only be done by faith, not by doubt or fear.

Jesus was able to demonstrate his perfect at-one-ment with the Father Creator throughout his three-year mission on Earth. This manifested itself in an array of ways: multiplying the molecular structure of a picnic lunch so that it was able to feed five thousand men, plus women and children, making a total of possibly double that number of people; walking on water; causing the boat in which the disciples were only about midway across Lake Galilee to instantly be at its destination, (Jn. 6:21), when rowing or sailing would have taken hours; calling souls back to the body from which they had departed (including his own tortured and mutilated body); releasing people from possession by earthbound souls; restoring mortal illness to health from a distance by saying the word – the list is endless.

Was there ever a moment in which he was fearful or doubtful? Just the one, according to the Gospel records: his own imminent torture and death on the cross. Yet, he did not run from this, when assuredly he could have easily done so; and having faced his fear and come through it back to strength and faith, he prevailed in his objectives: to demonstrate to mankind the illusion of 'death', and to get our attention.

Clearly, Jesus saw things of which most of us have no awareness. But this is not because those things are withheld from our vision by a partial God. It is because we – 'having eyes, see not; having ears, hear not', as Jesus reminded us – are asleep, in terms of our spiritual awareness. All the things Jesus saw and did, we also have the potential to see and do. If we *truly* seek and *earnestly* desire, that potential will come to fruition, *if only we can believe*. We do not have to wait for this to happen until either we have laid aside our body, or until a full, global manifestation of Jesus miraculously empowers us, because the Kingdom of God and the spiritual empowerment that our at-one-ment with it brings to us, is *within*. That 'within-ness' is in *us* – each and every one of us. *There are, and can be, no exceptions.* If we are lukewarm in our desire for, or fearful of, spiritual awakening, then we cannot become fully awake to that reality and our true nature as Papa's one, beloved, ever-living Son, with all the power of Creation that is available to us by faith, by believing.

So, summoning my faith I said to Papa, "We are empowered by faith to overcome all things, and so, by faith and trust in You, I command these fleas to be gone from this house, never to return."

As soon as I had spoken these words I saw columns of tiny fleas, following a human-size flea, walking out of the house, rather like the rats following the Pied Piper of Hamelin. As the big flea got alongside me it scowled at me as if to say, *'Bah, humbug, you have rumbled me and I have no power to resist your command.'* I considered the meaning of a 'giant flea' and eventually realised that this was 'flea consciousness' with which I had wrestled and, by faith, prevailed. The experience was so objectively real that I knew in my soul that the fleas would be, from that moment, gone – both from the animals and from the rest of the house.

And indeed, that was the case. For several weeks there was no scratching from the pets and no flea presence anywhere else in the home.

However, as the weeks went by, my faith and trust in what had happened as a Principle of Life of the Father, *in practice*, began to flake, and doubts crept in. Not doubts that this *was* a Principle of Life of the Father, in practice; a real experience, and that the fleas had gone – which they definitely *had* – but doubts in my own ability to *believe* that I had been the agency through which this occurred. *That* was where the doubt lay.

Every day I started looking for them again. Would Jesus have done that? Of course not, is the answer, because that was doubt manifesting itself, and Jesus did not doubt. He knew with a total certainty that when he asked for/called upon the wholeness, the balance of perfection that is the free gift of the Creator, it was always there for him. That is the temporary difference between where Jesus was/is and where most of the rest of us, his brethren in the Sonship, perceive ourselves as being.

Indeed, it would never have occurred to him that what he called upon from the Universal Source, Papa, for the benefit of the 'lost sheep of the house of Israel' (or anywhere else!) would not be granted; not as a favour, as if either he or the Jews – or anyone else – were 'special', to be granted privileges or benefits that the Creator Spirit would withhold from others because He didn't love them or see them in the same light. It never occurred to him, not because he had become arrogant or blasé, but because he could plainly see what others around him had withheld from their own discernment: that all creation is One; that all Life, in all its manifestations, is part of, indivisibly connected to, the Allness; for *". . . he is not far from any one of us: for in him we live and move and have our being"* (Acts 17: 27,28).

He knew that the Universal Life Force is one and the same within each and every one of us and every other living thing, from amoebae to blades of grass to olive trees to orang-utans and everything in-between. Jesus saw this and saw that the souls of those around him were in an illusory state of imbalance, disharmony and dis-ease with themselves and with the Allness of which they were part, and that even in their *apparently* dissonant state they could not *actually* become separated from Him.

By the attunement of Jesus with the Oneness by his faith, trust, obedience and commitment to the great mission he had sought and to which he had been anointed – declaring and establishing the foundation for bringing into manifestation the Kingdom of Heaven on Earth – he had become empowered to perform 'signs and wonders' by calling back into balance and harmony the discordant energies of his fellow-inhabitants of that strip of land at the eastern end of the Mediterranean.

These wondrous signs and miracles were an outflowing of the God-Power within him to those conflicting energies which manifested as various ailments in the mind and body of others, restoring them once more to oneness with Creation. Thus did he say to the paralytic he had healed at the pool of Bethesda, "Behold, thou art made whole: sin no more, lest a worse thing come unto thee" (Jn. 5:14). What he was effectively saying was, *Do not forget, again, Who you really are, or you will attract back into your presence some equally unserviceable condition.*

So, when the doubt – that great dismantler of faith – started to set in and I began looking for fleas again, sure enough, back they came – through the opening created conveniently for them by my own doubt. This was a big test of my faith; what I now call 'a self-assessment opportunity'. Was this – the reality of Eternity with which I had been walking for more than thirty years – nothing more than my imagination, a myth of my own creation? Was it that the Great Spirit did not exist after all? Or was it that He did exist but I had vainly imagined my at-one-ment with Him? Or was it that I had walked, albeit somewhat intermittently, in the reality but had 'failed' this 'test' of my faith? If this last possibility was the case, where did this leave me now? Surely, bereft, beset by uncertainty, about who I was, where I stood and where to go from here.

"We have power to prevail in the presence of adversity by transforming it, through faith, into fulfilment, 'that the works of God should be made manifest'."

At that moment, Papa was right beside me and spoke into

my right ear, *"Don't give up!!"* His words were so positive, so encouraging, so reassuring, so exhorting. Instantly my spirits were restored and soared to the heights in reaffirmation that as I had perceived originally, so is it: we have power to prevail in the presence of adversity by transforming it, *through faith*, into fulfilment, 'that the works of God should be made manifest' (in any and all of us).

At this, I felt re-empowered to cast out the fleas again in like manner, and this I did forthwith, with my faith strengthened beyond where it had been on the first occasion. The fleas disappeared, and although from time to time one did show up, picked up inevitably by Susie when coming in close contact with other dogs on our walks, they never again took hold and became established as an infestation.

* * *

Footnote: September 2011: August in southern England is an active time for fleas moving from one host to another. Although we no longer have dogs to exercise I still walk in the Cotswold Hills most days and there, encounter dogs and their keepers. In August 2011, I began to experience flea bites – for the first time since 1999. I had no doubt 'adopted' a flea, or fleas, from one of the hill-walking dogs. I thought, 'It is time to re-engage my God-given empowerment to cast them out.' But I found my mind was in a state of 'empowerment limbo' for this task. I couldn't think of anything to say, and neither spontaneously felt, nor could I summon, any focus or verve, any feeling of ability to perform this 'exorcism'.

I re-read the record of the process that had taken place in 1999 (above), thinking that might get me 'back on the wavelength', but felt no enlivening of mind or spirit for the task. However much I tried, I felt completely flat, and even though I went through the motions of casting them out – several times – I felt and knew that because I was unable to attune with the empowerment, it was not going to happen; a self-fulfilling prophesy, perhaps.

I knew that it is no use fighting what we cannot control with self-will or determination, so I did the only thing I could – place the entire matter in the care of the Holy Spirit, the higher, all-knowing, real Self of us all, and committed to *leaving* it There, knowing that by so doing the matter *would* be resolved in the perfect way at the perfect time, even though, at the moment of so doing, I hadn't a clue how it might happen. This didn't bother me because I knew Self knew, and that was good enough for me. I was facing another self-assessment opportunity, and resolved to pass the 'test', in the only way possible: by simply *allowing* the process to proceed and outwork under Holy Spirit control. I recalled to my conscious mind that when what looks like adversity shows up, it is really opportunity, so I resolved to view it as such.

Probably three or four weeks elapsed since the first flea bite and more were appearing, although it had not reached calamitous, panic-inducing proportions. Nevertheless, I could not help wondering, more or less daily, when or how the matter would be concluded. Still, I held my nerve and left the Holy Spirit in no doubt as to my commitment of the situation into His care.

Then, out of the blue, it dawned on me that my understanding of reality had grown exponentially since 1999, and I now realised that *everything* about egoland is unreality, including, of course, the fleas. If I tried to cast them out, this would be giving them reality in my own mind. No wonder my mind had been 'closed-down' with regard to that initial intention. This was Self, putting the lid on persona Brian's seeking solutions in the past. I had moved along and was ready to engage with Self at another, higher level of operation, even though it had taken me two or three weeks for the penny to drop. As Olga Park used to lament, "*Why are we so slow!?*"

Now, with right-mindedness re-engaged, I said to Self, Jesus, Papa – Whoever was listening – 'Fleas don't exist for me anymore because I am choosing steadfastly to Awaken to the truth of my Whole Being. So rather than try to cast out what is not there, I now *re*-mind myself that they are not there for me. The only reasonable thing to do with nothing is forget it, because it is impossible, in my right, or whole Mind, to be aware of anything but the truth of eternity, so that is what I now choose to do.'

Nothing outwardly dramatic happened, but I had an inner knowing that I had arrived at the answer to the situation, and that, now, the illusory fleas would be gone from my awareness and thus, from my experience. This has indeed been the case. As our beloved friend, the Teacher would say, "*We go forward.*"

10. An Open Letter

In the small hours of one morning in October 1996, I was gradually brought to waking consciousness by a growing awareness that Papa was speaking. I was very drowsy and was more eager to get back to sleep in that state than I was for discussion with Him! I tried to ignore it, thinking, *I can give this my attention in the morning.* But the Voice continued, and it became clear to me after a while that this was not going to stop until I gave it my full focus. I forced myself into full wakefulness, put on the light and got my notebook and pen. All the while I was doing this the Voice never stopped speaking in my head. As I was becoming gradually more awake and better able to be aware of what was being said, it dawned on me that the message was being repeated over and over, as if to say, 'I am going to keep repeating this until you take notice and record what I am saying'.

The message was actually not for me; I was to be the recorder and deliverer of it. I was instructed that this was an 'Open Letter to George Carey'. George Carey was, at that time, the incumbent at Lambeth Palace: the Archbishop of Canterbury, the supreme cleric of the Anglican and Episcopal Communions.

Here it is:

An Open Letter to George Carey

You have assumed the office of My servant Aaron, whom I called to keep himself holy unto the Lord.

Now I ask you, by whose authority is *your* office established – by the authority of Earth or of Heaven?

Have you not read My word; have you not listened to My messengers; have you not reverence for My beloved firstborn, in whose name you parade and strut so vainly?

Have you not recalled that I dwell in the high and holy place, with him also of a humble and contrite spirit, to revive the spirit of the humble and to revive the heart of the contrite ones?

Have you not held in the highest esteem My word through My beloved, that not all who say Lord, Lord shall enter the Kingdom, but he that does the will of the Father?

Have you not remembered his chastisement for righteousness' sake? Have you not pondered in your heart his words and his actions, that his zeal for his Father's house drove him to perform: 'My Father's house is a house of prayer but you have made it a den of thieves', and he drove them out?

Have you not held sacred in your heart My warning by My anointed, that he who offends against children, it would be better for him to be cast into the sea, tied to a millstone?

And yet, have you not equivocated and havered concerning these very matters in the outer court of My temple, over which you preside? Whose 'sin' do you believe is the lesser in My sight – that of traders in merchandise and changers of money or of pederasts and paedophiles?

Shall I spew you and yours out of My mouth, or shall I make you a pillar in My holy temple?

I say unto you, incline your ear unto Me and remember the fire that I placed in your heart.

My beloved messenger has opened the door to the Holy of Holies forever and no man shall shut it. Now goes out the cry, 'the bridegroom comes' and all are invited to the great banquet which it is My great joy to give to all who will enter in and receive of Me the unspotted garment.

Do you believe I am interested in the sullied sacrifices offered on the brazen altar of the outer court when all I crave from My little ones is their love and thanksgiving, offered upon the altar of their hearts?

It is my desire for *all* to enter the Holy of Holies, *trusting as little children*. For this reason have I sent messengers and My beloved and his beloved disciple to foretell of the things which are to be; how the great whore, drunk with the blood of the saints, falls because of her iniquity, and My angel calls out from her My people, that they be not partakers of her sins and receive not of her plagues.

My word has gone out and shall accomplish that for which it has been sent; it shall return unto Me fulfilled. Will you be within it, rejoicing? Will you sing My new song? Will you cry out, with Jerusalem, *'Baruch haba be'shem Adonai* – Blessed is he who comes in the name of the Lord'?

Think you that I rejoice in wrath? I draw My little ones to Me in Love, that I may embrace them and have with them joyful fellowship unto all eternity.

I AM the loving, eternal Papa of all the children of Earth.

In 1967, Olga wrote a treatise on the messages of the ascended Christ to the 'seven churches of Asia' (Revelation, chapters 1, 2 and 3) in which she posits that these messages are not just to be perceived as to seven congregations dotted around what is now Turkey at the time that John wrote of these manifestations, but applicable also to seven *phases* of the church during the period from that time through the entire Christian Era, or second measure of meal. This treatise reasons that two of these churches, Philadelphia and Laodicea, are applicable simultaneously to these times (the changeover between the end of the second measure and the beginning of the third measure of meal), and actually describe two very different churches.

The one, Laodicea, believes itself to be rich, and increased with goods, and have need of nothing, whereas it is in fact 'lukewarm, and neither cold nor hot; wretched, and miserable, and poor, and blind, and naked', so the Lord counsels it to 'buy of me gold tried in the fire (of Eternal Spirit), that they may be rich; and white raiment, that they may be clothed, and that the shame of their nakedness do not appear; and anoint their eyes with eye salve, that they may see' (Rev. 3:18). Further, Jesus says that *because* they are lukewarm he would spew them out of his mouth (Rev. 3:16).

To the other, Philadelphia, Jesus says he has set before them an open door that no man can shut, for they have a little strength, and have kept his word, and have not denied his name. He says he will bring others who are false believers to learn of them, and also that he will keep them from the hour of temptation, which shall come upon all the world. He counsels them to hold fast to that which they have, that no man take their crown; to those that 'overcome' he will make pillars in the temple of God, will write upon them the name of God, and the name of the city of God, and also his own, new name (Rev. 3:8-12).

Clearly there is much symbolism here, but the differences are that Jesus has a diatribe against Laodicea, and praise and encouragement for Philadelphia.

"The institutionalised church of today is perfectly described by Jesus as Laodicea: (spiritually) lukewarm, poor, blind, wretched, miserable and naked."

It is obvious to the objective observer that the institutionalised church of today is perfectly described by Jesus as Laodicea, and that Philadelphia is those congregations and individuals who have kept their love for Jesus and their earnest desire for the Kingdom alive in their hearts, regardless of whatever is going on within the institutionalised, denominational churches; have not allowed themselves to become blinded with rules and regulations and petty, sidetracking, irrelevant, ego-engendered arguments; that where necessary, they have abandoned 'Laodicea' in favour of free churches/congregations and home worship (entering into their closets); kept their loyalty to Jesus first and refused resolutely to let Laodicea stand between them and Jesus.

If a person is a 'citizen of Laodicea' and decides that this is no longer where he desires to be, it is entirely possible to 'emigrate to Philadelphia' simply by the act of so choosing and making the 'mental shift'. Jesus said to the Laodiceans:

> Behold, I stand at the door, and knock: if any man hear my voice, and open the door, I will come in to him, and will sup with him, and he with me. To him that overcometh will I grant to sit with me in my throne, even as I also overcame, and am set down with my Father in his throne. He that hath an ear, let him hear . . .
> (Rev. 3:20-22).

"Seek ye First the Kingdom ..."

There is a groundswell of 'emigration' from Laodicea actually taking place now, in these climactic times in the events of world spiritual awakening, encouraged by the Creator Spirit, Whose Angel says:

> Come out of her (Laodicea), my people, that ye be not partakers of her sins, and that ye receive not of her plagues (Rev. 18:4).

Would-be émigrés will be enheartened by the knowledge that Philadelphia is a substantially plague-free zone.

It is, of course, *spiritually* that the (Laodicean) church of today is lukewarm and it is *spiritually* that it is 'wretched, and miserable, and poor, and blind, and naked'. This has happened because the church has become institutionalised, and the purpose of an institution is to perpetuate itself. This is when the original objectives of its leaders have become lost in a mire of rules and regulations and administrators and petty politics and power struggles, and they now merely perpetuate the institution rather than being motivated by the fire of *spiritual* zeal for the great desire of Jesus: the Kingdom of Heaven on Earth. This is never mentioned in today's institutionalised churches because issues such as the ordination of women, and homosexuality, have become the consuming concerns, bogging the institution down in sidetracking detail – a characteristic ploy of ego. Such would do well instead to maintain focus upon the Principles of Life of the Father, which will keep souls in the Earth life on the right path – the Path of *Spiritual* Progress – through the maze of detail (never was there a truer adage than 'the devil's in the detail') and on course toward our destination: the Kingdom.

The same thing has happened with other institutions of today; government, education, the National Health Service, the judiciary, social services and a very substantial proportion of industry and commerce. Their objectives may not be overtly 'the Kingdom of Heaven on Earth', but they have still lost their way in terms of their respective objectives. This because again, they have not remained focused on the Principles of Universal Life and have allowed their institutions and regulations to get in the way and cloud their vision. This is summed up well by Jesus' statement to the Pharisees that the Sabbath was made for man, not man for the Sabbath.

The ever-increasing number of rules and regulations within all these institutions – and more – prevent those who have abdicated their God-given right to freedom of thought and creativity from expressing that freedom. This is what is meant by references in Revelation to being sealed on the forehead (their Earth-mind) with the mark of the beast (ego), blocking the awareness by those so marked of who they really are. They 'must abide by the rules' even where common sense and compassion – compassion is one of the great gifts of the Spirit in humanity – cry out for individual cases, situations and circumstances to be decided upon their individual merit. So, we are creating for ourselves a compassion-free society, at least in terms of the unwieldy institutions that hold sway over so much of life in the various cultures and nations of Earth.

Fortunately, compassion at the individual, personal level of the interrelationships of life can never become extinguished because each of us IS Love, and compassion is an inseparable facet of Love. To remember this, and allow it to hold greater – preferably, predominant – significance in our human relationships (including those relationships between individuals and groups brought into contact through the various institutions to which reference is made above) would be a giant step toward the Kingdom of Heaven on Earth.

One could imagine a scenario in which two Jesuses are travelling around Judæa, Samaria and Galilee teaching and healing. The first Jesus, seeing the multitude, was moved with compassion for them because they were sick and fainting and lost, as sheep without a shepherd; and he went amongst them and healed them of every sickness and disease. And after a long day, when his disciples wanted him to send them away so they could all get something to eat, he says *No, I will feed them*. And by faith, love and compassion, he transforms a picnic lunch into a banquet for more than five thousand souls, because he loves them all, unconditionally.

The second Jesus moves among the multitudes healing as many as come forward, and when hours have gone by, it's getting late and he is eager to conclude this tiresome, enervating business, he tells the people they must now go home because he has finished for the day, since there is only so much one can do in a day.

The first scenario is a kingdomly scenario indeed. The second scenario is more in harmony with the society we are creating in today's institutionalised world. Is the latter the society we really choose to create, in preference to the former? Many of us have read Jesus' words (perhaps, for many of us, more times than we can remember): "Inasmuch as ye have done it unto one of the least of these my brethren, ye have done it unto me." (Mt. 25:40) But still we so often fail to see the connection between the opportunities in our daily lives to 'do it unto these, our brethren' yet haven't the time, inclination, compassion, desire, heart, energy, will or whatever. This, while claiming to be his followers, going to church as regularly as clockwork but not applying our stated desire for Christ discipleship (or simply 'good citizenship') in the *living* of our daily lives amongst our fellows, many of whom are desperate for some reassurance, some encouragement, a friendly smile and caring word; even just to be *noticed*.

What has caused the institutionalised church to become confused is the fact that the purpose of God *goes forward*, continually, toward its conclusion. It is an evolutionary process, to do with the expanding, unfolding nature of awakening human spirituality, moved by the drawing power of the Creator Spirit. So, what was the perception of the Israelites under the spiritual leadership of Moses three thousand four hundred years ago as being suitable codes for life are not necessarily serviceable for humanity now, in the third millennium CE, because man, drawn *forward* by the Spirit of Life (God, if you prefer) has grown, and mankind's perspective has become enlarged as an inevitable result.

This does not mean that the law and the prophets of the Old Testament are wrong; it means that the Purpose *goes forward* and so everything moves along; everything *has* to move along, toward its ultimate destiny. Lessons in third grade are for third graders, but as those same souls move on through the system there is no purpose to be served by continuing with the lessons of third grade when they are in sixth, ninth or twelfth grade.

Jesus said plainly that he had not come to destroy the law and the prophets but to fulfil them. That fulfilment has happened

212

(he said on the cross, *It is finished*) in *eternal* reality but, like us being '*now* the sons of God but it doth not yet appear . . .', the fulfilment has not yet fully and perfectly manifested itself at the Earth life level of apparent physical 'reality'. It is happening now, just as described by the lead player of this three-act cosmic drama in the parable of the three measures of meal, with the proving activity of the leavening process taking place one step at a time, across a broad front.

And it will continue to happen because the structure has *already* been completed at the psycho-spiritual level of being, just as the oak tree is already grown in the etheric level of being at the germination of the acorn. Yes, a woodsman may come and chop down the oak when only part-grown at the physical level of manifestation, therefore thwarting the growth to *physical* fulfilment. The same thing *could* happen with the fulfilment of the manifestation of the Kingdom of Heaven (already completed in the etheric) on Earth if there is enough anti-Christ (ego) energy directed toward its destruction, or enough apathy amongst the children of Earth.

However, because *Jesus* has overcome the world (ego) we have *all* overcome the world in the only true reality – Eternity – because there is only one of us. All that was required was for 'one' to overcome and *all* have overcome. I have been told numerous times from the Realms of Light that the Great Rescue Programme is infallible and unstoppable. That is fairly convincing terminology, from any angle.

The bride of Christ (Revelation, chapter 21), a vast multitude of souls, have, over the last twenty centuries, espoused their lives to Jesus and his great desire for the Kingdom on Earth. Acting in unison of purpose with him, they are similarly empowered with all power in Heaven and Earth as vested in Jesus. A portion of these is in the etheric envelope of Earth and a portion is incarnate at this time of writing, or is in the process of incarnating. They are a mighty spiritual powerhouse for truth, with all the resources of Eternity – Heaven – at their disposal. This is an infallible, unstoppable, tireless, totally-committed-by-the-power-of-*unconditional*-love force for the fulfilment of the Kingdom of Heaven on Earth plan. This plan is fully and comprehensively understood by the bride of Christ in the etheric realms, but is not fully *consciously* understood by most of those souls in the Earth life who love the Lord Jesus, because they have been misled by the smokescreen of false dogmas and doctrines fabricated by the schismatic, ego-controlled, institutionalised churches.

So many of the leaders of those institutionalised denominational churches are lacking the light of spiritual discernment. They are therefore torn between trying to adhere to the scriptures written by and for peoples of very different times and cultures in order to be 'seen to be faithful to the Letter of the (religious) Law' on the one hand, and on the other to be seen to be 'up to date' with current social and cultural trends. They do this in order to try to hang on to the remnant of their congregations, to whom the Angel is calling, "*Come out of her, my people, that ye be not partakers of her sins, and that ye receive not of her plagues*" (Rev. 18:4).

And the people, drawn inexorably by the power of Spirit, like iron filings to a magnet, are indeed coming out of her, in droves. They are leaving even though they have no discernment at the Earth-life level of consciousness of the fact that it is the outworking of the Great Purpose of the Holy One (of Which all are inextricably, at the soul level of their being, an indivisible part) in their lives.

This dichotomy of the church – trying to be all things to all people in order to hang onto its now almost exhausted power *over* the people – is actually accomplishing the very two things it is so anxious to avoid: driving away the congregants because of the havering, equivocation and hypocrisy, and tearing itself asunder because of the division within caused by what the conservatives see as giving way to liberalism and the liberals see as hanging on too hard to conservatism.

The dyed in the wool (religionist) conservatives are – especially in America – becoming more and more radical and right wing in their fundamentalist beliefs, engendering perceptions that adherents to other faiths, and even other denominations of the Christian church, are the 'enemy'. This is at least in part because of the swing of others to liberalism. And the liberals are becoming more and more disenchanted with the institutionalised church, partly because of the shift to the right by the conservatives. This is ever-further polarising the mass of humanity calling itself Christian and practising that belief system through any and all denominational churches that are, in reality, Laodicean. This is because of their resolute adherence to ever greater numbers of rules and regulations which are holding them back instead of freeing them, as would be the case if they saw through the distracting detail and held fast to the Principles of Life of the Father. These Principles take care of the detail, if we are unequivocal, steadfast, in our focus upon them.

Many today believe the Roman Catholic Church is the great whore, Babylon the Great, the mother of harlots, so colourfully described in Revelation, chapters 17 and 18. The Roman Catholic Church fits the descriptions sufficiently to justify such perceptions; but such descriptions are not all exclusive to the Church of Rome. The Church of Canterbury, founded by Henry VIII as a breakaway from Rome, has been as full of intrigue, power-mongering, torture, mayhem and 'living deliciously with the kings of the Earth', albeit on a lesser scale, as Rome.

The message for George Carey (or whoever sits on that 'throne') is addressing the issue of paedophilia and pederasty. Acts of sexual indecency, especially unnatural acts such as pederasty (sodomy) committed by adults against children, is truly an abomination in the perception of all 'civilised' segments of society in virtually every race and culture on Earth. This is what Jesus had to say about it:

> But whoso shall offend one of these little ones (children) which believe in me, it were better for him that a millstone were hanged about his neck, and that he were drowned in the depth of the sea. Woe unto the world because of offences! for it must needs be that offences come; but woe to that man by whom the offence cometh! (Mt. 18:6,7)

These are issues confronting not only the Roman Catholic Church, with its unscripturally-founded enforcement of celibacy upon its clergy, so that the strongest urge of man (after survival) often finds an outlet in some ungodly behaviour, causing untold guilt, grief and misery upon the perpetrators of such acts as well as the choirboys, altar boys and whoever else are at the receiving end of such, when the clerics could be finding joy and fulfilment with a spouse and a family. There are plenty of acts of paedophilia and pederasty amongst clerics of the protestant churches also, even though in many cases the perpetrators may be married, with children of their own.

And when such acts come to public attention, the church (Protestant and Catholic) is so concerned with the perpetuation of the institution it has constructed around itself that it closes ranks and tries to cover it up. Instead it could do the kingdomly thing of being honest, openly acknowledging the issue and truly endeavouring to first redress it, and second, to work diligently to eliminate the *causes* of such behaviour, rather than simply sticking yet another finger in the dyke.

"Society at large becomes increasingly secular because of the hypocrisy of the church and the slippery slope down which it is heading."

Unless and until the church gets back to following the admonition of Jesus, to seek *first* the Kingdom of Heaven and to be concerned about only two commandments (love God and love your neighbour as yourself) the petty squabbles, the divisions, the lapses in seemly behaviour by its clergy and other dignitaries will continue to tear it apart. This rendering is causing it to be marginalised, ridiculed and even despised by society at large, which becomes increasingly secular precisely *because* of the hypocrisy of the church and the slippery slope down which it is heading. Hardly the way to achieve its objective of 'winning souls for Jesus', but assuring the fulfilment of the call in Revelation 18:4: *"Come out of her, my people, that ye be not partakers of her sins, and that ye receive not of her plagues."*

I asked Papa what He wished me to do with this message and was sure that the answer was to send it to the *Times* newspaper. I was very trepidatious about this because I had no desire for the possibility of hordes of journalists at my door twisting my motives, trying to dismiss the nature of the origin of my communication(s) by some 'rational, alternative explanation', most of which, in a faithless and perverse generation and without the light of spiritual discernment, are much more bizarre and far-fetched (*the elaborate theories of men*) than the real truth.

Nevertheless, having been told by Jesus on many occasions over the years that the operation of hiddenness that had been the nature of our solitary or near-solitary mystical communing with Christ for decades would become an operation of openness when the time was right, and that circumstances would bring about the change, I emailed this message to the religious affairs correspondent of the *Times* newspaper.

Nothing happened, so after some days I sent it again. Still nothing. Perhaps Papa had meant me to send it to the *Church Times*? There seemed to be some logic and reason to that so I faxed it to the editor. Nothing happened there either.

As I look back now, in the light of further understanding of the agendas of the various institutions (including the printed and electronic media), I see that it was inevitable that they would not respond; that they would do everything possible to pretend that no such communication could be authentic in its origins because 'God does not talk to people today; and if He did, it would surely not be to a nobody, without great theological learning from some august institution'.

And if He actually *did* speak to a nobody, calling into question the state of the religious establishment, how could they acknowledge that the 'nobody' messenger was delivering a message suggesting something was *wrong*; how could they possibly admit it to the world at large, and thus lose face? Exactly that dilemma faced the religious leaders in Jerusalem when they asked Jesus by what authority he performed his acts of healing. He said to them, "I will answer your question if first you answer my question: By what authority did John the Baptist baptise, that of Heaven or of men?" They reasoned amongst themselves, 'If we say of Heaven, he will say, Why then did you not believe him? And if we say, of men, the crowds will be upset with us because many of them believed John.' So they said to Jesus, 'We cannot tell'; just as Jesus *knew* they would have to. The religious (and all the other) establishment(s) of today 'cannot tell' whether any messenger today is delivering a bona fide message because it would question their position before the citizenry. So they must ignore it as long as they possibly can!

Olga Park received the following message on March 31, 1948:

The Thirsting Christ

It is I, the Christ, who speak,
The Christ whom men undiscerningly worship,
I, the Christ upon the cross,
From out the three-hour darkness
Wherein I did suffer in my soul of the sin that had been,
The sin of Israel and of her priests
Against Moses, and against the prophets,
And the sin that should be, the sin of my Beloved
Against me, her Christ.

I had felt its beginnings in the strivings by the way
Of those, my stewards, unto whom I must entrust my all,
My household, my sweet vineyard.
The spirit of the world was there already
Contending for my flesh: so I took and stripped myself
That they might know as indeed I had taught them often
That the body is more than raiment:
And I took a basin filled with water –
Emblem of my own pure springs, my own essence of life -
And I washed away the soil from their feet,
The uncleanness of their contentious self-desire
That so they might know to keep my household
Free and clean from the spirit of the world.

I had felt its threatenings
    in the judgement-spirit of John and James
Who desired that all who received me not
    should be destroyed by fire.
I had sensed its flabbiness
    in the conforming spirit of Simon Peter,
Who would have had me refuse the cross;
The treachery of its cupidity in Judas,
Who desired to serve both God and Mammon.

I had taught them by precept and by example
And by the influence of my spirit: I had done all,

And I had kept them unto the last
from the spirit of the world.
But there upon the cross I felt it enter in again –
The spirit that cried, "It is necessary
    that one should die for the people:
Away with him! Crucify him!"
And my spirit was driven forth into desert places.
Then I saw the spirit of reckoning
    standing in the place of faith;
And the spirit of the scribes had darkened
    the lamp of my truth;
And the meek and the poor in spirit,
The pure in heart and the peacemakers
Had their honour taken from them and given unto the
    rulers of Earthly kingdoms –
To the clever and the proud and the scornful,
And to mighty men of war:

And the stewards of my household did sell to the wealthy
Tablets of remembrance and windows of coloured crystal
    inscribed with their names;
And the light of heavenly wisdom had gone out.

And an altar was set up, and on it
Stood the symbol of Israel's shame, and
    countless thousands
Worshipped the symbol without understanding:

And kings crowned me afresh with thorns,
And soldiers mocked and spat upon me;
And authorities of Church and State nailed my hands
That I could no more bless the humble;
And my feet, that I could no more
    hasten to the healing of the sick;
And the dew of my life-essences was dried up,
And the whole body of my church was shrivelled:

The whole Earth is in darkness because of her
    and reels to and fro:

All her bones are broken! Let the sword pierce her heart
 until she cry with Israel
Eloi, Eloi, lama sabacthani – My God, my God,
 Why hast thou forsaken me?

Olga was so profoundly shocked by the message of this
lamentation that she hid it away for many years, showing it
to no-one. I have contemplated the message and its multi-
layered meanings since she first showed it to me in 1967.
Undoubtedly it will say many things to any who read it, and
the more contemplatively it is read and considered, the more
meaningfulness it will have for each individual.

It says two main things to me. First is that the so-called
Christian Church, at least in its main, institutionalised
manifestations at this changeover time between the second and
third measures of meal, has followed the same, ego-inspired
pattern as the religious authorities of Jesus' time on Earth. This
has been extensively discussed above.

Second and far more incisive for me has been the statement,
"Then I saw the spirit of reckoning standing in the place of faith."

This has much wider-reaching implications because it applies
both to sectarian *and* secular sections of today's world. The
dictionary defines 'reckoning' as the act of counting or calculating.
Today's secular, materialistic society discredits anything beyond
what can be seen, touched, analysed in a laboratory or detected
with a piece of electronic equipment. Further, it increasingly
marginalises people who display faith in, or profess any experience
of, eternal reality, always seeking an alternative explanation (*the
elaborate theories of men*, as Jesus described this to me) to reports of
happenings beyond the 'known' laws of physics (or chemistry or
biology), based on cold, hard calculating.

This is not how Jesus operated his life on Earth and it does
not have to be how we, the rest of the Sonship of God, operate
ours. Of course most of us are not yet awake to the place where
Jesus was in terms of our spiritual awareness, but we are *always*
at free choice as to which way we are headed on the spectrum
which has absolute reckoning at one end and absolute faith, trust,
obedience and commitment at the other. Even if we are at the
'reckoning end' because that is where our conditioning has led

us, we do not have to *stay* there. We can take a leap of faith.

---

*"We are loved, accepted and blessed, just as we are and
for what we are, and not judged by the Creator Spirit"*

We are known *in our entirety*, in every moment. We are loved, accepted and blessed, just as we are and for what we are, and not judged by the Creator Spirit, because we are His beloved Son. All that appears, at the Earth-life level of experience is simply an illusion and is not who or where we really are at all. And because it is an illusion, a dream, it is not real; so our 'sins' are not real, but simply mistakes, errors or misperceptions. Jesus knew this ("I and my Father are one"). He came to remind us that we are too. This is the Good News.

He, the Creator Spirit, does not expect, demand or require of us that we somehow, miraculously, without His help, instantly arrive at the Faith end of the spectrum before He finds us 'acceptable' and starts working with us to get our life moving onwards and upwards. But if we awaken to the point where we begin to find in our heart a deep and true and earnest desire to move in that direction – perhaps because we are beginning to realise that the Reckoning end is two-dimensional, hollow, flat, unenlivening, cold, hard, calculating(!), ruthless, soulless, uninspiring, exhausting . . . – and ask for help in making a leap of faith *into* Faith, we are *always* heard. We don't need to go to church to do this, or say a rosary, or confess to a priest, or invoke intercession of the Saints – although they will always be glad to assist! As we take that leap of faith we are *always* lovingly helped and guided. *Believing* this will be immeasurably beneficial in enabling that help to be received and *experienced*.

It will be serviceable if – when – we do make such a choice, to leave the calculator aside (metaphorically speaking) because a whole new dimension, or dynamic, of power starts to come into play that does not need or use a calculator. It is the power of the Spirit of *Livingness*. Calculators (including ready reckoners!) are not imbued with that Spirit.

All the calculations in this new dynamic are *automatic*, worked out for us by the benign Spirit of Life, which operates in and through

221

us, enlarging our awareness, restoring us to remembrance that this is who we really are; drawing us back toward and into Itself. And there are no accidents, no coincidences. What may seem like an amazing chance happening is part of the synchronistic plan for us, and of which we are all inextricable parts.

"Faith places us within the living, loving, perfect, beneficent, caring, helping dimension of Papa."

At first we will be functioning only *partly* in faith, but it is a start and is acceptable, placing us *within* help, not outside it, as is widely believed, due to some mistaken perceptions about worthiness. Faith places us within the living, loving, perfect, beneficent, caring, helping dimension of Papa. When we are wholly functioning from that place no calculator or spirit of reckoning will be required, but if we are not yet at that place it is not because the *potential* for us to be there does not already exist. It is innately within us, as God, the Spirit of Creation and all life, is indivisibly within us, and we in Him. But He will never prod us or try to force us into that place, because He has given His Son free will. And He means it; the free will, that is. He never retracts that gift because He has given His word and His word is eternal, unchangeable and inviolable.

In one sense we have all eternity to awaken spiritually; there is no rush, unless we suddenly feel a sense of urgency to go forward – perhaps because we have just started to become aware of this reality and it somehow appears pressing because we feel we have fallen behind. However, a word of caution because the old adage, *more haste, less speed* applies.

Balance is an integral quality of Creation and of Creativity. If we try to rush along the Path back Home – a route that unfolds at our feet one step at a time, and is invisible to our Earthly senses – we will find ourselves out of balance in some aspect or aspects of our being, which is a multi-faceted phenomenon. Such imbalance will not be comfortable, profitable or healthy and will lead us into a place called bewilderment! Papa said to me in November 2008:

"There is no rush to awaken. Eagerness, yes; but rushing

is of ego, and engenders frustration, anxiety, turmoil. Remember, *allow* it to happen; do not attempt to rush it. Rushing is ego attempting to re-establish control."

As mentioned previously, the Creator Spirit is benign (why would the Creator be other to that which He has created?) and it is His job, His purpose, His *desire*, to strengthen and restore His 'prodigal son', not to break him. So, embarking upon such an adventure – which is likely to take half a lifetime and possibly much more, depending upon where on that Path one is at the time of awakening to awareness of it – is not as daunting as it may seem, in the context of Eternity, as one is about to take the first step!

If one decides to approach it as a grand adventure, to be enjoyed, knowing one will move a step at a time into more and more creative, spiritual empowerment, and will experience love, joy, wonders and fulfilment beyond all 'spirit-of-reckoning consciousness', it will be quickly found to have been boundlessly worthwhile. One's perspective on Life will be utterly transformed. This will not happen for those who are not ready for such a leap of faith, and the way to know if you are ready is just the same as knowing if you wish to marry that person to whom you are so attracted: if you know of a *certainty* that fulfilment of your heart's desire cannot take place without that person, (or taking this leap of faith), then you are ready. Otherwise, you are not; and even if initial steps are taken, out of idle curiosity, it will not be long before the interest wanes and the attractions of time and place regain pole position in the attention stakes.

11. The Crucifixion: "I did it to get your attention."

One of the factors that were so beneficial to Theresa's healing from the trauma of her childhood, which caused her to have such a distorted self-perception, was counselling, lovingly given at a centre for Christian healing, to which she was introduced by a friendly soul from the office building where we had our business at that time. Over a period of about ten years Theresa regularly attended their Wednesday evening service of healing ministry, and perhaps once a year she stayed in-house for a week of intensive prayer-counselling. These sessions, the like of which are described in *Seeds of Redemption*, would bring enlightenment by the Spirit of Truth about the factors from her childhood that were still impacting her life and self-perception, enabling a releasing process to take place from the burdens of childhood conditioning.

This centre of Christian healing was of inestimable benefit to Theresa, and the counsellors and other volunteers and staff there had wonderful commitment to their calling and sincerity in carrying it out. However, in spite of their perceptions about spiritual healing (as distinct from spiritualist healing) being somewhat advanced compared with more conservative, orthodox Christian church-minded people, they had no awareness of those from the Realms of Light so closely attendant upon them *ministering unceasingly to the sick and fainting spirits of men.* Indeed, were one to have mentioned such and one's actual, conscious awareness of and intercourse with the same, one would have rapidly become *persona non grata.*

Nevertheless, because of their commitment and sincerity, much good work (aided and abetted from the Realms of Light in a much more palpable manner than they had any experiential awareness, even though they believed it as a matter of doctrine and faith) was accomplished, and Theresa was greatly helped by them over the years she attended.

From time to time I accompanied her to the Wednesday evening service. On one such occasion there was a talk given by the retired principal of a nearby Bible college. He spoke at length about the crucifixion, keeping well within the confines of orthodox Anglican perceptions of this pivotal historic event.

The Crucifixion – and, of course, the Resurrection – is, rightfully, a central aspect of all people professing the Christian faith, and I had thought about this momentous event countless times over the years since I had, as a young adult, given my life into the care, guiding and protection of Jesus. It had always seemed to me that there was something so deeply and profoundly mystical about it that it placed any comprehensive insight into the true depth of significance of the event for mankind well beyond the reach of Earth-mind perceptibility. This is fortified by the vast amount of ecclesiastical doctrine and mythology attached to the event and by which much of Western society is conditioned into limited and restrictive thought parameters.

I felt a longing to have a deeper insight into this crucial act in the purpose of Jesus' incarnation, and this was brought into focus by the homily of that evening. I sat there, partly listening to the speaker, but more, directing my focus on the living Jesus, who had been so much a reality in my adult life, asking him for greater discernment on this, the most spiritually significant occurrence in the history of mankind. Instantly he spoke, taking me by surprise with the rapidity of the response and the casual manner in which the words were so immediately impressed into my mind, but massively more so by the impact of the words, so utterly different was his response from anything I could have begun to imagine:

"I did it to get your attention."

It was a throw-away line. He might as well have been speaking about doing something as (relatively!) mundane as a bungee jump in today's world.

I sat there, stunned and yet also greatly excited. There was absolutely no doubt that this was the Master who had spoken, and it was further affirmed by the very characteristic nature of his response: designed to get my attention! Olga used to call him *the Master of Surprises* and I can attest to the validity of such a title.

This seven-word answer cut through all the mythology and doctrinal attachments of the institutionalised church. It brought the whole event down to Earth and made it something that anyone, regardless of their education, could accept, without any previous requirement to conform to any religious creed or doctrine. Jesus did not come to start a religion. He said, "I am come that they might have life, and that they might have it more abundantly. I am the good shepherd: the good shepherd giveth his life for the sheep" (Jn. 10:10,11). He is speaking as the Good Shepherd of his flock – mankind, lost in deep spiritual wilderness. Here, he tells us that he has come that we might have LIFE, abundantly; not religion and mythology and dogma and rules and regulations and doctrines.

Mankind was (still is) lost; we had (have) forgotten who we really are. He came to remind us and to lead us back to God in the eternity of Heaven, our true and only Home. In order to demonstrate his credentials that he was (is) the way, the truth and the life and therefore trustworthy to be followed, he had to do something that would grab our attention; not for a generation but for a full two millennia. This, so that he could, having got our attention, lead us, win our trust, our love, our willingness to follow so that he could show us that we are not just citizens of Eternity but citizens of the Kingdom of Heaven – because Eternity and the Kingdom of Heaven are one and the same. The Kingdom is a state of being one with Creation and of our Creator, to Whose wavelength we can attune *here*, now, in the illusory Earth life.

"God is not preventing our entry into the Kingdom.
The only obstacle to our 'entering in' is our self."

We don't have to wait until we 'die' and go through some judgement process which will, according to some arbitrary set of rules (which vary according to the religion and the sect or denomination within each religion) determine our readiness/ worthiness to become its citizens. God is not preventing our entry. The only obstacle to our 'entering in' is our self. We obstruct our entering in by not observing the *Way* to the Kingdom, or by observing it but choosing not to *follow* the Way.

There are those who say there are as many ways to the Kingdom (or nirvana or whatever one chooses to call it) as there are people. In the sense that we have all eternity in which to find it, that may be true because if we stumble around, spiritually blind, for long enough, the very fact that we, even in our blind state, are inextricably attached *to*, part *of*, one *in* the Creator Spirit, should indicate that we cannot but be drawn back to the Kingdom of which we are all citizens, however long that may take.

However, this does not take into account that ego is the antithesis of God and is therefore treacherous, lying and deceitful, and is deliberately using these negative, destructive qualities to keep us in the illusion of time and place, because ego's time is up when we awaken to the reality of Eternity and the remembrance that time and place is nothing more than a figment of our imagination. The ability of ego to mislead, confuse and shatter our confidence, trust, and one-pointed focus on eternal truth, should not be under-estimated; at least until we are totally certain – as Jesus was totally certain – of who we really are.

But in the Cosmic order of Life, those who are ahead on the Path of Progress back to Eternal Reality have an innate desire (not a wishy-washy, lukewarm, what's-in-it-for-me desire but an *absolute*, unequivocal, totally committed, selfless desire) to help forward those further back on the path. Jesus is such a soul who has attained the state of full awakening to remembrance of and oneness with, God, the Creator Spirit. This desire to help is born of Love; spiritual Love, agapé, unconditional, *Perfect* Love; Love which sees through the illusions in which we have allowed ego to dupe us into believing ourselves as being: sinners, failures, unworthy, guilty, unlovable, limited, mortal etc., etc. Jesus does not see us that way, and the reason he does not see us that way is because it is not the truth, and he sees only the truth. He sees us for who and what we *really* are: lost, mistaken, misled, confused, but his younger brothers and sisters nevertheless; all magnificent, innocent, guiltless Children of the Creator who are loved unconditionally, and beyond all Earth-mind imagining, by the Father from Whom he came because he loved us so totally, unconditionally, he simply could not stay away.

Nevertheless, the cosmic 'rules of engagement' stipulate that we do not, ever, force our true awareness of eternal reality on those who are not awake, or not ready to awaken to those realities. So Jesus stands at the door of our hearts and lives and knocks. If/

when we hear him and invite him in, he will accept our invitation and come into our lives and fellowship with us (Rev. 3:20). He is the perfect gentleman. He *longs* to enter our lives and he knocks at the door and waits with infinite patience, knowing that when the time is right for us we will become aware of that knocking and open to him.

But he NEVER says, 'Behold, I am charging at your door with a battering ram, so coming into your life, ready or not.' And what would be the point? His agenda is God's agenda and God's agenda is our agenda. That agenda is that we are here (in the words of St. Paul, Acts, chapter 17) to seek after God – even though He is not far from us – by our experiences in our earthly lives, until we find Him. Full stop. In reality, we will *never* find Him in the outer perceptions of Earth, because the physical universe is an ego-construct, all in the split-off-from-Truth part of the mind of God's Son, not a creation of God at all, so He, God, is not here, in the without.

Ego will keep up the prestidigitation, to hoodwink us into believing this is reality and that God can be found here, if we look long and hard enough. But we can and do begin to realise, one step at a time, that God is *not* here, and that will get us beginning to look elsewhere than in the without of the Earth physical; namely, in the *within*. There are no conditions to our seeking except free will. Others, with a religious agenda, will try to say there are conditions, but this is not as stated by he who, assuredly, knows: Jesus of Nazareth.

This is not an attempt to proselytise citizens of Earth into becoming Christians, followers of Jesus of Nazareth, and away from some other persuasion (religious, agnostic or atheistic). It is simply setting out my understanding, born of my experiences since the 1960s, that regardless of how many 'ways' there are/ may be to God, the way that I have found has been consistently trustworthy, reliable, loving and lovable, fun, joyful, rewarding, spiritually enlightening and illuminating, constant and steadfast, filled with life-transforming, empowering, spiritual, no-nonsense, take-it-or-leave-it truth.

It is not for me to try to persuade another free-spirit to follow the way I have followed. Indeed, first, each of us persuades our self which way to follow, led by an upwelling of desire from our own within; and second, anyone who wishes to try following the way described in this writing will find himself following a way which he will discover is uniquely *his* way, not mine. If he desires and chooses to ask Jesus to be his guide, the way along which Jesus will lead him and guide him will be the way Jesus knows is uniquely and perfectly right for him (the seeker), just as he did for me.

It cannot be otherwise, because each of us in time and place is unique, with our own individual potential to develop and fulfil. That is why we are here: to develop and fulfil the potential we have brought with us. That potential is, ultimately, spiritual, and is for the remembrance of who we really are, so that we can break the cycle of birth and death (what I call the carousel, or the not-so-merry-go-round) by forgiving ourself and our brethren, undoing ego and healing all the seemingly broken relationships that are keeping the karmic carousel going round and round, until at last all is restored to oneness in the Sonship. Then we will find ourselves as true Citizens of the Kingdom of Heaven on Earth. Jesus knows this because he has *remembered* all this, and his job is to help us remember it also.

"When an individual is ready to undergo an awakening experience, it will be in secret, with the 'still, small voice' speaking silently to and from his own within."

Congregational churches, with scores, hundreds or thousands of members can never be the mechanism by which we have awareness of, and communion with, the living Jesus, and the journey on which he will lead us 'back to God', to the Holy of Holies, to the Kingdom of Heaven. This is because the way, being mystical, is hidden from our earthly senses, and our journey is one-on-one with Jesus and/or the Holy Spirit, not in a disparate crowd. Events proceeding in the without, with a congregation of people, will divert our focus from the within, where we have our meeting place with God. Jesus' admonition "But thou, when thou prayest, enter into thy closet, and when thou hast shut thy door, pray to thy Father which is in secret; and thy Father which seeth in secret shall reward thee openly"

(Mt 6:6) will be entirely more serviceable to the fulfilling of our awakening desire for communion with Him. If a person is at the place where such mass-fellowship in the without is adequate for his personal, spiritual seeking, so be it. But when an individual is ready to undergo an awakening experience, it will be in secret, with the 'still, small voice', the Voice for God, speaking silently to and from his own within.

It will not be dependent upon his regular or occasional attendance in a mass gathering of souls for organised worship, and if such a Damascene awakening event were to take place in such a mass gathering, he will ultimately be led by the Spirit away into a secret place, where, and only where, he will be able to open his heart and mind to the mystical experiences and revelations awaiting him. And it will be only when he enters into the closet, 'alone', and shuts the door, and there opens the door of his inner being in secret that the living Jesus will respond to his invitation to enter and engage with him in loving, spiritual, mystical, joyous, uplifting, exhilarating, enlightening fellowship.

Jesus, he will discover, is a one-on-one person. That one-on-one experience can then be shared with brothers of like-minded readiness for such sharing, such as was the case with Theresa, Steve and me, but our ultimate mystical encounters with the Holy One are, at this stage of our spiritual awakening, of necessity, 'solitary'.

Meanwhile, in a mass-gathering of souls in a traditional church service, all the fellowship can and will be only in the without, 'horizontally', with the other congregants. Jesus, assuredly, will be there, *in the midst*, with them, loving, blessing and *ministering to the sick and fainting spirits of men,* but their focus will be too distracted by outer, horizontal-flowing energies to have vertical, *mystical* awareness of, and communion with, his living presence. Only those who are ready, spiritually, will be willing to hear and receive the blessing, new understanding and enlightenment that the sharing of such mystical awarenesses and experiences of his living presence in their midst brings.

12. The False Doctrine of Sacrifice as the Path to Salvation

One of the most significant instances of scripture having the potential to turn the practice of Judaism and orthodox Christianity on their respective heads is to be found in Jeremiah 7:22, for which the seventeenth century translation into English, known as the King James, or Authorised, Version (KJV) reads:

> "For I spake not unto your fathers, nor commanded them in the day that I brought them out of the land of Egypt, concerning burnt offerings or sacrifices."

This is an unequivocal statement by God to Jeremiah indicating that the very heart, the core, of Mosaic and Judaic religious tradition is founded on a false precept. This is further supported in Psalm 51:16, which states:

> "For thou desirest not sacrifice . . . thou delightest not in burnt offering . . ."

and verse 17 says:

> "The sacrifices (asked) of (by) God are a humble and contrite spirit."

Isaiah 57:15 supports this position by stating:

> "For thus saith the high and lofty One that inhabiteth eternity, whose name is Holy; I dwell in the high and holy place, with him also that is of a contrite and humble spirit, to revive the spirit of the humble, and to revive the heart of the contrite ones."

King David further says:

> "I will offer to thee the sacrifice of thanksgiving"
> (Ps. 116:17).

. . . clearly indicating that *thanksgiving* is entirely acceptable to God. If God required bloodletting to secure atonement, He would not countenance the dwelling with Him in the high and holy place those who 'simply' had a contrite and humble spirit.

It does not seem unreasonable to construe from these quotes that God does not require, and never has required, sacrifices or burnt offerings. It could not be stated plainer than this, from Jeremiah 6:20:

> ". . . your burnt offerings are not acceptable, nor your sacrifices sweet unto me."

The implications for orthodox Christian doctrine are staggering because this states that Jesus was/is the *blood sacrifice*, or atonement for all humanity, for all time, for their sins. This, as long as the sins are 'confessed' – thereby confirming those sins as 'real' – and forgiveness sought.

Romans 3:25 states:

> "[Jesus] Whom God hath set forth to be a propitiation through faith in his *blood* . . ."

There is great confusion about the use, here and elsewhere in the Bible, of the word *blood*, which is a Greek word for *life*. If *life* is substituted for *blood* in this and other similar statements, it completely alters the emphasis from Jesus saving us by the *crucifixion* (blood-shedding) to his *resurrection* to *life*, demonstrating the indestructibility of God's Son. According to Jesus, we are *all* God's Son; one, appearing as many in what is but a *dream* of separation.

Unless these belief-requirements about Jesus as our atonement by blood sacrifice are accepted and adhered to, so says Church doctrine, God will judge us and condemn us to outer darkness at least, or eternal burning in the fires of hell. In other words, a very conditional arrangement for a God also doctrinally declared to be the God of *unconditional* love. Orthodox Christian doctrine further states that this sacrifice of/by Jesus is the replacement, or substitute, for all the millions of Mosaic-tradition animal sacrifices that went before, and that subsequent to Jesus' sacrifice, no further animal sacrifices are required by God.

Yet, as clearly shown by the Old Testament references, above, God never required sacrifices. Verse 23 of Jeremiah 7 goes on to say:

> "But this thing commanded I them, saying, Obey my voice, and I will be your God, and ye shall be my people: and walk ye in all the ways that I have commanded you, that it may be well unto you."

Hosea 6:6 states:

> "For I desired mercy, and not sacrifice; and the knowledge of God more than burnt offerings."

Jesus quotes this verse to the Pharisees in Mt. 9:13, suggesting to them that they go away and learn what it means! No doubt their egos were cut to the quick by this uneducated, bastard son (as they saw him) of an itinerant Galilean tradesman telling them where to get off.

"If Jesus had believed his crucifixion was intended to be a once-and-for-all blood sacrifice, he assuredly would have taught to that effect, but he gave no such teaching."

Would Jesus have quoted this word from the Old Testament prophet, clearly indicating his position – and its oneness with that of God – if it was intended that he, himself, would soon end up as the sacrifice that most manifestations of the religion calling itself Christian state as the fundamental tenet of their faith? If Jesus had believed his crucifixion was intended to be a once-and-for-all blood sacrifice, he assuredly would have taught to that effect, but he gave no such teaching.

This is not intended to repudiate that his crucifixion took place. Instead, it is intended to indicate that his reasons for submitting himself to this brutal form of execution were entirely different from the church doctrines about it, as discussed in Vignette 11, above, and as explained in great detail by Jesus himself in *A Course in Miracles* (ACIM).

As stated in Gary Renard's book *Your Immortal Reality*,** 'The guiltless mind cannot suffer. It blows the whole idea of glorifying sacrifice right out of the water . . . pain is not a physical process, it's a mental process, and if you healed all the unconscious guilt in the mind, then you couldn't feel any pain. That changes the message of the Crucifixion from the idea of worshipping suffering and sacrifice to a demonstration that if you were healed, then it would be impossible for you to feel any pain or to suffer. But suffering, like people now believe J did, is a hallmark of the religion that he had nothing to do with, but that was founded in his name.'

Surely, the above quoted scripture references indicate unequivocally God's intentions toward His children. If God is the God of *unconditional* Love, which religionists agree He is, and nothing of time and place – including sin – exists, because it is merely a dream, an illusion (which is central to the theme of ACIM), there is nothing for God to renege on in respect of the unconditionality of His Love. As there is no atonement for sins required by God, sacrifice *cannot* be on His agenda. Indeed, the Old Testament contains literally hundreds of admonitions toward mercy (*not* sacrifice), most of which read, 'His mercy endureth forever.'

So, after more than three centuries of unequivocal statement (in the KJV bible) that animal sacrifices/burnt offerings were not the intention of the God of mercy – which seemed to have escaped the attention of (or been conveniently overlooked by) both orthodox Jews and Christians – along come a raft of new translations. Most of these agree with the KJV version of the statement in Jeremiah 7:22 – but with two very notable exceptions: The *New International Version* (NIV) and the *New Century*. In the NIV that pivotal verse has had one extra word added that causes the verse to imply the exact opposite meaning. That word is 'just':

For when I brought your forefathers out of Egypt and spoke to them, I did not *just* give them commands about burnt offerings and sacrifices.

The *New Century* translation adds the word *only* instead of *just*. I have software with sixteen Bible translations, and all the others agree with the intent of the KJV wording. Some might say that the NIV and *New Century* wording is making change for change's sake. Others might ask if, perhaps, they were made to comply with and thus give (false) validation to Jewish and orthodox Christian doctrines held for millennia.

The term used by institutionalised religion for this doctrine of sacrifice is 'Atonement'. In religious circles it is pronounced 'a-*tone*-ment'. The actual, *correct* pronunciation is 'at-*one*-ment', which derives not from Latin or Greek but from Anglo-Saxon, and literally means 'making at one'. This simple change of pronunciation helps to bring a totally different light of understanding to the whole confusion.

It is not the death of Jesus on the cross that 'makes us at one' with God but his *life* – and his demonstration of Life's indestructibleness by/through his resurrection – and leading us back to God by reminding us who we really are: eternal, immortal Beings of Light, God's perfect Son, all One within the Sonship.

As shown above, Bible scriptures completely negate the contrived, false, unauthorised-by-God-or-Jesus Christian Church doctrine that Jesus was sent by God (or volunteered) as a once and for all blood sacrifice to God as a propitiation for His wrathful, vengeful frame of mind for the 'sins of the world'. This, and everything to do with sacrifice and suffering 'for the good of the soul' is not from the Voice for God, but from the voice of antiChrist, the ego. This is made very comprehensively and unequivocally clear by Jesus (does anyone know better than he?) throughout ACIM.

He chose to demonstrate the illusory nature of make-believe's trump card – death – in a drama so intense that it would get our attention and hold it, for two thousand years, getting us to actually listen to him so that he could tell us the truth and we would have good reason to *believe* him. The fact that ego-mindedness caused most of us to misconstrue his demonstration and interpret it as a God-intended sacrifice (just to continue the old, *wrong* pattern in a new form) was of no consequence to Jesus, who knew perfectly well that this would happen, because he knew that this is the nature of ego.

Here is what Jesus tells us in ACIM* about the truth of our Being and the misperceptions we have made that got us into the spiritual darkness that hides this truth from our awareness:

"Hear, then, the one answer of the Holy Spirit to all

the questions the ego raises: You are a child of God, a priceless part of His Kingdom, which He created as part of Him. Nothing else exists and only this is real. You have chosen a sleep in which you have had bad dreams, but the sleep is not real and God calls you to awake. There will be nothing left of your dream when you hear Him, because you will awaken.

"Your dreams contain many of the ego's symbols and they have confused you. Yet that was only because you were asleep and did not know. When you wake you will see the truth around you and in you, and you will no longer believe in dreams because they will have no reality for you. Yet the Kingdom and all that you have created there will have great reality for you, because they are beautiful and true."

As stated in Vignette 5, Jesus teaches us in ACIM, page 401 of the "Workbook for Students":

"Forgiveness recognizes what you thought your brother did to you has not occurred. It does not pardon sins and [thus] make them real [as in 'false' forgiveness]. It sees there *was* no sin. And in that view are all your sins forgiven. What is sin, except a false idea about God's Son? Forgiveness merely sees its falsity, and therefore lets it go. What then is free to take its place is now the Will of God."

And as he says in Chapter 14 of the Text:[†]

"Unless you are guiltless you cannot know God, Whose Will is that you know Him. Therefore, you *must* be guiltless. Yet if you do not accept the necessary conditions [i.e. guiltlessness] for knowing Him, you have denied Him and do not recognize Him, though He is all around you. He cannot be known without His Son, whose guiltlessness is the condition for knowing Him. Accepting His Son as guilty is denial of the Father so complete, that knowledge is swept away from recognition in the very mind where God Himself has placed it."

If we believe Jesus died as a God-required blood sacrifice for our sins, we are making real what is false – nothing but a *dream* of guilt and sin – and thereby confirming our perception of guilt as real. This is clearly in direct contradiction of what Jesus is now teaching us in ACIM, to correct our misperceptions and thus set us free. We are now, as always, free to cease believing what isn't true.

ACIM Notes:
Section IV, *A Course in Miracles*, Second Edition:
* Chapter 6: "The Lessons of Love," p 100
† Chapter 14: "Teaching For Truth," p 278.

** Gary Renard, *Your Immortal Reality*, (California: Hay House, 2006)

13. A Mass Rescue and Healing

Jesus tells us that we are the light of the world (Mt. 5:14). John states: Beloved, now are we the sons of God, and it doth not yet appear what we shall be: but we know that, when he (Jesus) shall appear, we shall be like him; for we shall see him as he is (1Jn. 3:2). We are now in the time of the fulfilment of John's words. We are awakening to the remembrance that we are like, or the same as, Jesus.

Jesus is the saviour of the world and therefore, in truth, we also are, with him, the saviour of the world. He states plainly in *A Course in Miracles* that the world cannot be saved without our input, our involvement, because we are all, eternally, *indivisibly*, one. And so, unless and until we choose to join with him, the Sonship is incomplete, and therefore, not saved, or saveable.

Ego would have us believe all this is arrogance in the extreme; a heresy, blasphemy, apostasy. But that is its effort to hide the Truth from us and keep us on the carousel of birth and death. Do we believe Jesus was/is arrogant? There is no *need* of arrogance when one knows the Truth. Arrogance is bluster to cover fear and ignorance.

Ego is on very shaky ground because its foundation is built on a lie, an untruth, an unreality, and therefore has no substance to uphold it. So it is inevitable that the resistance of ego to this reality will fail and we shall remember the Truth of our Being, and our only purpose for appearing in time and place. This does not mean that any one of us must single-handedly take on the role of saviour, but when we begin to remember and accept our true, unlimited state of Being, we will actively *want* to participate in the saving process. Only our belief in the illusion of limitation denies our acceptance of this truth.

Theresa and I attended a 'Five-Day Intensive' entitled *Unconditional Love – the Place of Miracles* by Michael Roads.* During this five-day event participants were led by Michael in a series of 'Inner Experiences' in which the attendant group is prompted to close their eyes, relax and enter into their own beautiful, landscaped valley, where all is peace, love and joy. There, they can encounter whoever 'shows up'. This might be departed loved ones, or still-incarnate souls with whom we might have some outer conflict – major or minor. We are invited to join with such visitors for a healing, loving, sharing, joining experience.

There is a pool, into which a waterfall flows, but the pool and waterfall is Love and Light and when we enter, the Love Light washes away the cares, the hurts, the pain, the fear, the grievances, the unforgiveness and in their place inner peace, joy and unconditional love become the experience. I had no-one particular in mind who I wanted to turn up. Instead, to my surprise, I found myself in a sphere of Light, about the size of a small car, speeding through a large, dense forest at about the pace of a sprinting man. This went on for quite a long time – maybe a minute or two; time is illusory, especially in a non-physical experience.

I expected to arrive at a clearing in the forest, but this did not happen and the experience eventually faded out. Then I found myself back in the lawned area of the valley, near the pool of Light. A number of children – perhaps as many as twenty – appeared. I opened my arms and my heart and they came racing to me, clambering right into me as my heart opened and expanded to receive them. There was great love, joy and excitement.

Then, when it seemed all were 'aboard', a little boy of about three came stumbling/racing up, calling out, "Don't forget me; don't leave me out" and into my heart he climbed with all the other children. That little boy was me! Then, as I pondered this later, I realised that all the other children also were 'me' from other incarnations. They appeared as children because spiritually, that is what we, who are not yet conscious of being Awake, are. This was a healing, rejoining, reunifying of aspects of Self that have been appearing as fragmented, broken 'masquerade-costume' personas, the 'present' one of which appears in form as 'Brian'.

The scene then changed and these children/aspects of Self were playing joyfully in the pool and standing under the waterfall of Love and Light, immersing themselves in 'Showers of Joy' which were, at the same time, healing. In due course Michael announced that it was now time for event participants to leave our valleys and return to our bodies in the event room. As I began the return journey the children were a little reluctant to come with me because they were so happy playing in the pool. However, as I reminded them that we were all now 're-joyned' as one, they left the pool and came racing up to accompany me to the gate that led out of the valley.

As we walked toward the gate I became aware of untold numbers of African children amongst the trees that lined the edge of the valley. These children – all boys as far as I could detect – have been killed/died in the multitudinous wars raging around Africa in recent times, and still continuing in many countries. It brings new meaning to the term 'the dark continent'.

The children – ranging from age about six to about twelve – have been forced into the fighting and killing. The Love in that valley was so great that the fear and hatred that festers in their souls was sublimated by It and they were drawn to It. They were still trepidatious about coming out from the woods and joining us because trust is still an issue in them after all they have experienced, but the look on their faces (seared into their souls – and mine!) was a combination of, '*Please* can we join you? Will it really be safe to join you, as it appears to be? We are so desperately in need of love, comfort, succour, nurturing, LOVING, and we can see the Love radiating from you and in this beautiful place.'

But they were still tinged with doubt, uncertainty. I assured them they would be safe if they felt able to emerge from the dense woods, which was a place in which they believed they could hide, if need be, from more of what had been their wretched, terrified lives. But I felt that remaining focused on the reunifying process with the aspects of Self was the priority of the moment, in order not to become distracted and somehow 'lose contact with the process'. So I paused, looked deep into their souls and promised them I would not, *could* not, forget them; would be back for them *very* soon, and would bring help with me for them.

The next morning I returned, to assure them I had not forgotten them and would *never* abandon them. The following day, I went back and was aware that there were also thousands of girls there. They had been hiding further back in the woods on the two previous occasions. These girls, all also pre- or barely-adolescent, as far as I could see, had been brutally raped and otherwise abused, and murdered.

I had promised these children I would be back for them and

would bring them help to take them to a safer place; a place of Light, Love, Peace, Joy and healing of the terror, hatred, killing, abuse, murder that was all they had known. Yet the fact was, although I had total, unswerving commitment to help them, rescue them, bring them to Love, I had no idea whether I was empowered sufficiently for such a seemingly mammoth task, nor how to go about it.

Indeed, I knew that of myself I definitely could not accomplish this. Nevertheless, having made an absolute commitment to them, I had no intention of not going back. As I returned to them that third morning, the relief on their faces – the melting of doubt into hope – that I had not abandoned them was enough to melt the hardest heart. As I approached them to show them my love and benign intent, suddenly, Jesus was there, coming from behind me toward them.

As I became aware of this I realised that all that was needed of me was to reassure them, demonstrate to them that they *are* loved, *unconditionally*. This placed them at ease and *receptive* to loving help; indeed, *eager* for it and aware that it was possible, available, whereas until these encounters they were unaware of any hope at all. This establishes a preparedness in their hearts and minds (as is the case with any who are in desperate need of succour, or rescue from terrible experience) to receive the help. Without that it would not have been possible for them to be aware of Jesus' presence, because fear obscures the awareness of the Realms of Light.

"He opened his arms, wide enough to enfold the world, and these blessed children came rushing into those all-loving, all-embracing arms and heart."

The previous two encounters with them had enabled that preparedness, and their becoming aware of Jesus. Needless to say, I was profoundly grateful that he had come, because until that moment I hadn't a clue how to proceed from there. How characteristic of him to turn up at precisely the appointed moment! He squatted – to be at eye level with the children – and opened his arms, wide enough to enfold the world, and these blessed children came rushing out from the woods, into those all-loving, all-embracing arms and heart. They *knew* they were now safe and LOVED; that there would not, *could* not be any more terror, emptiness, loneliness, uncertainty.

It was a priceless, precious moment which I will never forget. To know there has now been established this 'bridge' between this dark place from where these precious souls have come, to the Light, to release, relief, and across which an indeterminate, limitless number of others will now be able to follow, is a great treasure, a 'pearl of great price'. Days later I realised that the journey through the forest in the sphere of Light was, in some way of which I was unaware at the time, to establish a connection with those African children who were hiding there.

I have a feeling that there must have been around half a million of these, our brothers in the Sonship of God. There are untold millions more, from every continent, lost, terrified, hopeless, helpless. Jesus would not leave one of us – you, me, them – without succour, help, rescue, healing, LOVE. We do not have to be fully Awake, Self-realised, to offer our assistance and thus each be, along with him, saviours of the world.

There are those who would say of themselves, 'How can I be a saviour of the world? I have not been authorised or empowered for such.' The only authority and empowerment required are desire, willingness and love for our fellows, our brothers. Jesus and/or the Spirit of Truth, our real, Whole Self, will accomplish all the rest for us.

---

[*] For more details on Michael Roads please visit www.michaelroads.com

14. "There is no light of discernment."

During the late 1980s and early 1990s, Steve and I usually met mid-week at a local hostelry, often one called The Little Owl, for a glass of ale and kingdomly fellowship. We have had many amazing experiences and encounters on these occasions, and the Master Jesus was almost always present to one degree or another of our awareness of him.

On one occasion, at the Little Owl, Steve had taken a comfort break, and as I sat there awaiting his return and looking around the bar area, across the room I saw a group of about half a dozen young men, early thirties, standing and quaffing their drinks, enjoying a light-hearted time together. As I casually watched this happening, I saw the Master Jesus walk across the room toward them. He came right up to them, put his arms around the shoulders of two of the men in the group (I feel sure that with his heart he embraced them all equally) and stood there in easy togetherness with them. Needless to say, none of these young men had any awareness of his presence in their midst. This did not distress the Master, of course, and he stayed with them for a few moments, radiating his unconditional love toward them. I feel certain that even if they had no conscious awareness of this, at the psychic level they will have felt it, and no doubt went home feeling that they had enjoyed precious, quality time together.

After maybe twenty or thirty seconds, Jesus turned his head toward me and said, indicating the young men, "There is no light of discernment." There was no dismay, disappointment, judgement or any negative vibration in his observation. It was a simple statement of fact, with barely the tiniest tinge of sadness, and in no way lessened his love for them all. I do feel sure that he would dearly have loved them to have been aware of him, but if they had, and had realised who he was, it would have put them ill-at-ease; and of course, that is the last thing the Master wishes to do with any of his 'little ones'.

On another occasion, Steve and I went to a hostelry at Tewkesbury, a charming, riverside town in north Gloucestershire with roots back to Roman times. There are many Tudor, Georgian,

Victorian and Edwardian buildings in the town and it has a rather timeless aura about it.

As we sat enjoying our ale and fellowship Steve suddenly said, "I have been aware of a man standing to my left and he seems to have been brought here by two angels. I didn't like this intrusion so I said to him, I command you, in the name and by the power of Jesus Christ of Nazareth, to go away and not to return."

"What happened?" I asked.

"He took a big step backwards and had a rather shocked look on his face," Steve replied. "But he didn't go away and the angels are still standing either side of him, upholding him."

"Do you believe this man to be evil?"

"No," he said, "just an unwanted intruder. No doubt he has problems, but so have we all, and who needs this interruption?"

I began to pick up on the vibes of what was going on and it became clear to me that this man had been brought to us for help, blessing and release from whatever condition was holding him back. There was no evil intent about him but he was clearly in distress.

I was well aware that in cosmic law, we go forward and are blessed ourselves by our acts of blessing and helping others to go forward, and I suggested to Steve that here was a soul who had been brought to us for our help; that this is a kingdomly thing to do and a true Christ service. The light dawned in Steve and he realised that this was indeed the case. His whole attitude changed toward the visitor, and together we blessed him for the peace of Heaven and release from his distress and going forward into the Light.

Later, as we stepped outside to make our way home, Steve told me he could see the street packed with souls from Edwardian, Victorian, Georgian, Tudor and all ages, each going about his business, completely oblivious to the presence of the people from all the other eras, walking right through each other. He could see the present day events, with electric street lights, Tarmac road; cobble-stone paving and gas lamps; unpaved, unlit street, all superimposed upon each other.

Clearly, they were still acting out the conditions of their earthly lives many years and even centuries after they have departed their earthly bodies. This is so even for those whose end to their incarnation was not traumatic, but are not yet at the place of awakening whereby they realise they have laid aside their body.

It was not just the half-dozen young men at the Little Owl for whom there is 'no light of discernment'. How needy the world is for a completely new understanding of who and where we all really are, and the spiritual source, origin and eternal, divine nature of our being. This will not just benefit the presently incarnate generation, but past and future generations also, because those from previous eras – who have, as the Master once said to me, ". . . left their Earth bodies behind but not their Earth mind" – can then be blessed for release from being stuck in their time-warp and go forward into a new phase of awakening on the path back to Eternity. Those of 'future' generations, meanwhile, will be able to receive more serviceable reminders from their elders about who they really are: citizens of Eternity, returning to Earth for another opportunity to resolve outstanding issues through the process of true forgiveness, and thus enable the hastening of their return Home, permanently, having dispelled ego and left behind any need for time and place in which to 'hide' from Papa.

15. Animals and Eternity

On our way back from one of our midweek evenings at the pub for spiritual fellowship, as we drove through the Gloucestershire countryside at about 11:00 p.m., I saw, in the light from the car's headlamps, a barn owl flying at tree-top height above us. Suddenly it swooped down at the car. Its head smashed into the windscreen right in front of my face and its eye burst on impact, spreading the vitreous humour over the glass, partially obscuring my vision.

The bird disappeared from view, presumably being tossed over the roof of the car. I stopped and Steve, very distressed – as was I also – by seeing this beautiful (endangered species of) bird mortally wounded, said, "I must see if I can find it" and got out to look for it.

"Steve," I said, "the poor creature could not have survived that impact; it is dead."

Nevertheless, he could not give up without a look. But it was an impossible task, in the country, no street lights, a thick hedge obscuring the view into the neighbouring field, and after a few minutes he got back into the car. Neither of us knew why this bird should have apparently deliberately swooped down from sixty feet in the air straight into the car, as if attacking it. Years afterward I was told that barn owls are very territorial and will attack anything they perceive as a threatening intruder into their area.

Later, as I got into bed, the experience was deeply embedded into my mind and I said to Papa, "I bless this beautiful creature for Your peace."

Instantly I saw Him, the owl cradled in His left arm and stroking it with His right hand, lovingly and tenderly. He said to me, "Many of My creatures will return to Me this night." Then, after a slight pause, "All are within My care."

Of course, at the intellectual level I knew this to be true but the experience of Papa showing me His precious love for this beautiful creature, nurtured in His arms like that and speaking those words, brought home to me in a very comforting and reassuring way, the *actuality* of His universal and yet always tender, caring, perfect LOVE.

* * *

Theresa and I had been visiting friends and family in Sussex one summer weekend in 2002. As we headed off for Gloucestershire through Ashdown Forest, where I had spent an idyllic childhood on the farm, we came round a bend and there, lying toward the side of the road was a deer. It had been hit by a car; there were bits of bumper and other vehicle debris in the road. This had happened only moments before our arrival on the scene. The driver had not stopped. The deer was mortally wounded but fully conscious, unable to move other than its head. There was blood and frothy sputum coming from its nose, and in its flank was a huge bulge, about the size of a rugby ball, and swelling visibly by the minute. My guess was that this was internal bleeding.

I felt absolutely helpless. Heart and soul overflowed with love and compassion for this beautiful creature, struck down in its prime, life ebbing swiftly away. After the experience with the barn owl a few years before, and remembering Papa's words, I cradled its head, looking into its eyes. They were completely calm and accepting. I gave thanks for its life and blessed it over and over and over, committing it into Papa's loving, precious care, all the while asking that He receive it quickly and bring a swift end to this distress. It seemed to take an interminable time, but after what was probably about five minutes it was gone, back to Papa. *Alleluia.*

* * *

The next morning, back at Gloucester, I sat at my desk attending to the day's events when suddenly, there beside me at my left was the deer, large as life. I reached out to stroke it and it nuzzled my hand. We communed silently for a few, loving moments, soul to soul, two individuations of Life, unified in this moment of eternity in mutual recognition that we are each part of the Oneness that is the Source of All. Then, instantly, it was gone, running free in peace and joy.

---

*"When humanity has awakened to the place of Oneness,
there will be no need for laws against activities
that deprive any of the other life forms of their
natural dignity and freedom."*

Truly, not only are we humans all children of the One God, brothers and sisters one and all, but all living things, in all their diverse forms of manifestation, are of the same, One Life. To become aware of this and to *experience* its reality is a blessing beyond any experience of the 'spirit of reckoning' consciousness, which perceives separateness as its reality. When humanity has awakened to the place where the experience of the Oneness becomes its reality, there will be no need for laws against cruelty to animals, factory farming and all the other activities of man that deprive any of the other life forms of their natural dignity and freedom.

16. Peter: "I came to clear the way for her."

In 1992, our older daughter went to Gloucestershire's college of agriculture to take a three-year course in equine management. She had been in love with horses from the time she was a toddler. My grandfather, Poppa, had been a horse breeder and Pop was also a horse lover but whilst I can admire a fine looking horse from the other side of a fence, horses do not seem to recognise me as their friend! So horse whispering skipped a generation with me, but it came back with the next generation. She took to the course like a duck to water, but it was to be short-lived.

The phone rang one day at lunch time. I was out walking the dog when Theresa took the call. It was the college calling to say, 'Just to tell you that the ambulance with your daughter on board has just left here on its way to the hospital', and then hung up. You can imagine the goings on from that moment, but to cut to the chase, she had been thrown from a skittish horse that had been overworked and had had enough for the day, had landed flat on her back and fractured two lumbar vertebrae. The fact that she ended up neither dead nor paralysed is a blessed act of Providence if ever there was one!

The ambulance paramedics were fantastic in every possible way: professional, kind, caring, gentle, loving, kept her spirits up; even visited her in the ward days afterwards.

Theresa got to the hospital about the same time as the ambulance carrying our daughter. At the hospital they gave her opiates for the pain. Theresa and I took it in turns visiting her while she was there for about ten days. During that time she made a truly spectacular recovery. She had to give up the Equine Management idea as a career prospect, but her life is largely unaffected by this experience, as demonstrated by the fact that her main sporting love is snowboarding.

One evening when I was visiting her in hospital the conversation somehow got onto the subject of her siblings in spirit; especially Peter, with whom she has always had a very close bond, through innumerable incarnations. Mark, the boyfriend of the time, wanted to know about Peter so I started to explain how he was her big brother, who had not made it through into this world because of the problem Theresa had had with the car accident at age eighteen causing a rotated pelvis, resulting in the womb being distorted, and his fœtus not having room to develop fully, thus ending in deformation, death and miscarriage of his developing body at thirty weeks of gestation.

Mark sat there taking all this in and was understandably quiet for a while, as were we all. During that silence I heard Peter, who had doubtless been with us all along, suddenly say, "*I came to clear the way for her.*"

The impact of that statement was electrifying and we were instantly welled-up with its implications. This meant that he knew it would not be possible for Theresa to carry a baby to full term in the displaced uterus (her rotated pelvis was re-positioned by a chiropractor when Theresa was two months into her second pregnancy) and had deliberately decided to take what he knew would be a body that could never survive, in order that it would grow and gradually push the womb back into a correct position so that his sibling could come through after him into this life. "*Greater love hath no man than this, that a man lay down his life for his friends*" (Jn. 15:13). Theresa wept when I told her of this revelation later that evening.

17. Religious Mythology

So much of biblical/religionist terminology is allegory, symbol and/or analogy. Jesus used symbols to create images so that the people of his time and these times could understand the *Principles of Life of the Father*. For example, use of the word 'fallen' to describe the state/condition of Earth-life humanity refers to a state of consciousness.

Most of us in the Earth life are conscious at a very limited level compared with our true, eternal, all-knowing awareness ('Now are we the sons of God but it doth not yet appear . . .'), so in that sense we are 'fallen'. It is nothing to do with fallen in the way it has been construed by mainstream Christian denominations, who perceive the word as meaning fallen into 'sin' – or 'out of Grace' with the Father Creator. That perception is religious mythology fabricated to obtain and maintain power over people by the consciousness of fear.

Similarly, the concept of evil, the devil and hell are mythological/allegorical constructs to explain ego, and project the guilt and fear away onto any person or thing outside the self.

Throughout most of my journey with Jesus he continued to use these symbols that he used during his Earth life – and that are part of biblical and religious terminology – in his leading me to a more spiritually awakened state of awareness. There is nothing wrong with the allegories; it is the limitation to growth of understanding that rigid maintenance of such terms as *literal* which is unserviceable to the spiritual awakening of humanity to the Truth of Eternity and our integral place in It.

18. The Not-So-Distant Shore

This experience came in the form of a dream. It was very vivid, and I was both witnessing it and participating in it at the same time.

On a well-populated, sandy beach of the island there is frequent talk about a fabled land across the sea. Some are convinced of its reality, others are undecided, and yet others are completely unwilling to believe.

Many – most, even – would like to escape from the island to this idyllic, Elysian place, which offers so much more than the island on which the people appear to be marooned, living barely an existence. A legend has developed that the distant place is the true home of these people; that the island is a temporary habitation only and this is why so many crowd the beach, hoping for a glimpse of their true home, so far away across the sea. But fear of the unknown keeps the people indecisive about seeking ways to reach their heart's desire, and so they remain wistfully on the beach, vainly hoping for a way to be opened for them.

From time to time someone ventures out into the sea, almost in desperation, as if to swim to their true home, unable to wait any longer. Many watch the venturer, with mixed emotions; some express great doubt and trepidation, and call him back, exhorting him to give up his hopeless quest. Others eagerly urge him on, willing him to succeed, perhaps against all reason or expectation, to reach the Promised Land, from whence he will, perhaps, return with great news of its reality and a safe passage there for the rest of the island dwellers.

Most who venture into the water turn back after a short distance, too unsure, discouraged by those on the beach calling to them that it is too hazardous, and they will never make it; and besides, who can be certain that the Elysian land is even there? Those venturers who are not tempted back by their fellow island dwellers and, out of unremitting hope, or perhaps, desperation, continue on their way, eventually disappear from view in the sea, and no-one knows if they have made a safe passage or have been lost forever. Sometimes a large wave appears to swamp the swimmer, and the watchers from the beach say, "There, it is much too hazardous; we dare not risk it. It would be suicide. We're better off staying here; at least it's what we know."

Much of the time the view across the water is hazy, and visibility is limited to only a few miles. But occasionally the haze clears and people strain to see if the distant shore can be detected. Sometimes it seems as if it *is* just visible, far out at the horizon, and a great gasp goes out amongst the people. Some excitedly cry out, "Look! There it is, there it is." Others, fearful, say, "No, it's a mirage; it's too faint . . . we cannot be certain." Then the haze returns to obscure the view and any possibility is lost, again, of the certainty being established that their much hoped-for homeland is there. The people resign themselves once more to remaining on the island.

Then, down onto the beach from the hinterland comes one of their number, who has said little, but in his heart of hearts has a deep, unshakeable, inner knowing of the distant shore's reality and that it is where he and his fellow island dwellers belong. He is determined to find a way to get there. He has long held this commitment but now, finally, it takes hold of his heart and mind, obscuring all thoughts to the contrary, and galvanises him into action that has brought him from inland to the beach. He looks around and there, part hidden in a cleft where the beach rises into steep, grassy banks, he spies a tiny, flimsy, pitch-covered coracle.

Without hesitation he picks up the coracle, walks out into the sea with it and clambers aboard. It is just big enough to hold him, seems barely seaworthy and entirely inadequate for a voyage of indeterminate duration into the unknown. But he has taken a leap of faith, and so one-pointed is his commitment that he is determined to reach his destination, come what may.

Outwardly, it seems foolhardy; certain to end in disaster, and such misgivings are loudly echoed by many of the onlookers on the beach, who call out, "Come back, you'll never make it; that thing is a death trap. It will be swamped by the first wave, before you get half a mile out. Besides, sharks will rip it to pieces and then you'll be a goner."

But in his heart he has a knowing, a certainty that, flimsy, unsafe and inadequate as the coracle outwardly appears to be, in direct proportion to his holding fast in faith, trust and commitment, he will be upheld and protected by an invisible hand, the Hand of Providence, and guided safely, regardless of the apparent hazards of the journey.

"He gives thanks, and his faith and trust grow until he feels he is soaring over the water, above the dangers, causing him to sense that he is no longer within their reach."

As each danger arises – high waves, boisterous winds, sharks circling menacingly – he reaffirms his faith in himself and his trust in the Guiding Hand, and as each threat passes without disaster, he gives thanks, and his faith and trust grow until he feels as if he is not paddling a tiny coracle, but soaring *over* the water, above the dangers, causing him to sense that he is no longer within their reach.

He notices that the breezes and the currents are now carrying him further and further from the island. His fellows on the beach become smaller and smaller; their voices warning of disaster fade into the distance until they are nothing. Now he is at the point of no return, but he is looking ahead only, with no thought of fear, no hankering for what he has left behind. The warm sun shines on his back and a shiver of anticipation and excitement courses through him. Gradually, the haze ahead thins out before him and there, suddenly, so near and welcoming is the beautiful-beyond-description, not-so-distant shore.

Upon it, waiting eagerly and lovingly to greet and embrace him into their midst are his loved ones, whom he has always known in his heart and soul were there for him, caring, exhorting, encouraging, blessing him every moment, regardless of where he was and what he was doing, until at last, by faith, he found his way home, rejoicing.

I had this dream in the 1990s. It was only in late 2005 that I began reading *A Course in Miracles* for the first time, and it was well into 2006 before I came to "Workbook for Students," Lesson 182, the first paragraph of which reads:

"This world you seem to live in is not home to you.

254

And somewhere in your mind you know that this is true. A memory of home keeps haunting you, as if there were a place that called you to return, although you do not recognize the voice, nor what it is the voice reminds you of. Yet still you feel an alien here, from somewhere all unknown. Nothing so definite that you could say with certainty you are an exile here. Just a persistent feeling, sometimes not more than a tiny throb, at other times hardly remembered, actively dismissed, but surely to return to mind again."

19. Ted's Passing, Rescue and Going Forward

In March 1994, Theresa's dad, Ted, laid aside his body. There had been bad feeling between him and us for years and he had disowned Theresa, the girls and me in 1988 after I had told him in a letter that his offensive behaviour toward us was unacceptable and it would no longer be convenient for him to visit us. We heard of his passing a few days after the event, by telephone.

Theresa and I stood in the kitchen discussing him and this event when I was suddenly aware of him standing two or three paces away, listening to what we were saying. He had his back toward us but his head was partly turned so he could hear us. It was clear from this body language that he was rejecting us, even though he was eager to hear what we were saying about him.

After a moment, during which I took in what was happening, I said to him, "Peace be with you." I might as well have given him an electric shock! He spun around so quickly it was almost a blur, and the look on his face indicated at once profound astonishment and incredulity. It was clear that he thought my attitude toward him would be identical to his toward me and that he had anticipated that, should his presence come to my attention – which assuredly he hoped would not be the case – I would say to him, "Rot in hell", or some equally unfriendly, dismissive term.

Yet he knew, because he could not deny the vibes that his soul picked-up from my words, and more importantly, the sincerity with which they were spoken, that I meant what had been said. Had he been in the Earth life he may have been able to deny the sincerity, but in the etheric/psychic body, the vibes are indisputable and he knew, unquestionably because he *felt* it, that this was spoken honestly – from the heart.

That moment was the beginning of the rescue of Ted from a dark and dismal place; a place of his own fabrication. Although we know practically no details, we understand that he had come from a dysfunctional childhood home and sadly, in spite of many lofty aspirations, his life had not worked out accordingly.

He had had grand ambitions for his offspring, but his controlling and brutal treatment of them drove them from his influence at the first opportunity. This had been obvious from the earliest visits to Theresa's family home back in 1968. His passing had been alone and lonely, and now, in the spirit world he was still alone and lonely, in spite of many years of involvement with spiritualism and a number of other occult groups.

At Communion on March 20th I wrote:

I had a sense that Edward (Ted), newly passed over, was watching (having been welcomed if he so wished). Gradually he warmed to the service, and certain parts were helpful and had special meaning for his circumstances.

At the offering of the bread he fell to his knees, overcome by the meaningfulness of the occasion and its pertinence for his life. There was a true sense of penitence emerging. At the offering of thanks for the bread he collapsed, as at the steps leading to a temple or cathedral, and a great emotional release set in, with uncontrollable sobbing. I saw his lips tremble as he began to go down. I sensed it was right to leave him to release his feelings. At the offering of the Wine of Christ Love for all in need, sorrow, sickness or any adversity, he grasped the chalice as if crazed by thirst, and drank deeply for a long time, taking great gulps and swallowing noisily. At the offering of thanks for the wine that converts tears into joy, death into life, I heard the Teacher say, "We go forward".

I told Ted that John was here and he was amazed, looking around to find him. John stepped forward from behind the altar. He threw his arms around his dad and gave him a great, long, enveloping hug. Ted stood there, his arms at his side, totally unresponsive to John's embrace. It was clear that Ted had no awareness whatever of John's presence.

I then told Ted that Thelma (Theresa's mother, who had laid aside her body in 1987) was also present and the response was somewhat more reserved. I sensed that Thelma, John and the others were 'tall' and that Ted was 'small'. No doubt he will go forward, rejoicing, in due course. I saw him with John's arm around his shoulder, standing, with John smiling and Ted looking a little unsure but hopeful, still unaware of John's presence.

I said, "Jesus, my blessed Lord and Master, thank you for the privilege of this joyous occasion and opportunity to serve the Kingdom purpose. Thank you also for what it teaches me – that forgiveness can and should be unreserved, and that time makes no difference."

He replied:

"My son, this is Unconditional Love and it is the stuff of which the Kingdom is made. It is the most abundant element in creation (manifest and unmanifest) so there is no shortage of it. Take freely of it and fill your heart, soul, life, that it occupy all parts of you, leaving space for no other, contrary, vibrations. It shall spontaneously combust the dross of 'Satan's harvest' and purify all your being, that life abundant shall be yours, and power anew to further perform the Will of the Father shall be yours also. Thus shall the little ones sullied by the way of the enemy be transformed. I say unto you, well done, thou good and faithful servant; power of many things shall be yours according to your diligent service, commitment and watching for the return of your Lord.

"I say also unto you, love and bless unreservedly, that the Kingdom may flow unrestrictedly through you into the Earth. Nevertheless, watch and guard, that evildoers have not their way with you. All is well; I am with you and have set my seal upon you, and my strong angel to guard your door. Peace be with you."

At Communion on April 17th, Steve and I were both aware of Ted as if he was in a pit, but eager to rise up. At the offering of the bread and wine he came very close, gripped my forearm with both hands and said, "Forgive me, Brian."

At the dedication hymn Ted said, "God was not at *my* departing, but sorrow and bitterness. I want to pray."

"I can't help you but Jesus can," I replied.

"Who's he?" he answered, sardonically. "What's he ever done for me?" This indicates the degree of his problem.

"You may think he's never done anything for you," I said, "but I can assure you, he has done *everything* for me."

It was clear Ted did not understand the Teacher's blessing ('So shall the Peace of Christ abide with us and Holy Spirit lead us in Eternal Truth') but Steve saw the Teacher rolling up his sleeves and saying, "I'll help him."

On April 24th Ted came in early in the service and was straining forward intently, trying to see what we were experiencing. I said it would benefit him to prayerfully and sincerely contemplate the words, and discernment would gradually come to him.

He said to Steve, "I want to speak! Help me say the right things. I *want* to see the God I know exists in my heart, but why Jesus? What has he ever accomplished for me in my life? I had a life of heartache and sorrow and not once did he come to my help. So why do I need him now? Let him come and help me here, *now*, if he will. I have no need of anyone but God. Show me that I need this Jesus, and I will turn to him. Okay?"

As I poured the grape juice onto the water in the chalice, in preparation for the consecration, I felt as if this was the Lord pouring his life and his love into the life of the children of Earth to blend with it and raise it up, quicken it, from *within*. I felt his tenderness toward his little ones in this, his act of selfless giving.

On May 1st Ted was here from the start, his door (to his inner being) 'bricked-up' and he is having difficulty letting go and opening the door. But his seeking and desiring eternal truth and reality is sincere; and the words of the service are having a loosening effect on the mortar of the brickwork. He has committed to coming again and again. The going forward process is underway, slowly but surely.

I said to him:

"Dear Ted, there has been a great deal of ill feeling and misunderstanding between us over the years and my attitude toward you has been negative, even as I know has yours to me. But you see and hear in the words of this service that all in the sight of God is positive – building, freeing, making new, making whole. It is my desire above all for my life to be made whole by attuning and becoming one with that love and giving. I know that cannot be unless and until I can expunge all the vestiges of my feelings and attitude toward you from the past. This is my sincere desire, to hold goodwill toward you. You see also how Theresa feels the same. Can we all be good friends and forgive and release our feelings from the past? This way we can all go forward, unencumbered."

Ted responded, "Brian, I know you are a good person; I see your sincerity in what you are doing. It has helped me already and I want to experience much more. It is very satisfying. I know many of my attitudes have been self-centred but this was actually because I believed what I was doing was right and I wanted the others to do it because I thought they would benefit by it. You are helping me to see that this was wrong. I am very, very sorry. I feel as if I need your forgiveness, and all the others too, for being so unbending. I want us to get on well. I see that what you are doing is more valuable than the ways of the world. You are helping me and I want to continue with this. Please be my friend now."

"Ted, I am glad we've had this healing chat. By the Lord's grace the barriers between us shall evaporate. You are welcome here always."

"Thank you; I see how much I need that."

On May 8th Ted said to Steve:

"I wish to speak. It is with deep regret that I look back on my life and the fiasco I have made of it and the lives of those I was supposed to love. I have caused unimaginable hurt and distress to my family and wish to make recompense for this. Show me the way, dear friend, for I can't seem to release myself from this pit. I feel as if I am sinking lower and lower. Dear God, help me get out of this place that I may make right all the wrongness I have caused. Dear God, forgive me. Show me this Light of Christ Jesus that you spoke of in your Service, and I will be willing to do whatever I can to make things right."

I, also, saw him in the same, circular pit I had seen him in before. It was about five or six paces across and about as deep as his own height. He was rather pathetically trying to get out, but his efforts lacked commitment and determination, and his tone of voice as he said, "I can't seem to get out of here, however much I try", clearly affirmed his lack of resolve, his demoralisation. It was apparent that he felt overwhelmed by the inadequacy of his ability to prevail in this situation.

At this point, Steve saw Ted turn around sorrowfully, and walk into a public lavatory as if that was where he lived. Steve asked the Lord how he could help him. The immediate response was, "He must help himself."

Ted visited several more times in the ensuing weekly Communion Services, and was up on some visits and down on others. Although he had ups and downs, there didn't seem to be any real forward progress, and I eventually said to John, "Your dad doesn't seem to be going forward and I am fresh out of ideas what to do or where to go from here. All I can do is say, 'over to you.' "

I didn't see or hear anything more of Ted for some weeks and rather wondered if there would ever be any further contact from him. Then, at Communion on August 28th I wrote:

This has been a remarkable Communion. Ted knocked diffidently at the door, pushed it partly open and said he had found a new friend and would it be all right to bring him along to the service? I of course said yes, and Ted entered, closely followed by his new friend, who I instantly recognised as John. He (John) was wearing plastic spectacle frames with an attached plastic nose, eyebrows and moustache! It was such a comical sight and it was so obvious to me who he was that I nearly burst out laughing, but he put his finger to his mouth in a gesture indicating to me that I should not give the game away. It was evident that Ted had no idea who this new friend really was. Assuredly John would have been properly disguised to the perception of his dad but this was neither required nor desired for me. The objective was to show me that he was disguised so that Ted would not know who he was – until the time was right to reveal it.

It was also evident that when I had said to John earlier in the year, "Over to you," he had indeed taken over (thank goodness) and I realised that he had shortly afterwards gone to visit Ted – who I had seen was living alone, dejected and bereft of hope and ambition, in a hovel in a grey and dismal landscape – disguised so that Ted would not recognise him. He had befriended this lost and lonely, bewildered soul, and gradually, rather like Jesus speaking to the two travellers on the road to Emmaus (Lk. 24:13ff), had, over a number of visits and a number of weeks (of Earth time, anyway!) been leading Ted, one step at a time, through the process of opening his eyes to the realities of Jesus and Eternal Truth.

John was carrying a small, fold-up picnic table (miniature banquet feast for two) with a large, tall, white enamel jug of wine. He unfolded the table and set the jug on the ground beside him, inviting Ted to join him at the table, which immediately became filled with good things to eat. Ted saw this and looked at John in astonishment, inquiring how he had done this, but John dismissed the matter as being nothing out of the ordinary. They sat at the table during the proceedings of the service, in convivial good fellowship, partaking of the banquet of good food and wine, which John poured for Ted from the jug every time Ted's glass got low.

At our October 2nd service, near the beginning, Ted came rushing excitedly in, straight up to me, gripped my left sleeve tightly in both hands and said, "I've found John! I have forgotten about all that nonsense (the past events), and I'm ready to go forward, unreservedly!"

He was twirling and dancing spontaneously with sheer joy and uncontainable excitement. I was reminded of King David leaping and dancing as the Ark of the Covenant, recovered from the Philistines, was brought back into Jerusalem (2 Samuel: chapter 2). All those present in spirit clapped and cheered, and Betty, my mother, who had laid aside her earthly body in May the same year, welcomed him to join her in the attendant gathering. John resumed his customary role as an Inner-Plane Sanctuary server but the others present called three cheers for him and sang, 'For he is a jolly good fellow', causing embarrassed remonstrations from John, who blushed pink at being the focus of so much loving attention.

"Provision has been made that all shall receive an invitation and shall be proffered a garment fitting for the wedding banquet."

I said, "Master Jesus, my beloved Lord and friend, thanks be to you and our Almighty heavenly Father for the wonders of Heaven and for the joy of all the company of the Kingdom and these blessed rescue missions, which by your love, grace and power are able to be effected. I know this is the time of much rescuing and that there are still untold numbers of souls, incarnate and excarnate, who are not aware of the Kingdom reality but who, if they were, would desire to be one with its joy, fellowship and fulfilment."

He replied:

"My beloved son and friend, fear not; all is well. Think you that I would leave one single soul, a child of my Father, out of the celebration? I assure you that provision has been made that all shall receive an invitation and shall be proffered a garment fitting for the wedding banquet. Have no concern for the ways and means by which men of goodwill shall be awakened in time. Rather, pray and commit all such into the loving care of the Holy One, by Whom comes all grace, righteousness and wholeness. Ponder all things of the Kingdom in your heart and let wisdom bring silence and humility, save where my spirit moves you to speak. Then shall the eternal, living word be adequate for each occasion as it arises.

"Go in peace and rejoice – now is the time."

October 9th was a Communion filled with joy. I saw the service structure as a vine that before my eyes sprouted new shoots in all directions, symbolising its value as the basis for spiritual awakening from which new growth is inevitable. Ted has been transformed and *is* unreserved in his new-found commitment to the Lord. He said:

"Brian, I have been wrong about so much, and this has caused grave misunderstanding, hurt and abuse. I cannot tell you how much I regret all the wrong, but John – God bless him – has shown me that the best and the only way to make up for the wrong is to work for good, and the best and only way to do that is by an absolute commitment to Jesus. Well I can tell you that this was something I would have run a mile from before, but you all have helped me to see, by your sincerity, commitment and the love and power of this Communion that Jesus *is* the way, the truth and the life. Forget the baloney of the Earth church doctrine and dogma, which I rejected many years ago for its lack of humility, lack of practising what it preached, and on and on.

"I realise I have a great deal to learn but I am now ready to start again from scratch. There's plenty to do and I want to give my total commitment to making good all the wrong. Thank you *all*, each of you, for your understanding, your forgiving nature and your acceptance of me in this brotherhood of Christian worship and praise. I am whole-heartedly with it. I want to help all who are lost, or stuck, or hurting. I know I can do that with your help and that you are willing parties to it. We can work to the greater good as a team. John and Peter have been telling me about teamwork. I am willing to learn all about the ways of the Lord; I see he is the only way. God bless you, Brian and you, Theresa, for your love and understanding.

"Your new friend, Ted. I had to get this off my chest."

On October 16th, at the beginning of the service, Ted stood up and sang the hymn, *Alleluia, sing to Jesus* . . ..What a transformation!

I said, "Beloved Jesus, Lord and Master, this transformation of Ted is as great a wonder and joy as any I can recall."

He spoke:

"My beloved friend, this is the power of love and commitment to Eternal Truth. It is all-encompassing and shall make *all things* new. It is in your life, one with you, part of you and you are part of it. It is *all* available to you for good, and by it shall be fulfilment of your heart's desire. What you see and experience is but the beginning for you. It is a gift, given freely. It cannot be abused, only used, in love and the spirit of goodwill for good works in my name for our Father. All that you ask in my name, believing, our Father will give.

"Have no fear, but be assured that all is well. Although the enemy is ever close, you are, by your commitment, within the aura of my protection. The enemy has no part in me, and you are protected absolutely by your oneness with me. Remember this as each opportunity to go forward arises, my son. You have entered in to the Inner Sanctuary, and from therein shall your service be rendered. Go not out, for the invitation is to all to enter in, and those who would do so shall receive of you the living word at the entranceway. Let the holy chalice also be offered, for you have seen how the wanderers in the wilderness crave its restoring liquid.

"I am your guide, and lead you in every step. Remain until I shine the lamp of eternal illumination at your feet to make sure and clear the path before you. Thus shall no distress be rendered unto you. You have trodden the narrow and straight path of service, my son; all is well for you and your beloved Companion of the Way. Rejoice; the banquet feast awaits."

Ted continued to be present and actively involved in our weekly services and there were many acts of rescue and succour for lost and bewildered souls, wandering in wilderness conditions, in which Ted played a vitally contributing role, showing much Christ-love, blessing and commitment.

Then, at Communion on the 28th of April 1996, I was marvelling at the changes beginning to take place in the hearts, lives and conditions of Theresa's sisters, and glory that this is the hand of the Lord, no doubt with committed input from John and Ted in spirit. John immediately spoke:

"This shows the power of Almighty God and how it can work for good in the lives of those who commit themselves to Him."

I said, "John, my dear and beloved friend and brother in Jesus Christ, I have known you and Ted would be beavering away for rescue of Laura and Margaret, as well as others."

Too excited to contain himself, Ted jumped in: "Brian, this service, your sincerity and commitment, have been the instruments of my rescue. Lord only knows how long I would have been in the pit of despair otherwise. Don't you think I know how my own bull-headedness (Taurus!) caused this almighty mess in the first place? Nevertheless, I have, by the grace of God, put all that self-punishment behind me, with untold help from countless people.

"And your and Theresa's lives and commitment to Jesus has been true inspiration to me, strengthening my commitment and resolve to do *everything* for my beloved family, as well as all else who are brought to me for help by the Lord. Yes, I know him; yes, I love him; yes, he is *my* Lord; Lord of my life. Glory be to God for all His ways of love and perfection. Remember how I sought perfection, even demanded it? Well now I've *truly* found it and it's all so much more *relaxing*. And I have John, my beloved son and friend. We are all – you and us – one great big *happy* family and we are overjoyed at your new status." (As grandparents.)

John begins again:

"Brian, Dad has, I think, stopped for breath, so I guess I can put in a word or two! It is not as hard over here to bring about changes in the lives of souls in the Earth as it is from within the Earth-life, at least not in the way of those who are outwardly in left field. This is immeasurably easier when we have the power and energy to help us generated by the prayers of Earth-life souls such as you and Titch (Theresa). It is all, as Dad says, by the grace of God. Not one soul who can be rescued is to be left behind. This is the Word of Command from Papa, through our Lord Jesus, and is echoed, reverberating around *all* the halls of Heaven. *It is accomplished* by the gift, the life of Jesus, and can now be implemented by the co-operation of all who love him.

"Papa wants us to respond *to opportunities,
not to try to create them."*

"In such opportunities as are being brought about shortly, all I ask is your awareness that it is God, our Father, who will perform the necessary transformation, and this can happen most readily by our willingness and commitment to allow *Him* to do it. It is such a strong temptation to jump in and take things head to head. Papa wants us to *respond* to opportunities, not to try to create them. *He* is the Creator and wants us to let Him attend to His work and for us to attend to ours. Watch this space for developments.

"And as for Titch. She is some courageous lady. I take off my hat to her. You *will* see the metamorphosis and she will emerge in full flight.* You knew she could do it and your faith in her has stood her in good stead. What a team!

"Peace and joy be with you all; remember, we are all one big family and family means commitment. Thanks from the bottom of my heart for everything."

"God bless and keep you, John and Ted."

---

* Earlier this week I saw Theresa as a giant, human-size chrysalis sitting on the sofa. Before my eyes a huge – human-size – white, radiant butterfly emerged and flew, without a moment's pausing, straight up, vertically, in the air. The emergence and taking of flight was a single, seamless movement, the folded wings as they emerged from the chrysalis case unfolding as the butterfly took off, and were fully extended by the time the first beat of the wings took place.

20. From Breaking Rocks to Breaking Bread

During Communion one Sunday in November 1994, we suddenly were in a huge cavern about sixty or eighty metres high and disappearing out of sight into the distance in front of us, with many thousands of souls, lost and labouring, breaking rocks with sledge-hammers, piling them up, loading them into wheelbarrows, moving them to another part of the cavern, unloading them into other, new piles. They appeared to be doing this almost in a state of trance, aimlessly engaged and actually achieving nothing. I realised that this symbolised the Earth-life activities of the vast majority of humanity.

The cavern is rough-hewn out of light-coloured, rusty brown rock. I found myself standing on a ledge at the mouth of an opening that was about two or three metres high and roughly circular, about eight or ten metres above the cavern floor, speaking the invitation to Commune with Christ. My speaking was carried by good acoustics (and sincerity) throughout the cavern and those toiling monotonously below looked up, seeing this stranger with arms outstretched, welcoming them to partake of bread and wine of eternal life and truth/wisdom and love, in joyous fellowship with our beloved Lord Jesus. I was aware of a pale, bluish-white light radiating outward into the cavern from behind me, and realised this would be from the mobile entrance – which is somewhat like a flexible, extendible, elevated tunnel that leads passengers to the doorway of an aircraft – (or 'Open Door') to the banquet chamber of the marriage feast to which *all* are invited. The marriage is, of course, between Heaven and Earth, or more precisely, the reunifying of the fragmented, self-limiting, time and place consciousness with the limitless, all-loving, all-knowing, eternal Christ Mind.

Some of those in the cavern responded eagerly, dropped their tools and came forward; others were more hesitant, while yet others indicated scepticism and returned to their labours.

At the offering of the bread and wine, my position had moved to one end, and at a level that appeared to be slightly below that of the main floor area of the cavern, so that those who came forward could look upon the events from a satisfactory vantage point. There was a chasm between their level and mine, preventing their crossing. Onto a huge screen was projected the image of the altar and the proceedings to those who were too far back to be able to look directly upon the scene.

As the offering was made to *all who, in need, sorrow, sickness and any adversity, seek Christ help by this Sanctuary*, some of those standing at the edge of the chasm, and who clearly were eager to partake, found themselves transported across the chasm as if by an unseen hand, where they were enthusiastically welcomed by the Inner Plane Sanctuary servers. These included Ted who, dressed in formal waiter's attire, passed energetically among them, offering trays of food and drink and reassuring the newcomers that he, too, was but recently rescued from a dreary place by this same invitation. His enthusiasm for his work was joy and wonder to behold! He especially commended to them the wine because of its restorative and uplifting qualities.

Those left behind were astonished to see their erstwhile colleagues transported across the chasm. Some made as if to launch themselves into space but were fearful of the gap. I explained to them that if they *desired* to partake of the banquet, they would be transported across the gap *by their own desire* and need 'do' nothing more. Individuals began suddenly to be uplifted and found themselves in the midst of the growing gathering of Inner Plane Servers and newcomers – which was rapidly becoming a great and joyful celebration. Others, still fearful, could not make the crossing but were being hailed by their former colleagues who had achieved the transition across the chasm, reassuring them that there was nothing to fear, and urging them to join them in this new and better place. So, more kept coming and this in itself helped to reassure those still left behind, so that they were able to gain confidence that desire alone would afford them safe passage.

Before this, at the contemplation of the symbols, as we sang one of the hymns, I saw about a dozen angels, flying around the walls of our, lower, approximately semi-circular end of the cavern, with the rough-hewn rock walls rising-up behind and to the sides of us. As the angels flew, they were gathering energies generated by the service, and fabricating gossamer curtains of living light, which rose up from the floor, covering the cavern walls, higher and higher, as the angels flew back and forth. They appeared to have wands, or sticks, in their hands, which seemed to be the points at which the living curtains came into being. It reminded me of how candy floss/cotton candy is created and gathered on a stick, except this was coming *from* the stick. At the point at which the curtains came into being – the top end, from where they grew upwards – they were amethyst coloured, but below that they were a milky white.

As I made the offering of the wine for those in need, etc., I felt and heard (but did not see) a man standing right in front of me, very close – only inches away. He said, in an urgent, agitated, confused voice, *I was a stock-broker, I don't know why I should be here!* (in the cavern, breaking rocks). It was clear from his tone of voice that he did not feel he should be reduced to such humble circumstances, but was totally powerless to effect his own release.

It was evident that this scene is symbolic of Earth-mind consciousness, where those who have not kept the lamp of their spiritual awareness lit and trimmed, who have been conscious only at the 'mammon' level, metaphorically breaking rocks (or making their 'living' only at the Adamic-consciousness or 'red-Earth' level of awareness), will remain conscious only at that level, including after they have passed over, continuing to go through an endless, monotonous, purposeless round of hacking and hewing, scrabbling and breaking, carrying from here to there and back again.* Such activity will continue from one incarnation through the next and indefinitely until they awaken, from their own within – but with help and encouragement ever present to those who seek it – and begin the journey Home to the joyous eternity of Heaven.

So, whether we are a stockbroker, a builder of skyscrapers, a seller of cars, a medical practitioner, a charity worker, a corporate-giant executive or digger of ditches, until we remember who we *really* are and why we are *really* here (and that the 'outer labels' we wear are not who we really are), we will continue the endless round symbolically represented here by the breaking and transporting of rocks. When we begin to remember who we really are, then we can begin to realise that breaking bread – sharing eternal, spiritual aspiration, values and truth – is of inestimably more value to ourself and to our fellows than breaking rocks.

Then will we realise that true forgiveness is not only possible but easy because we will have begun to see that all this is merely an illusion, a dream, and therefore none of the events for which we perceived forgiveness was necessary ever actually occurred. How easy it is to forgive what never happened in the first place! Nevertheless, forgiving enables us to *receive* the forgiveness that is rightfully *ours* and the absence of which has held us back from returning Home to Papa. The reason people feel unable to receive the forgiveness that is rightfully theirs is that, at a deep, unconscious level they believe they are guilty, sinners, and therefore, unworthy of forgiveness. Institutionalised religion has lost no opportunity to hammer home this misperception for many centuries, using the name of Jesus to give its spurious message counterfeit authenticity. Is it any wonder that people are fearful of Jesus and don't want to hear about him?

The cave dwellers were dressed in animal skins, symbolising a much lower level of spiritual evolution than the 'clever, the proud and the scornful' might consider themselves to be, yet as they were transported to the 'banquet reception' their attire was transformed to such as befitted the occasion, i.e. white raiment.

At the hymn, *Creator Spirit by whose word* . . . I saw the Teacher sitting in his 'chair of office' rearward and to the left of the Sanctuary table. He was presenting himself as if all was 'normal' and outwardly dignified and 'as befits a being of such exalted status'. But this could not be, nor was it, other than a scarcely veiled attempt at hiding what was all too easy to see – an excitement, bursting forth from within, that he could barely contain, and which he really had no desire to contain any longer than this humorous pretence at being seen as reserved and dignified inadequately portrayed. It was altogether an overwhelming, uplifting, exciting and enlightening experience.

I said to the Teacher: "Beloved Teacher, I'm so excited and overjoyed at this, our work for the Kingdom, really getting underway."

He responded, "My dear friend Brian, you rightly observe the great excitement that I cannot, nor do I wish to, hide. I do assure you that we go forward apace, with much rescue work.

Now is the time of readiness for this progress. I see you discern that the years of preparation have been necessary in order that your awareness of the reality of the eternal realms of spirit could grow in your Earth-life consciousness. There has been much for you to learn, to assimilate, in order that you could be brought to this place. It has been my joy to oversee your progress. Now do we all rejoice that the 'serious' work begins.

"I know I do not need to caution you to be constantly on guard against the wiles of the enemy, or to maintain your armour of defence against the darts of destruction. You know that the cloak of the Lord's protection – living in Him and always keeping your heart and life open to His presence – is the whole armour, and that no further contortions of mind or body are needful for such protection. The greatest threat of breach to such armour is complacency. Thus shall the practise of this ritual serve you well in reminding, renewing and restoring you in Christ humility, love and desire to serve. And thus shall the desire of your heart be fulfilled in joyous fellowship of Heaven. And thus shall there continue to be much rejoicing in Heaven, echoing and reverberating in the 'caverns' of Earth, as such become illuminated with the Light of the Kingdom, banishing away the darkness forever.

"Peace, joy and love be with you all, always."

---

* But such conditions can be transformed by the love of Jesus and those one-pointedly committed and espoused to him and the service of his Great Rescue Programme, and who live by and for his promise: "*Behold I make all things new.*"

21. Laser: Amplifying the Light for the Kingdom

During Communion Services in the summer of 1997, we became aware of vast multitudes of souls from all ages streaming toward Jerusalem – the City of Peace – from all directions, all corners of the world, as far as the eye could see. These included large numbers gathered at a very long, high railing fence to the east, pressing hard against it, trying to get through to where we were, on top of Mount Moriah, the 'Hill of the Lord' in the city, where the temples, first of Solomon and later, Herod, stood. There was a turnstile in the fence and the people were crowding to get through. Steve saw a man, who was clearly in charge of the turnstile, walking amongst them, telling them of the need for orderliness and to attune with the aura of peace and tranquillity of the sanctuary in order to be permitted entry. This created, amongst those waiting to come through, a contemplative attitude as they walked past him, and they became focused upon the rarefied conditions created by our desire for, and attunement with, the Kingdom.

Then I suddenly realised this man, controlling the turnstile, was John the Baptist, and the turnstile/fence is symbolic of the River Jordan; that all who seek entry into the presence of the Lord on the Holy Hill must cross over the Jordan from east to west, and as they cross, to be baptised freely with the Waters of Life. The Teacher said, "We go forward."

At the offering I felt as if John the Baptist (JB) was relaying the words I was speaking from the order of service out 'beyond the Jordan', to all who dwell in the wilderness, as if he is accustomed to such conditions and can act as a channel for my speaking, as officiant, of the words of the Communion Service and all the pure desire energy generated by that which we do. This seems to be necessary because Jesus has counselled me not to go out (into the wilderness) but to remain at the entranceway to the banquet chamber, to welcome in all who would enter.

I said to him, "Beloved Lord, one step at a time our heart's desire awakens within us – and in sync with this, the operation that you have in place as it unfolds before us."

He replied, "My son, your heart's desire is not something that is *becoming*; a faltering, chance, haphazard development. It is a strong, well-established creation, as I have already said, forged in the fire of the Holy Spirit, in pure harmony with eternal reality. It is unfolding before you *in your earthly life* as you go forward upon the Path, led by me, your guide to Eternity, motivated from within by that strong desire. Therefore it is no coincidence that what you describe is so, for it is in fulfilment of your desire, harmonised aforetime with those of like desire, with whom you are in close association *because* of like desires.

"This is how you are in close association with me. That is not a chance happening; why should association with JB or any other of my beloveds, including my beloved disciple (the Teacher), be surprising? My plan is all encompassing; every opportunity is catered for, according to the power of the Spirit of Truth. No event in my earthly life was 'chance' fulfilment of prophecy. So also is the fulfilment of your birth vision because you have committed your life into my care.

"Let no one say to you there is no joy in such commitment of life, for I am the Lord of the Purple Ray – the perfect blend of Earth-life and fulfilment with eternal truth and reality. The joy of Heaven is thus yours in the Earth-life and by no other means is this possible. So is it with all who come to me."

"Lord, it seems so impossible that it could be as you have described, not just for us who love you and have been brought into alignment with your power and activity, but for the billions of souls whose lives and karma are in such a horrendous snarl, like a mass of tangled cables or spaghetti."

"This is not a problem because I am operating from the *within* of all my little ones; like fibre-optic cable, it can transmit the Light even round corners and entanglements."

On August 27, 1997 I wrote:
During recent months I have had a growing inner awareness that that which we do, that to which we espouse ourselves, our service of Mystical Communion with Christ, is 'a beacon of Light on the Hill of the Lord', sending out the Light into wilderness

places to draw all who will near to the Lord. Also, our prayers and blessings for all in need, I have felt, should be a receiving of Papa's freely given love and blessing to us, amplified in our hearts and minds by our love for Him and for all His little ones, our desire for the Kingdom and His righteousness and justice for all, and sending out that amplified love and blessing to those for whom we pray.

As we focused on this during our morning time of attunement and Theresa said it was 'like a lighthouse', I suddenly *knew* that this was not just shining and reflecting light, but *amplifying* it. This is according, it all suddenly came in, to the same principle as the LASER; Light Amplification by Stimulated Emission of Radiation. This bounces, amplifies by stimulated emission of radiation, light inside a ruby (a jewel) until it bursts out, hugely powerful, focused and concentrated enough to cut through carbon steel.

Sir Oliver Lodge (the famous British physicist, 1851-1940), who I realised had come near and put this awareness into my mind, said, "*Much* more powerful than *that*; powerful enough to penetrate the darkest hell." He also said our Communion is 'The Light Factory'.

Then, at our Communion on August 31st I had the awareness that Oliver had brought in a giant, prototype laser, and people were crowding round to see it, with great excitement. It was about the size of a large car, or van. This event was atop Mount Moriah, the 'Hill of the Lord', the site of Solomon's Temple in Jerusalem. We were facing east, toward the River Jordan, the north end of the Dead Sea and beyond that, to the mountains east of the Jordan in which the Ammonites lived in Old Testament times. The Ammonites were descendants of Lot from an incestuously produced offspring, Ben-Ammi, with Lot's younger daughter. The Old Testament describes how these people were a frequent thorn in the flesh of the Jews.

It became clear that the objective was to fire the laser at the mountains in which the Ammonites live(d) and that it would disintegrate them (the mountains, not the Ammonites!). "*Every valley shall be exalted and the mountains and hills laid low*" (Isa. 40:4) came immediately to mind. Surely, by the laser of our *desire for the Kingdom of love, righteousness and justice,* the (self) exalted shall be abased and the (self) abased shall be exalted. Jesus said:

"Well discerned, my son. As you naturally observed and as I subsequently taught you, all creation is according to principles, and all operate at different levels of manifestation. You rightly observe that the power of spiritual truth is the *great leveller* and will bring all things and all people to the place where they belong. This is inevitable and inexorable. It is Almighty God, so nothing can resist it indefinitely, though many try. All opposition is, by nature, of time and place operation only, so *must* come to an end. Papa does not intervene because it is His law not to, but also because He does not need to. What He does do and what I do with Him, coincidently, is to outwork the Great Rescue Programme.

"Thus the little ones of Earth, with time and place perception, perceive the time and place operation, which is discord, disarray and destruction according to the disharmonious ray of the 'Prince of time and place'. 'He' dresses things up in masquerade costume and my little ones perceive glister and glamour. This achieves its objective of deception. But my Father works, and I work, for the eternal objective of life abundant and life everlasting, filled with joy, full measure, pressed down. The oil shall never expire and the bread shall feed all my Father's children. (See 1 Kings 17:14.)

"This is why I say, have no thought nor concern for the enemy's plan; it is of none-effect save deception and corruption. Focus rather upon Eternity; there shall all your visions be fulfilled. I am able; all is accomplished."

"The Lord whom ye seek shall suddenly come to His Temple. Be thou always ready to receive Him, rejoicing."

At the end of the dedication hymn, Papa said, "The Lord whom ye seek shall suddenly come to His Temple. Be thou always ready to receive Him, rejoicing."

Oliver fired the laser and I saw it strike the mountains where the Ammonites lived, and they disintegrated, the landscape being levelled to that of the surrounding plain. After a few minutes, during which the dust settled, I saw the Ammonites come streaming in multiple columns, like ants, toward the Jordan, heading for Jerusalem – the City of Peace – to ascend the Hill of the Lord.

As the multitude coming from east of Jordan gathered and increased in numbers I wondered how John the Baptist could cope, and he immediately said, "I have the help of angels and of men" and I instantly saw Ted acting as one of his helpers.

I realised that we become living, human lasers. Jesus has often spoken of us, and all committed to kingdomly work, as jewels, and so this fits the analogy perfectly. Papa shines his light into us; we receive it into ourselves, and by the earnestness of our burning desire for the Kingdom of Heaven on Earth, that light bounces around inside us, being amplified by the stimulation of our emitting this great desire in the form of the Living Word (as expressed in or by the words of the Communion Service), love, blessing and all kingdomly radiations, until it cannot be contained any longer, and bursts from us hugely amplified, powerful, focused and concentrated; *powerful enough to penetrate the darkest hell*. Truly, a 'light factory' for the Kingdom.

Here, on the Temple Mount, we were beaming out our laser Light toward the wilderness, and on this occasion (with the help of Oliver), especially east of the Jordan and the Dead Sea, at the dwelling place of the Ammonites. I heard the Archangel Gabriel call out from the heights of Heaven, *Let the sons of Ammon join the throng and enter in*. Alleluia!

It is important in this parable-in-action to be aware of the importance of the symbolism involved, and its meaning. For example, if one takes the purpose of God in Israel as being the positive side of the polarity (PP) and those who are opposing it as the negative side of the polarity (NP), one can then readily see why the laser was directed at the Ammonites (NP), who were constantly having a go at the Israelites (PP). In this parable, we, with Oliver Lodge, were located at the epicentre of the PP, being on the Temple Mount in the City of Peace, Jerusalem, the focal point of the purpose of the Israel people in the Great Rescue Programme. The laser represents the Light of that purpose, amplified by the stimulating power of our desire for the Kingdom on Earth, and fired – emitted, not in anger but in agapé Love – at the NP. That amplified, stimulated Light of kingdomly Love, strategically emitted and radiated toward the 'power-base' of the NP clearly exerted a transforming energy on the negative polarity, causing a turn-around and an attraction of its proponents, drawing them toward the positive polarity Light/Love source, into which they are openly welcomed.

This is truly a parable in action of how the Kingdom of Heaven is being and will be created and manifested on Earth: by the transforming power of agapé Love on all the negative polarity energies and activities that are present and pervasive in today's world. Those negative polarities are not either side of a geographical, political or ideological divide; they are in our very own hearts and minds, manifesting themselves as fear, jealousy, greed, judgemental attitudes, grievances, separation consciousness (holding the illusion of the 'them and us' perception of our fellows and all other aspects of time and place). In other words, the works of 'the enemy': ego.

We are at freedom to choose, at any and every moment, to change those negative polarities into positive polarities by the transforming power of Love, true forgiveness and blessing. That may be difficult at first, if we have held negative attitudes or feelings toward another, perhaps for some hurt or slight, whether intentional or otherwise, but it becomes possible and easier if we are willing to make the commitment to true forgiveness and keep choosing that commitment to transforming NPs into PPs.

I said to the Master, "Beloved Lord Jesus, the Glory of all this is yours, according to the prophecies of the long ago."

"My son, the Glory is Papa's, and we all are illuminated and radiate His light according to our desire for His good and perfect Will, and our attunement with Him by FTOC (Faith, Trust, Obedience * and Commitment). He gives us, freely, lovingly, the *gift* of His Glory and so, in that sense, it is mine, as it is yours also, according to His eternal principles.

"Let neither false humility cloud the reality, for nothing can progress in such due to loss of sight of the Path (home to Eternity), nor let pride (ego) overtake you, for of yourself none of these things can be. I tell you truly therefore, let *true* humility and thanksgiving be in your heart, for Papa loves you so, and it is His great, good desire and pleasure to bestow upon you more wondrous and awesome *gifts* than you can receive or comprehend at this time.

"However, be thou faithful, as you have been faithful, and

keep on in this way, and He shall reveal to you, as He grows you in your ability to receive, all that He has in store for you. And this is His plan for all His children. I tell you, my son, this is what you shall reveal to all your brethren, even as I reveal it to you, because it is your heart's desire. Did I not promise you that in you would be fulfilled your heart's desire? I know you do not doubt the word of your Lord, for I am your beloved friend also! Joy of Heaven be yours, now and eternally."

---

* This means obedience to our own, inner Self, shining the Light of eternal truth into our mind.

22. Jim, Ship's Doctor

One of the Inner Plane servers who watched lovingly and caringly over Olga was, according to her description of him, a ship's doctor in the days of wooden sailing ships. In fact we believe he served with Admiral Lord Nelson at the Battle of Trafalgar in 1805. He was, so said Olga, Scottish and she usually referred to him, when speaking of him to Theresa and me, as *the Scottish Doctor* or *the Ship's Doctor*. He would say to her if she was trying to rush at getting something done, *One step at a time, Lassie,* or, *Tak' it easy, Lassie,* in his lilting Scottish brogue. We now have come to know that his name is Hamish (Scottish form of James), though he is most often referred to as Jim.

After we returned to England and our lives here continued to unfold and progress spiritually as well as materially, we had occasional awarenesses of him, with his famous catchphrases. Although he is clearly an unassuming soul who, by natural inclination, speaks fewer words rather than more, he is utterly genuine and sincere, with a total commitment for Jesus and the Kingdom of Heaven on Earth.

Various encounters we have had with him tell of his steadfastness and readiness to help anyone in distress.

One, in 1994, was when my brother Mike, Theresa and I had taken Pop, who was in a residential care home for the elderly (Ma had laid aside her body not long previously), for a pint and some lunch at a hostelry near Pop's care-home. As we sat there enjoying our drink and good familial fellowship, Mike suddenly let out a yell and grabbed his foot, clearly in agony. We asked what was the matter, and between gasps of pain he told us that occasionally his big toe suddenly dislocated, for no apparent reason; that often it would take him considerable time to get it back in joint and other times it went back in with little difficulty.

He was in great distress and we all looked on, feeling helpless. Then I thought about Jim and, silently in my head called out to him, asking his help for Mike. In a flash he was there. This was only the second time I had seen him, although I had been aware of his presence and heard him speaking his admonitions to *Tak' it easy* or *One step at a time, Laddie* on numerous previous occasions. He showed himself as he no doubt would have been in his earthly life. He looked about mid forties, bald on top with a rim of short, grey hair round the back and sides, wore circular-lens steel-rimmed glasses, was about five feet six inches tall and of a wiry build. He had a black leather doctor's bag with him.

He quickly got down on one knee on the floor in front of Mike and took his foot in his hand. Mike, meantime, was in excruciating pain, not daring to move for it, and had no idea that he was receiving skilled medical assistance at that very moment! I could see Jim gingerly feeling Mike's foot and toe for a few moments, then manipulating it deftly. Suddenly, Mike let out another yell, swiftly followed by "Ooh! That's better!"

"What's happened?" I asked him.

"It's gone back in suddenly," he said, quite astonished. "It usually takes a lot longer than that."

I said nothing to Mike about Jim because Mike is not outwardly a believer in the realms of life beyond this one, but acknowledging Jim, I silently said to him as he stood up and picked up his black bag, "Thank you for your help Jim; God bless you". As he turned to walk away he inclined his head toward me in acknowledgement of my thanks, grinned broadly and was gone. There have been no further dislocations since.

On another encounter with him, Theresa and I had arranged a dinner engagement with Steve and Sara, who was to become Steve's wife in a few months. The venue was a country pub about twenty minutes' drive from Gloucester.

We arrived about 7:00 p.m. and saw Steve and Sara through the window as we walked toward the entrance. However, no sooner had we got inside than they – who are both qualified hospital nurses – went rushing out! As they went by they hurriedly explained that they had heard from another person who had just arrived at the pub that there had been a terrible car crash a few hundred yards down the country road and they were going to see if there was anything they could do to help before the ambulance arrived. They said, "Wait here and we'll be back – whenever!"

> *"The blessing force began to emerge from us and quick as*
> *lightning Jim grabbed it and was gone, straight out*
> *through the wall – which was at least two feet thick!"*

We got a drink and sat at the table wondering how bad the accident was. Suddenly I became aware of Jim standing near our table, looking agitated, black bag in hand. I wondered what he was doing and why he was waiting here when his help could have been used down the road. Then it dawned upon me what he was after. He was seeking our love and blessing, our heartfelt outpouring of help, for those hurt in the accident. This engenders an emission of ectoplasm, or psychic life force that is part way between physical and spirit substance. I told Theresa what was happening and together we silently and earnestly prayed for the souls in the accident, blessing them and committing them into the care of the Almighty. As we did this, I saw the blessing force begin to emerge from us, and quick as lightning Jim grabbed it and was gone, straight out through the wall – which was at least two feet thick! I could see the blessing force going from us through the wall, like a white, spirit-substance rope, with Jim at one end and us at the other. This acted as a line of blessing-power between us and Jim, who would be able to call upon it as he worked with the injured at the accident.

What a joy it was that we were able to help in such a palpable way, even though we had no medical training, and never even left the pub! No wonder Scripture exhorts us so frequently to bless and curse not, for blessing is a healing, renewing, constructive, life-affirming energy, and cursing is a destructive, dishonouring energy.

At Communion a day or two later Jim came in and said:

"Brian, my friend, you have been aware of my presence twice now, these last few days. My desire for the Lord's perfect plan and wisdom to be outworked in the Earth is unflinching, although you have perhaps thought of me more as a pragmatist. This is, of course, true and I am one for getting on with the task at hand and then moving on to whatever next can use some assistance.

But I see also that this is the *modus operandi* of our Lord Jesus and my respect, admiration, commitment to and love for him is equal to any. Indeed, all who know him – and it is a great and joyful blessing – cannot help but love him with a great and abiding love.

"So, I bring to you this greeting of joy and fellowship in his blessed name. Any time you need help with matters to do with health, for yourself or any other soul, send out a prayer of commitment to the Master and think of me. I will be there in a trice, even as you have seen. Never doubt that it is in the Master's name and by his authority that I come; for my commitment is absolute and total. I have seen your commitment and the desire of your heart, and believe me, this conviction is a great influence for the going forward to similar commitment in the hearts and lives of sincere seekers this side of the 'veil'.

"For they can see the radiating energy of your aura, and it attracts souls of a sincere and honourable disposition. In fact many who would not have thought themselves such have discovered it within after coming close in Communion, or at other times, attracted by the light and uplifting power created by your desire and sincerity. It was ever thus with your beloved godmother, Olga, years ago, and I know the impact she made on you. Was it not her sincerity and commitment which drew you again and again? And so is it with all who desire Truth.

"Normally I am a man of few words, but a kindred spirit draws openness from even us more circumspect souls. So, God bless you, you band of troops for the Lord. Keep on keeping on, one step at a time. You are greatly loved, blessed and watched over. And I am never more than a cry for help away. In Jesus' name I am your friend and helper."

23. Exorcising Possessing Spirits

One weekend in 1999, while Theresa was away on a weekend course on Healing Ministry at the Christian Healing Centre, someone well known to us for many years (no names will be mentioned here to respect privacy) who had been travelling, came to stay at our house. This person knew about our Communion practice, albeit not in much detail. On the Sunday morning, she was in a highly agitated state and asked if she could attend the service with me. I was not eager for this because she would be coming to it 'cold' in the sense that there would be no time to explain, in sufficient depth, the background to it. She would be unfamiliar with the procedure and this would not be helpful to her or the vibrations of the service. Further, because I knew she was psychic and surrounded by a lot of negative psychic energy, I felt very uneasy about her involvement.

Nevertheless, she was in such a distressed state and had such an obvious desire, verging on desperation, for spiritual support and fellowship that I felt great compassion for her and remained with her, talking for several hours about kingdomly matters and her problems. She eventually asked if we could pray together.

We prayed for some time and after a while she said to me, "I feel as if there is something stuck in my gullet. I feel as if I want to vomit it up and get rid of it, but it seems to be resisting." She was greatly agitated, like someone who is violently ill and about to throw up. I got a bowl for her and she sat there retching for a few minutes, but nothing came out. She then told me that she felt that what was there and resisting coming out was a possessing spirit. I already realised this because I had seen the symptoms before and they were well represented in the film *The Exorcist*. However, I felt strongly that it was not for me to tell her that this is what I believed because, if she was not ready to hear what for most people would be such a shocking and frightening thing, it could distress her very much more and perhaps cause some even deeper emotional difficulties. Having *her* tell *me* that she believed this is what it was, however, created the opportunity to proceed with an exorcism without causing her panic (any more than might have already been the case!).

I held up a Bible and began to command this spirit in the name and by the authority of Jesus Christ of Nazareth to come out of her and to go to the place prepared for him, and never to return to her. There was a great choking, growling, gurgling, sub-human noise, augmented by the characteristic sounds of a person retching, emanating from her throat. She told me between gasps for air that it felt as if there was something stuck in her solar plexus that was triangular-shaped. I prayed more and repeated the command, in the most authoritative tone I could muster, for him to come out of her, in the name of Jesus Christ of Nazareth. Then, amidst much choking and retching and clasping at her throat, there was a rushing sound and the throwing up of sputum into the bowl, followed by a great calm and a return very quickly to normal colour. There was no doubt in my mind that the possessing spirit had been ejected.

We sat there giving thanks and discussing this for a while, but gradually she began to get distressed again. She told me she felt as if there was another possessing spirit welling-up in her and that she wanted to expel it, but it was, as before, resisting. I took the Bible in my hand again and spoke to this second spirit, telling it that her body was sacred to her exclusively and that he had no right to take habitation of it surreptitiously and without permission; that he belonged elsewhere and that again, in the name and by the authority of Jesus Christ of Nazareth, which he was powerless to resist, I commanded him to come out of her. The same process of retching and growling and choking took place and shortly, this second spirit came out.

Again we sat there giving thanks and rejoicing at the power and authority of Jesus' name and that this was a great purging of her; that she could now go forward freely in spiritual growth, released from such insidious interference. But this was once more to be short-lived because the presence of yet a third inhabiting spirit soon began to rise to the surface of her awareness, just as had been the case with the previous two. I began to wonder if this was going to become a 'Legion' experience, like Jesus' exorcising of the man at Gadara: "*And Jesus asked* (the spirit), *saying, What is thy name? And he said, Legion: because many devils were entered into him* (the Gadarene) (Lk. 8:17).

We went through the same process a third time and the third spirit came out in like manner. A third time we gave thanks and blessed the departing spirit as we sent it on its way.

That seemed to be all there were in the offing and so we carried on with our spiritual fellowship, and after lunch Theresa arrived back. We shared the news with her and all of us rejoiced and celebrated again at the exorcising and the release it had brought. But then, with Theresa present, lo and behold, there was yet *another* earthbound soul rising to the surface from somewhere deep within her. I thought, with Theresa here adding power and light to the mix this should be much easier to exorcise but in fact it was much harder, took much longer and was a real struggle. Nevertheless, following the procedure described above but with the additional presence of Theresa, this soul finally was ejected. Much further rejoicing and thanksgiving ensued, but again that was short-lived because there was still a fifth presence in our guest! This time a real tug of war began and we were a whisker from success, but eventually this soul refused to come out of her. There were all the noises and gurgling – louder and more violent than the other four – and in spite of invoking the name, power and authority of Jesus, he hung on and remained in place.

So, Theresa, inspired, stood over our guest with Bible aloft and prayed that this soul be *bound* within her and held powerless until more resources could be engaged in the exorcising, at a later date. It seemed clear to me that the four who had been removed were, in order of ejection, easiest first, and each being harder to remove until this last soul. I had the impression that he was the ringleader.

It is worth considering the words of Jesus on this matter:

When the unclean spirit is gone out of a man, he walketh through dry (i.e., desert, or wilderness) places, seeking rest, and findeth none. Then he saith, I will return into my house from whence I came out; and when he is come, he findeth it empty, swept, and garnished. Then goeth he, and taketh with himself seven other spirits more wicked than himself, and they enter in and dwell there: and the last state of that man is worse than the first. Even so shall it be also unto this wicked generation (Mt. 12:43-45).

The inference that can be drawn from this is that we will do well to be aware of the process and guard ourselves against such *re*-possession by earthbound ('unclean') spirits. How, one may enquire, can one do this? The answer is that like attracts like, and life is a matter of vibrations or frequencies or wavelengths. If one is on the wavelength of iniquity and intemperance, * that signal will involuntarily and unwittingly be transmitted out into the ether, and iniquity and intemperance will be attracted. The person emitting such signals may not be aware that a spirit stuck on such a wavelength has arrived in response to the signals he has sent out – indeed, most souls possessed by an 'unclean' or earthbound spirit have no conscious awareness that they are possessed. The phenomenon of possession was not restricted to New Testament times; it is massively widespread today and is a significant contributor to such social and medical malaises as road rage, drug abuse, schizophrenia, multiple personality disorder and all sorts of emotional, mental and physical conditions.

This is possible because the society we have collectively created over centuries, grossly influenced and impacted by religious persuasion that we are all 'sinners, *there is no health in us* (actual words from the Anglican Church's Book of Common Prayer, Morning Service), unworthy, destined for eternal hellfire', etc., has significantly contributed to a calamitously low level of self-esteem and self-worth; a calumny of catastrophic proportions. It is only by a mass transformation of self-perception by mankind back to the awareness that we are *all* citizens of Eternity, created by the Creator in His likeness; His beloved Son; God incarnate, capable of manifesting magnificence to unlimited potential; the light of the world, (all things we are told by Holy Scripture but conveniently ignored by religious teachers, who would be out of a job if they told the truth); that vast multitudes of incarnate souls can create, each one for himself, not only a 'house that is empty, swept and garnished' but a house into which no earthbound spirit, stuck on a wavelength of iniquity and intemperance will be attracted.

And, blessedly and ultimately, when we have collectively (albeit, individually) achieved such a mass transformation (by the help and drawing power of the overshadowing spirit of the Holy One), there will be so many incarnate souls aware of the etheric realms to which we are so closely and inextricably linked, with a truly enlightened attitude toward our fellows (like Hugh Dowding), that any souls left in despair and darkness in the etheric realms will be helped, released from their fear and mistaken perceptions, just as was Rachel, the Dutch Jewess in 1969, and find themselves instantly transported, and, indeed, transformed, into the Realms of Light where we all, of course, truly belong, because we *are* the Light.

"The emanations of love for all creation from such souls will be picked up by the other creatures that share our temporary, illusory home – Earth – and they will lose their conditioned fear of mankind"

Love, blessing, goodwill, doing unto others as we would be done by (the Golden Rule that Jesus emphasised) will send out such vibrations into the ether and will assuredly attract like vibrations back, both in the form of other souls of like desire and commitment, and simply positive and uplifting energies and events. Rather than such attracted souls and energies being a curse, they will be a blessed enrichment of one's life and wellbeing, just as all our loved ones in spirit, with whom Theresa and I have enjoyed such wondrous intercourse, have been in our lives. The emanations of love for all creation from such souls will be picked up by the other life-forms that share our present, temporary, illusory home – Earth – and they will lose their conditioned fear of mankind, and will no longer run or fly away when a human appears, because there will no longer be anything to fear. This will not happen overnight but it *will* happen, gradually. It is *already* happening for those who are at – or are consciously choosing to move into – that place of enlightenment, here, in the Earth-life, now.

Such enlightened souls visiting from spirit will never take possession of an incarnate soul's body without permission, other than in a situation of dire emergency, and then only for good, altruistic things to be accomplished. A classic example of this was the case when a man accidentally ran over a child who dashed in front of his car. He made an emergency stop but the vehicle came to rest with the rear wheels on the child's body. The driver was so deeply shocked that he literally froze and remained rigid, his hands clenching the steering wheel immovably and his foot pressed hard on the brake pedal. A passing nurse (female) saw this happen and when she could not get the deeply shocked driver to move the car, she went to the back and single-handedly lifted up the rear of the car by the bumper so that other passers-by arriving at the scene could remove the badly injured but still living boy from under the wheels. Clearly, there are very few men who could do this, let alone women. Assuredly, she 'found' super-human strength because she was helped from spirit by loving, caring, kingdomly souls.

Had the passerby been someone on the wavelength of iniquity and intemperance there would have been little inclination by such a one to help, and any spirit entities close to that wavelength would be similarly disinclined. This event is a real experience, fully documented and witnessed by many non-collaborating observers. There are countless others displaying the same process in multifarious circumstances.

As with all things, we are always at free choice about whether we attune to the light, love, goodwill, the positive end of the spectrum of life, or to darkness, fear, self-centredness, the negative, ego end of the spectrum of time and place. Jesus has said to me many times over the decades since the 1960s, "*Espouse good, eschew evil.*" Such counsel is highly serviceable to us all if we desire a life filled with love, peace, joy, altruism, good health and freedom from fear.

Theresa, our guest and I sat talking of matters spiritual and discussing how this possession might have taken place. As we prayed about this and our visitor became more at peace within herself again she began to cast her mind back to childhood. There had been many dark activities involving so-called 'friends' of her parents, and she began to recall one such man who had engaged her – aged no more than eight – in paedophilic activities. It was all very distressing.

Later she went to the Christian Healing Centre where exorcism is a well-established practice, and this possessing spirit was finally removed. They had talked to this soul and enquired of his name. He said he was Basil and that our visitor 'belonged' to him because, during the paedophile incidents which had occurred with him when she was eight he had claimed her as his possession. The Healing Centre counsellors explained to him how inappropriate this perception was and this helped in enabling them to cast him out. Clearly this was why we had not found it possible to expel Basil at our home; he felt the body of the little eight-year old girl he had abused all those years ago *belonged to him*, so why should he give up what was 'rightfully' his now? When it was explained to him that this was a mistaken perception, he was more amenable to departing.

What this – along with all the other experiences of possession I have encountered over the years – tells me is that there is no such thing as an 'evil spirit', or a 'demon'. Rather, there are souls who have departed this life in various states of unawareness or forgetfulness about who they really are, which is the pinnacle of God's creative glory – His beloved Son – created in His likeness, who have forgotten this during one (or more) sojourn in time, and become misled, mistaken about many of the truths and Principles of Life of the Father; become deeply lost in the spiritual wilderness – like the rest of us to a greater or lesser degree – and unable to find the way out.

"The more people wander, looking for a way out, the deeper they get into the wilderness and the more they become lost."

As with most people lost in the wilderness, the more they wander, looking for a way out, the deeper they get into the wilderness and the more they become lost. And, of course, in a world where there is no light of spiritual discernment or leadership from church or state, there are plenty who will give false directions along the way of their meanderings. So, they come to the point where their vehicle of expression at the physical level – their body – is worn out and they leave it behind, or they are separated from it by getting killed. They find themselves in a place where they are bewildered about their true estate and wander about the etheric envelope of the Earth, in the lower astral planes.

Those who, in their earthly lives, have been caught up in

addictions to such things as pornography, paedophilia, alcohol, cocaine, gambling etc. – iniquity and intemperance – are not magically released from such by the act of departing from their earthly bodies. They no longer have a 'vehicle' through which to find temporary gratification for their lusts and addictions, so in their wanderings in the lower astral plane wilderness they come upon souls still incarnate but whose psychic door is open, enabling them to latch-on to such hapless, incarnate souls. In most instances such 'latchees' are completely unaware that this has taken place. They will find themselves being drawn into a state of consciousness, and what the church calls 'sins of the flesh', resonant with the possessing spirit because that is the state of consciousness of the interloper, who is overshadowing the psyche of the possessed person in order to find vicarious satiation of his unenlightened desires.

There will be some sort of affinity between the possessor and the possessed before possession takes place and it is that resonance which draws the would-be possessor to the unwitting possessee. It may not necessarily be that the possessee is consciously afflicted with the same addiction(s) but to use the example of child molesting, you might have the molester, let us call him character *A* and the child who is molested, character *B*.

The two characters might be of the same gender, as with pederasty, or of opposite genders. So *A* has been a molester for much of his life and then 'died', remaining in his lustful desires after his demise. Then, character *B* is a soul who has been molested in childhood, perhaps multiple times, perhaps by the same molester – even a parent. *B* has grown up utterly bereft of self worth, believing – wrongly – that he was at fault in the molestation events of his childhood, feeling morbid, haunting, overwhelming guilt and shame for the dreadful experiences and being unable to tell anyone – due to a deep (but misplaced) sense of shame and guilt – of this awful burden.

The psyche of *B* will be – invisibly to his Earth-sense perceptions and those of others around him – radiating energy on that frequency out into the ether around himself. He has no conscious awareness that this is what he is doing, but it is happening all the same. *A*, meanwhile, wandering, lost in the lower astral planes, still clasped in the vise of his self-allowed

lusts and obsessions, will be drawn to the vibrations emitted by
B, like a vulture drawn from miles away to the emanations of a
corpse, or a shark to a drop of blood in the water, from similar
distances.

The very last thing B believes he wants is the attentions of
another molester. He believes, in his Earth-mind perceptions, that
at least all that is behind him physically, even if the terrible guilt
and shame continue to plague his every moment. In that sense
B is also *ob*sessed and it is this condition that is transmitting its
signal out into the cosmos and has attracted discarnate A to him,
resulting in possession.

Of course this becomes a self-perpetuating cycle, from
generation to generation. It can be broken by first desiring it to
be so, then by understanding the process, and then by having
the insight into how to break it. Remembering who we really are,
and reclaiming our spiritual empowerment through that process
of remembering, will make this possible. Meanwhile, placing our
lives within the loving, *trustworthy* protection of another who
has remembered who he is – Jesus of Nazareth is the most loving
and trustworthy such, and his credentials are impeccable – and is
thus spiritually empowered to help others, will be immeasurably
helpful.

It should be borne in mind that such empowered souls will
never give that help except in response to a genuine and sincere
desire, and *asking* for it. So, if a soul obsessed by lusts which
cause him to feel ill-at-ease with himself ('unclean') asks for and
receives help from such a Being of the Light and then chooses
to return to his obsessive condition, the Enlightened One will
allow him the freedom to so return. The Enlightened One has *not*
abandoned him. He has, of his own free will, left the protective
help of the Enlightened One. At such time as he chooses to return
to the protective help, the Enlightened One will still be there and
his help will still be available. That is what Unconditional Love
means – *unconditional*. It is as Jesus reminds us, to forgive our
fellows seventy times seven.

---

* *The Reader's Digest Wordpower Dictionary* defines 'intemperate' as: "Lacking self-
control characterised by excessive indulgence, especially (but not exclusively) in
alcohol." It is this broad definition that is intended here.

24. Religious Misperceptions of Duty

Many institutionalised religions inculcate a sense of 'duty' toward their religious sect into the minds of their followers. This can be an entrapment of those who feel a sense of religious commitment toward the God of their belief system, but if Love – unconditional, *Perfect* Love – is not the central, overriding factor in our motivation toward any sense of commitment or duty, then following such a path will become the slippery slope to spiritual darkness.

"Religious institutions that remain espoused to the separation consciousness, and insist that their followers adhere to that misperception, will wither and die"

If religious fervour is not motivated by love, blessing, peace, goodwill, heartfelt joy, a willingness to accept and honour the differences of other races, cultures and belief systems, an awareness that in the sight of the Creator Spirit we are all One – created in His likeness – then we will end up being deceived into a state of 'separation consciousness', or the misperception that we are *not* all One.

Religious institutions that remain espoused to the separation consciousness, and insist that their followers adhere to that misperception, will wither and die as we now move into the time when the Creator Spirit draws the hearts, minds and souls of the Created (humankind; the fragmented, one Son of God, appearing as many in time and place) ever forward and upward toward true and full, complete awareness, or realisation, of Self. Such revelations are from and through the Living Spirit *within* us, not from institutionalised structures, and will be personal to each who truly seeks and earnestly desires. As stated in the book of Joel: *"And it shall come to pass afterward, that I will pour out my spirit upon all flesh; and your sons and your daughters shall prophesy, your old men shall dream dreams, your young men shall see visions: And also upon the servants and upon the handmaids in those days will I pour out my spirit"* (Joel 2: 28,29).

We are now, as we move deeper into the third millennium CE, in the time of fulfilment of Joel's prophecy twenty-two centuries ago. We are free to choose to be part of it and grow with it, become spiritually enlightened by it ('it' being the outpouring of God's spirit). Or we can remain static within the strictures of religious structures that adhere to rules, regulations, doctrines and dogmas set out three thousand four hundred years ago (by Moses), nineteen centuries ago (by Paul), sixteen centuries ago (Council of Nicæa), fifteen centuries ago (Council of Constantinople), and five centuries ago (Council of Trent) – to name but a few of many such convocations.

Each of these, having been led by egoic control motivation, rather than the Spirit of Truth, distorted, removed and separated various aspects of the actual message of Jesus, replacing it with their own agendas and doctrines, which had no foundation in commitment to be inspired and led by the Light of spiritual discernment. But whatever our individual choice, it will make no difference to the outworking and fulfilment of that prophecy for humanity, which goes forward cosmically, unfolding from the within into the without, just as does all life in the physical universe.

Like a travelator, those who are on it will arrive at their destination with it, less fatigued, stressed, and more relaxed and comfortable. Those who choose not to be 'aboard' it and therefore not travelling with it, will still arrive, but more fatigued and by a more circuitous, less comfortable route. They will inevitably arrive because they are being drawn by the Spirit of the Holy One, in Whose likeness they are created, however vigorously their upside-down, ego-contorted mind may scream to the contrary. Ego is only of time and place; the Son of God is of Eternity, just like His Father.

293

25. The Gathering of the Clans

During a Communion Service in August 1992, we were, in the dual consciousness, on Mount Moriah again, looking down across the Jordan Valley. Millions of fragments of the Sonship, from all races, colours and creeds were streaming toward the Hill of the Lord, where we were in the presence of individuals who seemed to symbolise spiritual, or some other form of natural leadership of each respective group, or race. The Diary entry for this date describes the event:

Holy Communion, August 23, 1992:
Representatives of all the races have been here, drawn by the Light, and have joined in with the spirit of life and joy and upliftment that this Service brings. At the offering, the Life of the Father in the bread and wine radiated out to and through these peoples, stretching out and away into the distance behind them, as far as the eye could see. There were countless millions of souls.

The Jewish religious leaders have gone forward * somewhat; Chief Sitting Bull said a loud 'Amen' at the asking of the Lord's continual help that we may be faithful stewards. This was met with *much* enthusiasm from the Inner Plane Servers. Jack and Bobby Kennedy stood to one side, to my right, observing all these proceedings, and I heard Jack whisper to Bobby, 'This is what I have been praying for.'

Winston Churchill was also there, along with Martin Luther King and many other leaders of different races and groups of peoples. At the offering of the wine, Mohandas (Mahatma) Gandhi came in. He is a *great* light, effulgent as the sun, and his power and love filled me to overflowing. He stood facing me, smiling a smile of indescribable, ineffable, rapturous joy and with great happiness at what is taking place. He was inches away from me and he stretched out his arms and touched his fingertips to mine. The surge of spiritual power – which is love, joy, peace and wisdom of Eternity – that flowed from his fingertips into mine and through me, was immense, *overwhelming*, as if I had been plugged into the National Grid. I will never forget the radiant, uplifting power, beauty and glory of his smile.

I said, "Beloved Teacher, this is indeed a universal wayside altar for all travellers to seek light, truth, peace, reconciliation, renewal and all the good gifts of the Father."

---

*"there is no difference in the soul of man; all are one,
brothers and sisters in Christ Jesus our Lord,
and children of one Father Creator."*

He replied: "Brian, give freely to all who are drawn – there is no difference in the soul of man; all are one, brothers and sisters in Christ Jesus our Lord, and children of one Father Creator. All are here in the Earth conditions that they may come into oneness together in full and joyful brotherhood, and go forward to the House of the Eternal Father. This is the beginning.

"You also have gone forward this day. It is necessary for each one of you Earth-life servers and officiants of this Sanctuary to come to the place of spiritual growth whereby the desire of your hearts is that this, the Father's Will, be done in the lives of all the children of Earth. Thus it is the spirit of your own awakened desire-thought and conscious awareness of His programme for His little ones that leads the Service ritual.

"I am your appointed helper to guide you to that place, but ultimately the crown of authority and fulfilment shall be for each and all of you. This is my glory and fulfilment – that it be so for you all. For this reason has the ritual Communion Service been devised and for this reason have you been chosen to serve. As your heart's desire grows and awakens and strengthens, and your one-pointed commitment becomes united, so do we all become united in the fulfilling of our individual path of service by Jesus Christ, Lord of all mankind. We shall manifestly become brothers, equal in stature and Sonship.

"Meanwhile you progress as officiant and the reins † are gradually given into your hands. Have no fear; all is according to cosmic law and can only be according to the Will and Way of the Father.

"Peace and joy be yours, that you may give freely to all who will receive of this precious gift of the Father. This is the path to eternal Life."

At the time of this event we had little or no awareness of how this was becoming manifest in the Earth, but now, as I write this comment, nineteen years later, the signs of it are everywhere, and growing in strength, power, *certainty* of becoming the established order for life – the Kingdom of Heaven on Earth – even though ego still *appears* to hold sway in so many arenas of life. Assuredly, the Great Rescue Programme is taking hold in time and place, providing encouragement – for all who truly seek and earnestly desire the Kingdom – that the whole is, now *discernibly*, leavening.

---

* This refers to recent awareness of a group of orthodox, Mosaic tradition, Jewish religious leaders who were focused upon their traditional doctrinal procedures. They suddenly became aware of us and our Service. They observed but were stuck in their perceptions and not willing to receive the Light that was emanating from the Mystical Christ Communion. Nevertheless, it was evident that it made an impact upon them and they no doubt had been pondering this and returned for further 'inspection'.

† Reins are symbols of empowerment, authority and control over life energies.

26. Tyndale the Translator

During the early 1990s I became interested in William Tyndale, born around 1494 in Gloucestershire. He was the first to translate the Bible into English from the original Greek and Hebrew. He was murdered by the Roman Catholic Church, by papal decree, for so doing. In spite of the endeavours to suppress his work, it survived.

"I made a huge, spontaneous, involuntary intake of breath and shuddered as Will came close and overshadowed me with his presence."

A modern printing of his translation had recently come available, and I was given a copy of the *Tyndale New Testament* for Christmas 1993. On Christmas Day, as I removed the wrapping paper and saw what it was, I made a huge, spontaneous, involuntary intake of breath and shuddered as Will (as I came to know him) came close and overshadowed me with his presence. There was great power, commitment, humility, wisdom and love in his vibration. At our first Communion after that, January 2nd 1994, I was immediately aware of his presence. The exchange between us is shown below as the Diary entry for that date.

Holy Communion January 2, 1994:
I said, "Dear William Tyndale, your New Testament translation has got me excited, and the Christmas Day experience has brought me the realisation that you are close, to help with inspiration on the Living Word. I see from your writing that you are of unquestionable sincerity in your commitment to our beloved Jesus, Spiritual Lord and Master of this planet. If you are able and willing to speak on this in his name and by his authority, I shall be overjoyed."

Will responded, "Dear Brian, fellow servant of Jesus Christ, I also perceive your sincerity and commitment and this, dear friend, I assure you, attracts many souls who desire something more than pleasantness. It does also, of course, attract many souls (this service ritual of Christ commitment and communion) who are in dark and dreadful places. It is a power base in the Earth-life wherein those from on high and those in need of uplift who are ready to go forward can be brought together in a place and condition of harmonising of the life energies.

"Because this is a good and desirable thing and is clearly a part of our Lord's great and wonderful plan for the world, its progress and influence is needful of expansion. This can be accomplished by continuing growth of the Living Word in the fructifying soil of your conscious, dedicated life. I have been asked – and it is my desire also – to be an agent for expansion of the Truth in Scripture in your life, so that this that you do can continue to grow in serviceableness unto the Lord, our beloved Jesus. I see also that your mind and mine do harmonise well, for you also see the importance of language and structure for building new understanding.

"So, I hereby make myself available for service in the name and by the authorising of our blessed Jesus Christ, who I do see is much beloved of you, as also of me. For I, along with many others, having been drawn by the light and joy of this ritual, have been observing its process for a goodly while.

"And I will, while you are engaged in prayerful study and contemplation of the Living Word, if you accept my presence, bring such thoughts and inspiration as are serviceable and appropriate to illuminate your discernment, for the greater understanding. Thus shall all benefit by the going forward of that which we do in Christ's blessed name."

"Dear Will, I welcome you most warmly and enthusiastically into this new and inspiring experience and relationship. I thank you humbly for your commitment, and look forward to many uplifting and rewarding revelations that will be serviceable to the Lord and his purpose in our working together. God bless you and reward you richly."

"Thank you, sir, for your blessing; my reward is rich indeed in fellowship of Christ service, for this is all I desire. I see this is your desire also and do give you my blessing in the name of God our Father, Jesus Christ his beloved Son and also the Holy Spirit, the Comforter."

It is clear now, eighteen years on, that Will has indeed been very close – even though my conscious awareness of him has been limited – because the understanding of many Old and New Testament scriptures have become clear during that interval, and still are becoming today, of which I had previously little or no illumination.

Another way I have of knowing his close proximity is how often a particular quote from the Bible will suddenly be presented in my thoughts during various writing activities which is entirely apposite to the subject matter, and adds substantially to the meaning and value of that writing.

A few weeks after this initial encounter with Will I was speaking on the phone with our friend Pauline, who lived with her husband, Bob, in British Columbia, and telling her of the event. She said, "Bob told me a few minutes before you called that he has just finished reading an article about William Tyndale in the *Anglican Journal*, which is the newspaper of the Anglican Church of Canada. I will cut it out and send it to you." Here is another example of how our loved ones in the Realms of Light can organise these wonderful synchronicities, to demonstrate how closely, lovingly, purposefully we are watched over and guided in the outworking of our birth vision.

27. Jesus in Bedrock Hell Fastening the Escape Ladder to the Floor

This wondrous experience/event can best be described by copying the record of it from two successive Communion Services in early 1997.

Holy Communion February 16, 1997:
At the beginning I saw a ladder/stairway stretching from highest Heaven to darkest, deepest hell. It disappeared out of vision into the light above and the darkness below. Our Communion Sanctuary was like a 'staging post' about halfway up the ladder. I felt as if the words concerning the Lord's eternalness and His great God-mission for all mankind were being broadcast down to all levels and we were an amplifying/relaying station, via what we do and our commitment, into the depths below.

"I could see him and what he was doing because he was radiating light from his own within."

Later I saw the Master, at 'bedrock' of Hades (after his death on the cross and descent into hell). He had his right knee on the ground and the other knee up by his shoulder, in the absolute darkness of this place. I could see him and what he was doing because he was radiating light from his own within. He looked just as he would have looked as the Galilean carpenter in the long ago. There was no indication of any effects from the brutal torture and execution he had just experienced. He was securely fastening the base of the stairway to a solid, black-as-coal rock floor with large nuts threaded on to sturdy studs set into the floor. It was clear that this fastening was intended to *stay*, and would be immovable by an enemy once he had completed his task. It was also clear that this man knew exactly what he was doing and was working with the ease and accomplishment of great experience in his trade.

He looked up at me standing close by watching him in amazement, smiled quizzically as if to say, 'Why are you looking puzzled to see me doing this?' and then *actually* said, "I was a carpenter!"

"Master, I love you and I rejoice at this revelation."

"My son, my friend, your heart's desire is known to me. I am aware of your deep desire to serve in rescue work. Yes, this is according to my parables of the lost sheep and invitation to the halt, maimed and blind – for *all* who will to be invited into the wedding banquet for a feast of joy for all the senses. And he who follows me shall not walk in darkness.

"I had to establish contact through all the 'mansions' so that, having prepared a place in my Father's House, I could *return* to receive my little ones, my lost sheep, from the darkest wilderness, and restore them to their rightful home.

"Yes, there will be rebuking and chastening, pruning of unfruitful wood. This is not your work; leave it to those authorised by Papa. All are assigned according to their various gifts. You are assigned for door duty at the entrance to the banquet chamber. It is needful that you ensure all who arrive are provided with suitable raiment. Hold fast to that in which you have been tutored. Let no false messengers turn you away from this duty. All is well."

"By your commitment and one-pointedness is your perception unfettered from the 'bedrock' of Earth life literal-mindedness."

Holy Communion February 23, 1997:

At the beginning I saw the ladder again, and multitudes of people were walking toward its base and beginning the long ascent. Then I saw angels flying around, providing protection for all on the ladder. Then I realised that the Lord *is* the ladder!

"Lord and Master, you are all things for us, your little ones: the Good Shepherd, the banquet feast, the ladder upon which we ascend to the Father, and untold other mystical realities. I love you for your *all* sufficiency, Lord."

"My son, by your commitment and one-pointedness is your perception unfettered from the 'bedrock' of Earth life literal-mindedness. The mammon consciousness, which is entrapped in fear, feels more secure in restricting itself to the belief that all that is is all it can understand. The truth is that creation and creativity of the Mind of Papa has no bounds. You begin to attune with that.

"Your heart's sincere desire gives a surge of uplift to those on the path, even as my love for you gives you buoyancy. My love lifts you up because I gather you into my arms and into my heart. So does your love for those to whom you send blessings. (I saw those on the ladder make a sudden and rapid move upward, as on an escalator, as my heart filled with love and blessing for them at the offering of the wine.)

"Rejoice most of all that your names are written in Heaven rather than for anything that you see or hear or experience. Let this always be the focus of your rejoicing. Bless all your fellows that they may become aware that their names also are so written, from the least to the greatest among men. This is the Law of the Lord and it is wondrous to behold."

Needless to say, this event, unfolded over two successive weeks' Communion Services, was easy to discern as being of major significance, and has much more than is immediately to be observed by way of implication for humanity. It was worthy of much pondering, and I have pondered it muchly.

"The angels I saw were watching over the souls who were beginning the long ascent from the bottom of the ladder."

I was reminded of the Old Testament story of Jacob's ladder (Gen. 28:12) but with a number of significant differences. The ladder I saw went not just from Earth to Heaven but from bedrock hell – which it could be argued lies, metaphorically at least, somewhere 'below' the Earth-life experience – to Heaven. Our sanctuary of Mystical Communion with Christ was placed on a circular platform through which the ladder passed on its way up to Heaven. The angels I saw were not descending and ascending using the ladder (as in the Jacob's ladder narrative) but were flying around it, guarding or watching over those who were, in response to our broadcast invitation (in the Lord's name) from the staging post, beginning the long ascent from the bottom of the ladder. It was one-way traffic only: up!

That Jesus was a carpenter and was crucified on a wooden cross are hugely significant in this allegory. He used the wooden cross as his means of getting down to the bedrock hell – the lowest level of consciousness to which man can become degraded/have existence at the soul level – in which such a vast number of souls are stuck, with no light of spiritual discernment. Jesus came into the Earth life from a place of Great Light – the Source of All. Those from such a place of spiritual enlightenment are not visible to their brothers in 'outer (or lower) darkness'. He needed, as a deep-sea diver needs weighted boots, something to 'weigh him down' (spiritually) so that he could descend discernibly into the depths.

This was the 'sins of the world' laid upon him (or, taken upon himself); a burden he was easily able to bear, and which, for him, were as nothing at all, because he knew the truth: that all of time and place is but a dream, from which he is here to waken us. This is for 'practical' reasons, just as a diver puts-on weighted boots for practical reasons. It has nothing to do with a 'wrathful' God insisting on a scapegoat or 'once and for all blood sacrifice' for the 'sins' of all humanity from Adam and Eve through to the end of the world. The only one, true God, the Creator Spirit, is Love; unconditional, *Perfect* Love. The spirit of vengefulness and retribution has no place in the heart of the Holy One. That is a contrivance of literal-minded, Earth-conscious, control-hungry, fear-driven, hidden-agenda, ego-misled man.

Jesus used the cross for many reasons, symbolic and 'practical'. Practical is in quote marks because they are not necessarily all practical at the purely physical, Earth-mind level of perception, but more realistically at a mystical, spiritual, metaphysical, esoteric level of reality. At a strictly Earth-mind level of perception it could be said that he used the cross like a fireman uses a pole: to convey himself rapidly from one level to a lower level. None of this is said with tongue in cheek or in an irreverent manner. On the contrary, it is said in the utmost respect and in honour of Jesus the Christ, the Anointed Messenger of the Holy One, who so loves us – all of us without exception; that's what *unconditional* love is – that he descended from the utmost heights of spiritual awareness, reality and oneness with the Creator Spirit, into the

Earth-life realm, to be with us and bring us back to the Truth of Eternal Reality.

The Truth of Eternal Reality is that we are all eternal, living Spirit, coming from Eternity and returning to Eternity by the Path that unfolds at our feet, by faith, and is the free gift of The Creator Spirit, Papa. We are at free choice at every moment of our lives to espouse good and eschew 'evil'; or put another way, to seek/choose/espouse the *Light* and reject/turn away from/repudiate the *darkness*, or the absence of Light. 'Light' has an initial capital because this is the Light of Spirit, and is indivisible from the *Life* and *Love* of the Creator Spirit.

It helps in understanding all this if one can move back and forth between metaphor/symbol and 'physical-world actualities' in one's perception of these explanations. If the Creator Spirit is (the Source of All) Light and we are moving toward Him, then the place behind us – away from which we are moving – is darkness. The closer we move toward the Light, the more in the Light, or enlightened, we become. If we turn around 180 degrees and begin moving away from the Light toward the darkness, then we have the Light behind us and this will cause a shadow – our *own* shadow – to fall upon the path in front of us.

This is why Jesus called upon the people to "*Repent*, for the Kingdom of Heaven is at hand" (Mt. 4:17). The word *repent* means, literally, *turn around, 180 degrees*. Jesus was saying, "You are going in the wrong direction; you are heading away from the Light and out into darkness (outer darkness). Turn around 180 degrees and follow me; I will lead you back to God/the Source of the Light. This way you will become enlightened, see who you really are and *choose* the Light because the Light is who and what *you* really are (created in the likeness of God, the Source of All Light)."

So, he incarnated and spent his three-year mission in three main kingdomly activities: Healing the sick; casting-out possessing spirits; preaching the Good News – 'Gospel' – that the Kingdom of Heaven is at hand. The miracles and exorcisms were to establish his 'credentials'; evidence that he had, literally, overcome the world (ego), and bore true witness to his teachings about God, himself and the Kingdom. Nevertheless, it should be understood that he did not perform miracles to induce belief; he knew that would happen anyway, and serve his overall objectives, but his motivation for performing them was unconditional, perfect Love.

However, none of these activities was the real, *primary* purpose for his incarnation. That purpose was to bring down the Holy Spirit into the Earth-life consciousness of the seemingly separated, fragmented Sonship of God. The Holy Spirit (or Holy Ghost in KJV terminology) is the Voice for God, the Spirit of Truth, the Holy Breath; our true, eternal, unlimited, all-empowered (just like Jesus) Higher Self.

How the rescue, the salvation, by but one Awakened Brother, of all the rest of his identity-confused brothers is possible – indeed, inevitable – is by calling down the Holy Spirit into the world. All else for which Jesus is renowned – the teaching ('Never man spake like this man' [Jn. 7:46]) the miracles, the crucifixion, the resurrection – were to get our attention; to demonstrate that he knew something the rest of us clearly did not; to indicate he was worthwhile listening to, so that we would take notice of him and at least some of us would aspire to follow him.

He said in John 15:10-11: "...if ye keep my commandments..." [i.e., advice, spiritual counsel and guidance, and thus, become like him] "ye shall abide in my love ..." and " . . .that my joy might remain in you, and that your joy might be full" [i.e., complete, constant, eternal]. It is noteworthy that by abiding in his Love our *Joy* is full. When we 'fall in love' we experience great joy, but the joy of which Jesus speaks is of a dimension – spiritual, mystical – far, far beyond time and place, 'Earth-mind' comprehension or experience, although it *can* be experienced in time and place – by following, or keeping, his commandments. Such mystical Love and Joy are hand-in-glove, along with Peace, and all indivisible from each other.

Jesus incarnated to be an embodiment, or manifestation, of the Holy Spirit, or Spirit of Truth, the Voice for God. In other words, to bring the Spirit of Truth into the dimension to which his slumbering brethren have limited themselves so that he could demonstrate Its Reality to us, right 'here' in unreality.

The confused, bewildered mind of the fragmented Sonship had closed itself off to the presence of the Holy One, symbolised by the Holy of Holies in Solomon's Jerusalem Temple. The Holy of Holies, or Most Holy Place, and the Holy Place are adjoining chambers in the Temple, but separated, or divided off from each other by a veil. This symbolises the veil we have drawn over our vision, causing us to believe we are separated, unaware of the Light that is our Father and by extension, our Self. That veil only has as much reality, as much power to blind us, as we accord it. But to Jesus it had no power at all, and its 'rending in twain from the top to the bottom' (Mt. 27:51) demonstrated this; whether physically or metaphorically makes no difference because all the events and objects were and are outer *symbols* of an immeasurably greater *reality* behind them all.

This Voice for God has always been with us, but because we have been listening to the voice that believes the separation is real – ego, the voice of judgement, grievance and unforgiveness – this has misled and confused us, and drowned-out from our awareness the still, small Voice for God within our mind. Jesus heard, listened to and followed this Voice, Which led him to the place of full Awakening to remembrance of his True being as Papa's beloved, all-loving, all-empowered Son. And so he came at the start of the second measure of meal to manifest and anchor that Voice in time and place so that we could hear It also, *if we are willing to listen.*

The first record we have of him activating this process is in Jn. 20:22, when he appeared to the disciples in the upper room during the evening of the day of his resurrection: "... **he breathed on them**, and saith unto them, **Receive ye the Holy Ghost.**" The next record is from Acts, chapter 1, also shortly after the resurrection, when the disciples were still in Jerusalem and he appeared to them again:

> And, being assembled together with them, (he) commanded them that they should not depart from Jerusalem, but wait for the promise of the Father, which, saith he, ye have heard of me. For John truly baptized with water; but ye shall be baptized with the Holy Ghost not many days hence . . . ye shall receive power, after that the Holy Ghost is come upon you . . .

This coming upon them took place at the event called Pentecost, fifty days after the resurrection, as described in Acts, chapter 2. The disciples were greatly empowered by this wondrous experience, performed many miracles and spoke with the authority of the Spirit of Truth within them. In due course all this was lost to the awareness of subsequent generations of most of the followers of Jesus because an institution grew up following those early years, purporting to be established in his name and his representative on Earth.

But this institution became engulfed in distracting detail at the time and place level of consciousness. This institution was taken over by ego, and lived by the spirit of reckoning instead of remaining in the place of faith. Truly spoken are the words, 'The devil is in the detail.' According to the internet there are approaching forty-thousand different so-called Christian sects in today's world and this number is very far from static, as less than twenty years ago there were estimated to be around half that number. Divide and subdivide is ego's mantra.

The Son of God perceives himself separated from, blind to and bereft of God, but is actually as close to Papa as it is possible to be. It is impossible for the Son of God to not be the Son of God, regardless of his dream of separation from his Father and himself, broken into fragments of self-disempowered littleness; one, appearing as many in the valley of the shadow of death. And the leavening, the uplifting, the healing of the split-off mind of the Son is taking place. The 'dead' inhabitants of that valley are being resurrected, raised up, leavened, restored to Life, or Wholeness of Being.

Thereafter, during the leavening process that is the Great Rescue Programme, it could extend, like ripples on a pond, until the whole fragmented Sonship is raised up to awareness of Its Wholeness (Holiness) within.

Then each fragment can be led from his own *within* back to true Vision – as symbolised by the rending of the Temple veil, and the dispelling of the illusory separation of the Holy of Holies (Papa) from the Holy Place (the Sonship).

The path of incarnation by Jesus from the 'Highest Heaven' to Earth was one step – a considerable enough downward step at that. But the advantage of having taken that giant step for mankind (with apologies to Neil Armstrong) was that it brought him, as it were, 'halfway to Hades'.

Knowing the Master Jesus and his love for mankind – *all*

mankind – his commitment was to find every single lost sheep and place it lovingly upon his shoulders and return it safely to the fold (Lk. 15:5). Why would this not include those who, at any time, past, present or future, find themselves in outer darkness or the lowest depths of Hades, the pit? It assuredly does not apply only to those incarnate at the time of Jesus' earthly life, or to any other time before or since. Therefore, it must apply to *all* his brethren in the Sonship, wherever they are – incarnate or excarnate.

If that is the case, he had to have access to the excarnate souls who were in places of darkness. Why would Jesus, with his unconditional love for all humanity, individually, choose, in some arbitrary manner, to have some 'cut-off point' beyond which he would not go – in terms of the degree of darkness, the wilderness in which any soul/lost sheep might find himself – to search and rescue such a soul? Rather, he would be seeking souls at the very lowest point of darkness possible, in accord with his own words:

> They that be whole need not a physician, but they that are sick (Mt. 9:12),

and also:

> What man of you, having an hundred sheep, if he lose one of them, doth not leave the ninety and nine in the wilderness, and go after that which is lost, until he find it? And when he hath found it, he layeth it on his shoulders, rejoicing. And when he cometh home, he calleth together his friends and neighbours, saying unto them, Rejoice with me; for I have found my sheep which was lost. I say unto you, that likewise joy shall be in Heaven over one sinner that repenteth, more than over ninety and nine just persons, which need no repentance (Lk. 15:3-7).

Note that the record states: ". . . until he *find* it . . ." It does not say: 'until he has searched so far and no further'. Jesus, the anointed messenger of the Holy One, does not give up on *any* of us. Ever. That is the way it is with the Holy One. Commitment. Total and absolute. Is there one amongst us who would have it any other way?

Those who have sunk so low find it very hard – impossible,

actually – to rise up on their own, and the selfless giving, outpouring of great love, blessing and practical help toward such are all of inestimable benefit. It demonstrates in a practical, palpable way that they actually *are* 'worthy' of being loved. The objective of Jesus at the end of his mission in the 'halfway house of Earth-life habitation' was to visit the 'basement flats' and construct an escape ladder for those dwelling there. The cross was a highly serviceable mechanism, not only for getting him down there (using it as a fireman's pole) – it was the instrument of his separation from his physical body (a pre-requisite, one could argue, to such a journey!) and it was embedded in the ground, thus facilitating a 'downward progression' to the basement. Once there he, being a carpenter, could readily transform the material of the wooden cross into a wooden ladder-cum-staircase.

A pole is very difficult to ascend; a rigidly fastened, sturdy ladder with a deep tread that makes it more like a staircase is much easier. Fastening the base of the ladder – a single, seamless structure providing means of uninterrupted ascent from the basement of the Father's House right to the very top floor, the penthouse suite, with its banquet chamber – immovably to the bedrock of the basement was what he was engaged upon when I encountered him there.

It does not matter to Jesus what depths or degree of darkness any of us *appear* to enter or descend into; to him there is no place from which we are irredeemable. All that is required is desire – *our desire* – and willingness. Until a messenger comes along and reminds us that we are heading in the wrong direction, many of us sojourning in the Earth life get on a path that has the Light shining at our back and casting our shadow on the path ahead of us. Some may say, for a span (which could be a few years, a lifetime or an indeterminate number of lifetimes), 'That's fine, I am happy exploring this path out into the wilderness.' If so, they will continue and efforts by other well-meaning souls to persuade them otherwise will be to little avail. The desire to change direction, to shrug off ego-mind and be restored to the One-Mindedness of Christ, Papa's beloved Son, must come from the *within* of the individual.

When such souls have ventured far enough into the wilderness, and often when they have become lost and frightened of the dark, fearful shadows, they decide they have had enough and want out of there. That is when the trouble becomes apparent, because there is no-one to tell them *how* to get out, how to turn back, how to turn around 180 degrees, or 'repent'.

Jesus came to do that, but the literal-mindedness of ego-controlled, institutionalised religions, with their perceptions of a vengeful, wrathful God and their own (rather than God's) agendas of power over (rather than power with) the people, has, over scores of generations, caused many to believe they *will* go to hell, so when they depart their earthly bodies they go to such a place that their highly creative imaginations have fabricated for them.

Others didn't believe the message from Jesus because the institutionalised religions distorted its unconditionally-loving, forgiving, original substance with all the literal-minded, mistakenly-perceived images of wrath, vengeance and eternal hell-fire and destruction which have taken precedence over the real message of love and forgiveness. Thus have untold numbers of fragments of the Sonship abandoned the message because of its inaccurate, distorted delivery, and find themselves without a *true* message with which they can resonate gladly, joyfully, upliftingly at a deep, heart-mind level.

In the context of Eternity, all this is fine because the purpose of God moves inexorably along and we are in the time of the fulfilment of the prophecies, and harbingers, messengers, heralds of the Great Rescue Programme of Jesus are announcing this to the people of Earth, *right now*. There are thousands of them, with more incarnating every day, each with their own facet of the message. This is the true interpretation of this quote from Revelation:

> And I John saw the holy city, new Jerusalem, coming down from God out of heaven, prepared as a bride adorned for her husband (Rev. 21:2).

These facets, like the facets of a diamond, reflect the Light of Spiritual Truth in all directions and at all angles, to catch the eye of people of all persuasions if they are sincere in their desire for inner peace, goodwill, the brotherhood of man – all the kingdomly qualities of Eternity – rather than temporal, expedient

310

paths to material gain that are at the expense of their fellows. "For what is a man profited, if he shall gain the whole world, and lose his own soul? or what shall a man give in exchange for his soul?" (Mt. 16:26).

If we first, last and always choose to discern the message as having its foundation in eternal, unchangeable, unconditional, perfect Love – thereby refusing to take any words or doctrines to the contrary at face value – then we can start to separate the wheat of Eternal Truth in Holy Scriptures from the chaff placed there by mistaken perceptions or hidden agendas, of which there have been a lack of neither within the institutionalised religions established in the names of messengers from the Holy One over the millennia.

Then will we be well on our Way Home. That journey starts with us here, on Earth – time and place – because it is of an existence on Earth that we are dreaming. Jesus taught that the Kingdom of Heaven is at hand, all around us – though most of his brethren, then and now, were/still are, unaware of it. We cannot be transformed into Kingdom-awareness in Heaven from an ego-conditioned state of misperception (wrong-mindedness) without a total retraining of our minds to kingdomly desire and understanding. That retraining will bring us to the place of awareness where we will be ready and willing to leave the Earth and its duality, separation-consciousness ways behind us. This is a co-operative process between Jesus and/or Holy Spirit and us; it is not something to which They will help us awaken until and unless we ask and are willing to *receive*, and accept unto ourself, that Kingdom awareness. That can only happen here, on Earth, so that we are prepared, *made ready*, for a smooth, joyful (unencumbered by fear or guilt) transition to full, eternal Kingdom reality – in Heaven.

Ego, that split-off-from-Truth part of the mind of the Son of God, made the physical universe as a hiding place from God. To return to the Light, we (the fragmented Sonship) must be restored to at-one-ment in our true, unified reality *as* the Sonship, by a willingness to allow, and co-operate with, the Spirit of Truth, our highest Self, in undoing, dispelling ego from our mind, so that it can be healed and restored to wholeness. Then, and only then, will we no longer be on the ego-mind wavelength. Then we will have no awareness of ego or its construct, the physical universe.

That construct will then cease to appear to have any existence, because we will be in our right mind, our Christ Mind, in which ego and its constructs have no part. This means that the Great Rescue Programme will first restore us to Kingdom awareness here on Earth – the Kingdom of Heaven on Earth – and then we will be ready, all of us, together as one, to be uplifted by God Himself to our final and permanent Home in Eternity, the Kingdom of Heaven in Heaven; One, again, in Papa, the Creator Spirit, our eternal, perfectly-loving heavenly Father.

Finis

---

* It is important to understand that this does not imply judgement or punishment, but correction of erroneous thinking, beliefs and perception, which in turn lead to erroneous understanding and actions, keeping us on the carousel of birth and death. All such have to be 'pruned', or shone away by the Light of Eternal Truth.

AFTERWORD

There has been so much synchronicity involved in the events that have led to this writing coming before you, the reader, that I feel prompted to share some of it with you.

Throughout the decades of my journey with Jesus he has said to me many times, 'Freely have you received, freely give', and this has gladly been my approach to sharing the events, inspiration and revelations that this journey has brought to me. In the 1990s and early noughties (the first decade of the new century) I was acutely aware that there had been so many blessings that if I came to the end of my sojourn in time as Brian without at least making the effort to share some of them with my brothers in the Sonship, I would be left with an overriding sense of profound regret at a missed opportunity.

So, in the early noughties I began writing the story, and felt the title *Synchronicity, for Goodness' Sake* (SFGS) was apposite, at least unless or until I was guided/inspired otherwise. However, Jesus had also told me over the years that the devotional Service of Mystical Communion with Christ (SMCC) in which I had been instructed by Olga Park in 1967, and which Theresa and I, and others, had subsequently practised – and the enlightenment and guidance I (and others) received as a result of this practise – was 'an operation of hiddenness'; that when the time was right it would become 'an operation of openness'.

This is in accord with the principle that governs the emergence of new life from a seed. In February 1992, the Teacher said to me:

"The seed has fallen upon fructifying soil. It has entered into the dark and secret place wherein it has imbibed of the waters of life. These waters have caused its own life to be stirred into an unfolding of its purpose from deep in its own *within*. Thus has the seed germinated and grown in the secret place. In due time shall the seedling emerge from the secret place into the open and shall put forth branches and leaves and flowers and fruit. Therefore I counsel you, that your life be in harmony with the Spirit *within*, that you may be protected from those who would peck at the tender shoots and who would burrow within your structure and weaken and distort your growth."

Jesus told me that the switch-over from hiddenness to openness would be by circumstances not of my choosing, and that when it happened, I would know of a certainty that it was the time.

In the small hours of June 5, 2005, my 61st birthday, I was wakened by the Inner Voice speaking to me what I later entitled *The Caterpillars and the Butterfly* and subsequently subtitled *An allegory of human spiritual life*. This was so clearly and powerfully impressed into my mind that when I got up a few hours later I was able to type it out verbatim. I emailed it to a few people, including Owen Waters, who administers a website called *Infinite Being*, without any explanation about how it came to be written, or even who had written it.

Within a few hours Owen emailed back saying how good it was, and could he please use it as one of his weekly articles that he emails to a sizeable mailing list. I had had no thought that he would respond in this manner, but as soon as I got his reply I 'knew' that this was the moment of the switch-over from hiddenness to openness. I of course said go ahead, and in the exchanges that followed I happened to mention I had written a manuscript of my experiences, and was intending to publish this on a website in due course (this happened about seven or eight months later, after I went to night-school to learn how to develop and install a website!).

To my amazement and delight, Owen said he would gladly tell recipients of the allegory article that this was written by me and that I had also written a manuscript of the experiences of my journey with Jesus; that I would happily email it free to anyone who was interested. During the days that followed Owen's sending of the allegory to everyone on his mailing list, I was inundated with messages saying how enlightening the allegory was, and how it had helped provide a much clearer understanding of who Jesus really is, and our relationship to him; and further, would I please send them the manuscript.

This I gladly did, and received numerous messages back expressing deep gratitude for it. Many shared mystical experiences they had had. Correspondence developed and I began sending occasional articles I was prompted from within to write, and accompanied by entries from the records of the messages from Jesus and others in the Realms of Light, which I dubbed *Diary of a Christ Communicant* (DCC). *

By the time I finally got the website up and running in early 2006, I was finding that the articles were flowing from within such that this became a weekly feature, even though I had never had such a conscious intention. By this time, I was realising that if the Spirit of Truth is in charge, it is best to go with the flow. Indeed, Jesus had warned me on a number of occasions over the years to be ready for anything at a moment's notice, so if this was the way things were heading, who was I to stand in the way?

The website took shape and I uploaded the manuscript under the title initially selected. Things continued and progressed for several years and there were correspondence from people around the world. The web stats indicated that there were thousands of hits on the Honest2goodness (HTG) site each month from well over one hundred countries. Many hits were from countries that were unidentifiable by the stats compilers, so I assumed this would be countries such as China and Saudi Arabia.

I have long since realised that monitoring web stats was the Holy Spirit's job, not mine, so have not checked them since. Jesus told me my job was to *deliver* the message and not to concern myself over how it is *received*; that this was his job, along with the Holy Spirit. I was entirely relieved at this; it took all responsibility for it and how it might increase out of my hands!

Over the years a number of people asked me if I had ever thought of having SFGS published, and I replied with what Jesus had told me about freely giving as I had freely received. Then, in June 2010, we had friends visiting from Vancouver.

Peter knew all about my writing but when he indicated he didn't know something that was in the book I was surprised and asked if he had read it. He said he had read snippets here and there, but reading off a website, or a computer monitor was not always convenient; he told me people like to hold a book in their hands, pick it up, read some, and later, read more, wherever they might be; that this is not possible online. His point came across loud and clear. I printed a copy for him to take back to Vancouver and he told me he read it on the plane, with great enthusiasm, and said I *really* needed a publisher.

I had assumed that the Holy Spirit would be firing people up to read it off the website or download it and print it out for reading elsewhere.

I had experienced how difficult it is to get a publisher to publish a book by an unknown author when we tried to get Theresa's book *Seeds of Redemption* published, but it was becoming clear that the Holy Spirit was moving things along, and it now seemed the time was approaching for SFGS to be brought into print format. So I said to the Holy Spirit, 'Over to You. If You want this to get published, so be it. I leave it in Your hands.' If His intent is there, it will happen, but as time is an illusion, I am content to leave the 'when' in His able care.

Money is not a primary motivation in this labour of love; it is an ego distraction, to keep us focused in the without. Jesus tells us: ". . . take no thought, saying, What shall we eat? or, What shall we drink? or, Wherewithal shall we be clothed? . . . for your heavenly Father knoweth that ye have need of all these things. *But seek ye first the kingdom of God, and his righteousness;* and all these things shall be added unto you" (from Mt. 6), and in Mt.16: "For what is a man profited, if he shall gain the whole world, and lose his own soul? or what shall a man give in exchange for his soul?"

* * *

During 2011, I was prompted to add several new Vignettes in Part Two from the DCC records and to generally tidy up the manuscript and provide more details about some of the events recounted. It is not that the events changed, but one's understanding of the meaning behind the events grows over time, and so I have been able to share some more of that enhanced, clarified understanding.

One of the most synchronistic events that took place during 2011 is that the title changed. It emerged during discussions that practically everyone felt the title – *Synchronicity, for Goodness'*

Sake – was not 'powerful enough' and did not do justice to the message. No-one had wanted to tell me because they didn't want to hurt my feelings! Meanwhile, my friend Michael Roads, author of *Through the Eyes of Love* (books *One* and *Two* and *Three*), who had read the manuscript, wrote so positively of his feeling about it:

> "An inspiring book. Brian is a living, dynamic challenge to the old, pre-digested version of Christianity. In his journey and dialogue with the real Jesus, he opens the door to a whole new way of resurrecting declining religious perceptions into vibrant, living spirituality. *Seek ye first the kingdom of God*, becomes truly meaningful as you follow Brian and Theresa on a journey taking them ever deeper into that very kingdom. Insightful, uplifting and profound, I thoroughly recommend this book."

Well, as soon as we read what Michael said about '*Seek ye first the Kingdom* . . .' it became immediately clear to us that this was the 'right' title for the book. So did it to everyone else to whom we mentioned this. All agreed it is the powerful title it needs. Michael also suggested the addition of the subtitle, 'One man's journey with the living Jesus'. Thank you, Michael, for your wise, incisive discernment. And when combined with the inspired cover design that goes with it, created by Lana Carolan, who is an inspiration in herself, it all just falls into place. I very much felt the Spirit of Truth has been in charge of all these activities. I certainly asked Him to be, and ultimately it will be the reader who perhaps can best decide for him- or herself.

Peace and joy be with us all as we travel the 'journey without distance' together back to the Kingdom of Heaven within us all.

Love and blessings, always,

Brian Longhurst

---

* Please visit www.honest2goodness.org.uk for full details.

ACKNOWLEDGEMENTS

There are many without whom this work could never have been brought before its readers. For this, and all involved, I wish to express heartfelt thanks and grateful acknowledgement. First and foremost is our Heavenly Father, the Creator Spirit, 'Papa'. Where would we be without Him? Truly Jesus spoke when he said of his relationship with Him, *Of myself I can do nothing.* He is the Source of All, in Whom we live and move and have our being. To You, beloved Papa, I am eternally grateful.

Then, it will be no surprise to the reader, comes Jesus, Papa's *Anointed Messenger*. He has befriended me, tutored me, loved me completely, unconditionally, led me with infinite patience, and won my total trust, loyalty, following, devotion and love. How wonderful will be the day when we are all brothers to each other as he has been to me, and in truth, is to us all. On that day will the Kingdom of Heaven be well and truly operational on Earth.

I have no idea how to acknowledge the Holy Spirit. All I know is that my heart impels me to acknowledge Him. For He is the true, Whole (Holy) Self of us all, the Highest part of our mind; the Voice for God within us; the Voice that reminds us that we are, along with Jesus, one in the Sonship of God; the Voice that will speak with us of the Truth of Eternity, if we are willing to be still and listen. *Ssshhh!*

Now, my beloved wife, Theresa. In 1967, I asked Jesus to bring to me a Companion of the Way. Within four months he fulfilled my request by bringing us together in the unlikeliest of circumstances. Steadfast, long-suffering to a fault and stalwart are terms that come to mind to describe Theresa. But more than that, her support, patience and contribution in proofing and making suggestions for improving the manuscript and a thousand other ways as I worked on it, all have been invaluable, and in which I am truly blessed. Thank you, Darling, my beloved Companion of the Way.

Thanks also to Laurie Pentell, without whose dedicated, tireless, diligent editing this writing could never have been brought to resemble anything like a professional presentation.

And all without too much kicking and screaming from me, such was her flair for, and diplomacy in, suggesting, recommending some alternative ways of saying what I was trying to express.

To me, a kindergarten child in the world of computers, Tim is an unsung hero, who cannot go without mention here. Whenever a need for help with computers arose, since the mid-1990s, Tim has been there for us. And there has never been an issue that his indomitable approach to every challenge was not able to resolve, usually in two shakes of a lamb's tail. Thank you, Tim; please do not emigrate!

I am blessed to count Lana Carolan amongst my friends. She is a gifted artist, designer and illustrator, and I was overjoyed when she volunteered to design, illustrate and lay out the cover. Cometh the project, cometh Lana. Lana radiates love, joy, peace and goodwill. Thank you, Lana, for being the Light that you are.

Last, but by no means least, is Denise Williams of Six Degrees Publishing Group. It is completely evident that you are a consummate professional; diligent, competent, committed, comprehensive in your communications and to fulfilling your role as publisher to the last detail, yet with great empathy and sensitivity toward the perspective of the author. Altogether, Denise, you are a pleasure and breath of fresh air to work with.

ABOUT THE AUTHOR

Brian Longhurst has been aware of the reality of the spirit realms since childhood. Born in England, he moved to Canada as a young man, where he began what was to become an enduring, personal relationship with Jesus, who manifested in glory to him when Brian was twenty-two. Jesus told him he had come to lead him back to God. From then, his encounters with the living Jesus began in earnest, with a decades-long journey of spiritual awakening.

After marrying, Brian returned to live in England. He now resides in Gloucestershire with his wife, Theresa.

Read More . . .

More writings of Brian Longhurst, including his *Messages of Encouragement* (MoEs), *Diary of a Christ Communicant*, and a Forum page, in which all are invited to share their Christ-awarenesses, or ask questions about Eternal Reality, are available at:

http://www.honest2goodness.org.uk/

Recommended by Brian:

Any who feel inspired to enter in and climb the inner stairway to the Upper Room of personal, one-on-one Communion with the living Jesus will find this website most beneficial:

http://www.members.shaw.ca/communion/

Lightning Source UK Ltd.
Milton Keynes UK
UKHW021858130121
376964UK00010B/818